GEORGE WASHINGTON

GEORGE WASHINGTON

WOODROW WILSON

Introduction by Marcus Cunliffe

SCHOCKEN BOOKS • NEW YORK

TO

E. A. W.

WITHOUT WHOSE SYMPATHY AND COUNSEL

LITERARY WORK WOULD LACK

INSPIRATION

First published 1896

First SCHOCKEN edition 1969

Introduction copyright © 1969 by Schocken Books Inc.

Library of Congress Catalog Card No. 69–14803

Manufactured in the United States of America

INTRODUCTION TO THE 1969 EDITION

WOODROW WILSON'S *GEORGE WASHINGTON*

IT MUST BE at once conceded that Woodrow Wilson's biography of George Washington is no masterpiece. Rather, read in the context of Wilson's own life, this biography tells us at least as much about the twenty-eighth President of the United States as about the first.

The great work he dreamed of during his academic years, on "The Philosophy of Politics," remained unwritten. Instead, having won an early success with *Congressional Government* (1885), he came dangerously close to being a hack author. At least this is how much of his output looks in retrospect. He produced a flow of magazine articles, collected subsequently as *An Old Master* (1893) and *Mere Literature* (1896). His historical books were written at the suggestion of various editors; unlike his friend Frederick Jackson Turner, he was hardly a historian's historian. A harsh verdict would be that he published not because he had something to say, but because he felt he had to say something. An as-yet unfocussed ambition drove him on. Editors warmed to Professor Woodrow Wilson of Johns Hopkins (1883–85), Bryn Mawr (1885–88), Wesleyan (1888–90), and Princeton (1890–1902) for good editorial reasons: he was fluent, he was industrious, he was amenable to advice, and he was becoming a "name." So he wrote a textbook, *Division and Reunion, 1829–1889* (1893), for Albert Bushnell Hart's series on "Epochs of American History." Well-received, it stimulated other editors to approach him. His most ambitious endeavor, *A History of the American People* (1902), was serialized in *Harper's Magazine*. He earned $12,000 from the

v

magazine installments, and considerably more from sales in book form. Wilson refused several invitations to contribute unpaid reviews to the *American Historical Review*. "I know you will deem me a churl," he candidly admitted, "but really the thing is impossible, honorable as I should feel to find a place in the *Review* to be. The fact is, that the editors of the popular monthlies offer me such prices nowadays that I am corrupted." No wonder that a Princeton colleague later dismissed the *History of the American People* as a "gilt-edged potboiler." [1]

A similar epithet could be applied to Wilson's treatment of George Washington, also serialized in *Harper's Magazine* in 1895–96, and published as a book in 1896. Working under pressure and during vacations, he had no opportunity and indeed no particular impulse to pursue original research. He drew upon secondary material. His portrait of Washington was conventional. To judge from later references, he did not even go closely enough into his hero's career to discover that it was Thomas Jefferson, not Washington, who spoke of "entangling alliances." [2] And while serial publication may have obliged him to chop his book into narrative blocks of

[1] Henry Wilkinson Bragdon, *Woodrow Wilson: The Academic Years* (Cambridge, Mass., 1967), pp. 247, 251. Much of my material has been drawn from Mr. Bragdon's excellent study; see especially chap. 12, "Literary Historian." There are briefer accounts of Wilson's historical work in Arthur S. Link, *Wilson: The Road to the White House* (Princeton, N.J., 1947), pp. 29–35, and Arthur Walworth, *Woodrow Wilson* (2d ed., Boston, 1965), pp. 63–66. An older discussion by Louis M. Sears in William T. Hutchinson, ed., *Marcus W. Jernegan Essays in American Historiography* (Chicago, 1937), pp. 102–21, is still of value. Marjorie L. Daniel, "Woodrow Wilson—Historian," *Mississippi Valley Historical Review*, XXI (December, 1934), 361–74, is of less use and does not deal with Wilson's *George Washington*.

[2] "We still read Washington's immortal warning against 'entangling alliances' with full comprehension and an answering purpose": speech in New York, September 27, 1918. There is a similar allusion in a Wilson address of September 19, 1919. See Donald Day, ed., *Woodrow Wilson's Own Story* (Boston, 1952), pp. 287, 347.

equal length, the result is curiously disproportionate. Too
much preliminary space is devoted to an evocation of Virginia
colonial life. Throughout the work there is an excess of general narrative, a dearth of genuine biography. The last ten
years of Washington's life are perfunctorily handled; the
chapter contains little indication that one future President
had meditated upon the presidential office.

Critics have been especially irritated by his overindulgence
in archaisms. Dozens of sentences begin with " 'Twas"; he
uses "but" for "only," "ere" for "before," awkward inver-
sions, superfluously picturesque adjectives. A couple of examples show Wilson at his stylistic worst:

> But with Washington it was a different matter. There
> was that in his proud eyes and gentleman's bearing that
> marked him a man to be made friends with and re-
> spected. A good comrade he proved, without pretence
> or bravado, but an ill man to scorn, as he went his way
> among them, lithe and alert, full six feet in his boots,
> with that strong gait as of a backwoodsman, and that
> haughty carriage as of a man born to have his will.

> [Contrecoeur] was staking everything, as it was, upon
> this encounter on the way. If the English should shake
> the savages off, as he deemed they would, he must no
> doubt withdraw as he could ere the lines of siege were
> closed about him. He never dreamed of such largess of
> good fortune as came pouring in upon him. The Eng-
> lish were not only checked, but beaten. They had never
> seen business like this. 'Twas a pitiful, shameful
> slaughter—men shot like beasts in a pen there where
> they cowered close in their scarlet ranks. Their first
> blazing volleys had sent the craven Canadians scam-
> pering back the way they had come.

Costume-prose of this sort makes one sympathetic with the
plea of a cinema owner to his distributor: "Don't send me
no more pictures where the hero signs his name with a

feather." Wilson, according to one critic, "only added to the steel-engraving status of the Father of his Country"; "rather fourth-state stuff," concluded another.[3]

Such criticism, however, requires qualification. The first point to emphasize is that Woodrow Wilson was quite highly esteemed by the majority of his academic contemporaries. They did not feel he was merely churning out historical pablum for the sake of the money. J. Franklin Jamieson, the editor who kept pressing him to write for the *American Historical Review,* was a man of rigorous standards. Jamieson and others had seen from *Congressional Government* and from some of Wilson's book reviews in the monthly magazines that, given a suitable subject, he could be an incisive commentator. The chapter that Wilson undertook for Lord Acton's *Cambridge Modern History,* on "State Rights, 1850–1861," so pleased the editors that they tried to persuade Wilson to do three more chapters of United States history.

A second mitigation is that Washington biography has always posed problems for the biographers. There is the snag that little is known of Washington's early life, though plenty is known about the Virginia of his day. One way of overcoming the absence of personal material is to indulge in supposition, or to stretch out apocryphal anecdotes—as was notoriously done by Parson Weems of "cherry tree" fame. Alternatively, the biographer is led into a broad survey of the "times" in which Washington is apt almost to disappear from view. Later periods of Washington's life, as commander-in-chief and as president, carry a similar tendency, because his existence and that of his country seem inseparably intertwined. Again, every Washington biographer for a very long period has endeavored to avoid hero worship, to disclose the real man behind the chorus of adulation. The effort gained fresh impetus toward the end of the nineteenth century, en-

[3] William E. Dodd and William Allen White, quoted in Sears, *Jernegan Essays,* p. 112.

couraged by the emergence of professionalism in historical writing. A typical title, of a book published in the same year as Wilson's, was Paul Leicester Ford's *The True George Washington*. Henry Cabot Lodge, who produced a two-volume life of Washington in 1889, had been trained in Harvard's postgraduate school with Germanic strictness. His biography took a severe attitude to the sentimental inventions of Weems, "a man destitute of historical sense, training, or morals." Yet every biographer, except for a small minority of soured debunkers, found himself reproducing the traditional Washington portrait, in the conviction that this must after all be the "true" George Washington.[4] The more readable the treatment, the less professionally sound it was apt to be : *The Seven Ages of Washington* (1907), by the novelist Owen Wister, is an example. Conversely, the more scholarly, the less readable : an example of this failing is the substantial yet colorless two-volume life of Washington (1900) by Worthington C. Ford. Henry Cabot Lodge's attempt was on the whole no better than Wilson's. Lodge tackled the task earnestly, and possessed a vigorous style. But he presented Washington very much as a Federalist politician ; and his confident analysis of Washington's military career rested on a shaky grasp of tactics and strategy.[5] The historical profession of the 1890's, while fond of the notion that history was or might become an exact science, was still markedly patriotic and literary in outlook. In his 1898 presidential

[4] For an analysis of the problems of Washington biography, see the introduction by Marcus Cunliffe to *The Life of Washington* by Mason L. Weems (John Harvard Library, Cambridge, Mass., 1962). On Lodge, see especially pp. xxxii–xxxiv.

[5] Senator Lodge's bitter enmity to President Wilson is a matter of common knowledge, and indeed of great importance in the shaping of American foreign policy. It is tempting to argue that their rivalry began as early as the 1880's, when they were two ambitious young academics, competing for eminence in the same field and sometimes in the same magazines. *Harper's Magazine* ran a Lodge article in one of the 1896 issues that also contained an installment of Wilson's *Washington*.

address to the American Historical Association, George P. Fisher, the author of a much-admired work on *The Colonial Era* (1892), maintained that if a choice had to be made, hero worship was preferable to iconoclasm. There was nothing to be gained from searching out the flaws (if any) in the character of a George Washington; every nation needed at least one sacred personage "justly enshrined in popular veneration." [6]

The style in which Wilson garbed his narrative has not worn well. But it is worth remembering that his biography was written in a period when historical romance and glamorous make-believe were in vogue. Realistic and naturalistic prose was confined to a handful of writers such as Stephen Crane and Frank Norris, and even they were not entirely consistent. The most widely praised fiction of the decade leaned toward the tinted and the exotic. The taste of readers was formed upon such novels as Anthony Hope's *The Prisoner of Zenda* (1894), Frances Hodgson Burnett's *A Lady of Quality* (1896) and *His Grace of Osmonde* (1897), and S. Weir Mitchell's story of the American Revolution, *Hugh Wynne, Free Quaker* (1898). Mitchell's was one of a number of historical novels that deferentially introduced the personage of George Washington. So it would be wrong to suppose that Woodrow Wilson was guilty of any worse literary sin than writing in the idiom of his time, or at least that approved by the educated middle class. This will be apparent to anyone who glances through the issues of *Harper's Magazine* which contain Wilson's *Washington*. Wilson's style differed little from that of Theodore Roosevelt, for example, whose account of the winning of the West was being featured at the same period. More surprisingly perhaps, there were certain affinities in the prose of Mark Twain. Twain's serialized *Personal Recollections of Joan of Arc*, a

---

[6] Herman Ausubel, *Historians and Their Craft: A Study of the Presidential Addresses of the American Historical Association, 1884–1945* (New York, 1950), p. 268.

much-praised book that he himself took very seriously,
is couched in a "historical" vocabulary, with deliberate
archaisms:

> It was vexatious to see what a to-do the whole town,
> and next the whole country, made over the news!

That sentence could easily have come from Wilson's
Washington.[7]

Wilson was far inferior to Twain as a writer. Like Twain,
however, he was casting about for an appropriate narrative
method. It is arguable that unlike Twain he never found one.
An early attempt at a "psychoanalytic study" of Wilson,
William B. Hale's *The Story of a Style* (1920), interpreted
the increasing pomposity and obscurity of Wilson's prose as
evidence of a progressive deterioration of intellect:

> Mr. Wilson does not concur, he entirely concurs; he is
> seldom gratified, he is profoundly gratified; he does not
> feel pleasure, he experiences unaffected pleasure; he
> seldom says anything, but he is always privileged to say,
> or, speaking from his heart, says, or in all frankness
> says.[8]

[7] Grant C. Knight, *The Critical Period in American Literature*
(Chapel Hill, N.C., 1951), pp. 95–98, 124–25. The Twain quotation
is to be found in *Harper's Magazine*, XCII (December, 1895), 135.
The same issue included, together with the first installment of Wood-
row Wilson's *George Washington*, a short story entitled "The Last
Sonnet of Princivalle di Cembino."

[8] Hale, a well-known journalist, was a former friend of Wilson. His
tract against Wilsonian rhetoric is described by his son William
Harlan Hale, "President Wilson, Dr. Freud, and 'The Story of a
Style,'" *The Reporter*, June 26, 1958, pp. 28–30. Freud's com-
ments to William B. Hale are interesting in the light of his subse-
quent collaboration with William C. Bullitt (*Thomas Woodrow
Wilson . . . A Psychological Study* [Boston, 1967]). Freud admitted
to Hale his detestation of Wilson, but also said: "Mr. Wilson is a
living personality and not a product of political phantasy. . . . In my
opinion, psychoanalysis should never be used as a weapon in literary
or political polemics. . . . Psychoanalysis should be not practiced on
a living subject . . . unless he submits to it. I am not in the habit of
killing my own patients."

Yet before he entered politics, Woodrow Wilson was pre-
occupied with words and their uses. "I have imagined a
style," he wrote to his fiancée Ellen Axson in January, 1884,
"clear, bold, fresh, and facile [W. B. Hale might have said
that "facile" gave the game away] ; a style flexible but always
strong, capable of light touches or of heavy blows; . . . a
style full of life, of colour and vivacity." He added: "Is it
any wonder that I am disgusted with the stiff, dry, mechani-
cal, monotonous sentences in which my meagre thoughts are
compelled to masquerade." Eleven years later, insisting to
his wife that he was still no true man of letters, he lamented:
"If I could only write prose that was delicate, imaginative,
full at once of grace, force, and distinction, that would be
something: my thoughts would at least go clad like aristo-
crats. But alas! I shall but wear my soul out trying." In
1897 he dwelt on the deficiencies of his literary essays, in a
letter to a friend. The phrasing, he said, was "too elaborate"; it lacked the "easy pace of simplicity."

Despite Wilson's capacity for self-criticism, there was
perhaps a basic flaw in his desire to improve his prose. His
real aim, that is, was oratorical rather than literary. He
wanted to achieve glory, victory, immortality; he dreamed of
great occasions and instantaneous acclaim. Indeed, oratory
sometimes yielded him such triumph, notably in a commem-
orative address delivered at Princeton in 1896. *Belles lettres*
and historical writing could hardly bear such a burden of
expectation, especially since (he informed Ellen Axson in
1885) he had "no patience for the tedious toil of what is
known as 'research'." [9]

Yet he had a point, in the historical milieu of the late
nineteenth century. The emphasis on professionalism, the
belief that history was or might become a science, led to a
marked improvement in the technical competence of American historical writing. Johns Hopkins University furnished a

[9] Donald Day, ed., *Woodrow Wilson's Own Story*, pp. 25, 30; R. S.
Baker, *Woodrow Wilson: Life and Letters*, I, pp. 109–14.

dignified entry to the life of scholarship for Wilson as for
Frederick Jackson Turner and many another budding professor. But Wilson clung stubbornly to an older ideal—of
history as an art, a branch of literature. "Style is not much
studied here," he informed his fiancée in October, 1883. At
Hopkins, "*ideas* are supposed to be everything—their vehicle
comparatively nothing. But you and I know that there can be
no greater mistake . . ." [10] Whatever may be said in dispraise
of Wilson's historical work, it is no more dead, and considerably more readable, than most of the monographs produced
according to the dictates of the new professionalism. Missing
in Wilson was the dedication, the passion for facts, the intellectual curiosity of some of his academic contemporaries.
Missing in them was the imaginative excitement, the passionate if ambiguous determination to make history *live,* that
linked Wilson with such amateurs as Theodore Roosevelt. He
was a historian in the mould of Roosevelt, or perhaps of Sir
Winston Churchill. He wrote, in other words, not as the
culmination of arduous research, but rapidly, fluently, for
ulterior though not necessarily unworthy motives: to stimu-
late patriotic enthusiasm, to reach the ear of the public, to
gratify concealed autobiographical impulses, to arm himself
for future activity in some larger, public sphere.

The main value for us of Wilson's *George Washington* lies
therefore in the clues it offers to his temperament during the
pre-political stage of his development. Certain of the clues
are negative. They hint either at limitations that were to per-
sist throughout Wilson's career, or at conventional opinions
he was later to revise or repudiate.

The book confirms that up to the age of forty Woodrow
Wilson was still orthodoxly conservative in outlook. George

[10] Day, *Wilson's Own Story,* p. 24. These ideas are most fully expressed in "On the Writing of History," an 1895 contribution to the
Century Magazine: see Bragdon, *Woodrow Wilson: The Academic
Years,* p. 243. Lodge and Roosevelt expressed almost identical views:
see John A. Garraty, *Henry Cabot Lodge* (New York, 1953), p. 57.

Washington figures as a "thoroughbred gentleman" of Virginia. Washington's Americanness is that of the good sturdy
sort of Englishmen who took Wilson's intermittently Anglo-
phile fancy. By contrast, Thomas Jefferson is too Frenchified,
too affected by "demagogues and philosophers," to be altogether reliable. Wilson had decided in 1894 that while Washington was truly a great American, Jefferson could not quite
qualify on account of "the strain of French philosophy that
weakened and permeated his thought." As a Democratic
political leader Wilson subsequently overcame all such doubts.
His initial response had been, as it chanced, quite close to
that of Theodore Roosevelt.

Wilson's cordial adoption of Turner's idea on the importance of the American West, noticeable in his previous book
Division and Reunion, finds little outlet in *George Washington.* This is hardly surprising. In his Turnerian "Calendar
of Great Americans" (1894), Wilson proclaimed that "the
typical Americans have all been western men, with the ex-
ception of Washington." Rather than seek to explain how the
exceptional could be also typical, he falls back in the biography upon a conventionally genteel admiration for Washington the exemplary aristocrat-leader (with an occasional
hint at "backwoodsman's" qualities).

The brief, trite summary of Washington's presidency
shows that in the 1890's Wilson had no clear conception of
the role of the nation's chief executive, and of practical
politics. Or rather, his picture was clear but was too simple
and theoretical. He offered various Emersonian observations
on leadership—for example, an address at the University of
Tennessee in June, 1890: "I do not conceive the leader a
trimmer, weak to yield what clamor claims, but the deeply
human man, quick to know and to do the things that the hour
and his nation need." At the age of forty-five, in 1902,
shortly before he became president of Princeton University,
Wilson wrote to Frederick J. Turner, "I was born a politician and must be at the task for which, by means of my

historical writing, I have been all these years in training." [11]
The task he referred to, however, was that of settling down
to compose his *magnum opus* on the "Philosophy of Politics."
His destiny was vaguely conceived: he might sway men by
means of oratory or eloquent printed arguments, but he had
as yet gone no further than commencement commonplaces.
The actual mechanisms of politics were remote to him, and
in a way would always remain so.

Some scholars have traced Wilson's vision of a powerful
executive further back than 1900. Even in his first published
article of 1879, and more fully in *Congressional Government*
(1885), he had stressed the importance of bold, efficient
direction of national affairs. In an *Atlantic Monthly* article
of July, 1897, pointing to the examples set by Andrew Jackson and Abraham Lincoln, he demanded a new "national
leadership"; and in a lecture delivered shortly afterward to
a group of lawyers he defined the American system as a
"Leaderless Government." But in such pronouncements Wilson was still thinking of a partnership, more or less on the
British model, between the president, his cabinet, and Congress. Power, he seemed to assume, resided in Congressional
committees, or among the executive officers. The president
could not master enough of the complex mass of business,
even with a reformed method of federal administration, to
be more than a kind of board chairman. In short, "leadership"
appeared in practice to be a collective activity, not that of one
man; by "executive" he understood the whole executive
branch, rather than the president as "chief executive." The
introduction he wrote in 1900 for a new edition of *Congressional Government* proved that he had begun to take note
of a fresh political climate, involving a dramatic extension of

[11] Note the echo (*must be at the task*) from the New Testament.
The young Jesus was found by his parents in the temple, *sitting in
the midst of the doctors, both hearing them, and asking them ques-
tions. And all that heard him were astonished at his understanding.*
When his worried mother chided him, Jesus replied: *wist ye not that
I must be about my Father's business?* (Luke 2:49).

presidential power. It was however a fact to be recognized, not a transformation he had predicted or urged. True, in the 1880's and 1890's he admired the courage of the Democratic president Grover Cleveland. But it cannot be demonstrated that Professor Wilson foretold the resurgent presidency that started to emerge after the Spanish-American War of 1898.[12]

On the other hand, there are in Wilson's *George Washington* plenty of generalized clues to his own inchoate visions of greatness. Washington had been drawn into public life by the demands of the age. So might that other Virginian Woodrow Wilson, who in 1885 complained in an intimate letter that he had been "shut out from my heart's *first*—primary— ambition and purpose, which was, to take an active, if possible a leading part in public life, and strike out for myself, if I had the ability, a *statesman's* career." Washington as a young soldier displays the "haughty carriage . . . of a man born to have his will." Compare Wilson's avowal to Ellen Axson, on the acceptance of his first book (December, 1884) : "I feel as I suppose a general does who has gained a . . . foothold in the enemy's country. . . . My rejoicing . . . has in it a great deal that is stern and sober, like that of the strong man to run a race." Washington's firmness of purpose and his ability to meet additional responsibilities are stressed in the biography. We hear too of his "old passion for suc- cess"; and of the ardent, almost violent emotions held under control by the Mount Vernon planter-aristocrat. Compare again Wilson's confession to his fiancée (December, 1884) : "It isn't pleasant or convenient to have strong passions. I

[12] See August Heckscher, ed., *The Politics of Woodrow Wilson* (New York, 1956), pp. 40–48; Woodrow Wilson, *Congressional Government* (Cleveland, 1965), with an introduction by Walter Lipp- mann which maintains that as early as 1884, when he was writing the book, Wilson began to take a new view of the presidency under the inspiration of Grover Cleveland. James M. Burns, *Presidential Government* (Boston, 1956), pp. 94–95, shows that Lippmann's theory is unsound: Wilson sent the manuscript of *Congressional Government* to the publisher in October, 1884, before Cleveland had even been elected president.

have the uncomfortable feeling that I am carrying a volcano about with me." [13]

Other parallels could not have been anticipated by Wilson the academic. It is reasonable though to assume that within Wilson the president, toward the end of his heartbreaking White House years, there may have stirred the memory of things he had once written about the nation's first chief executive. The picture of Washington coolly withstanding the clamor for war in 1793 might seem to prefigure Wilson's own insistence on high-minded neutrality. There is the sense of a parallel sequence thereafter. Washington faces controversy ("Strong measures bred strong opposition"). Congressional opponents stir up trouble ("the opposition slowly pulled itself together . . . to concert a definite policy of action"). Washington remains serene (confident that "the right view will prevail; that the 'standard to which the wise and honest will repair' is also the standard to which the whole people will rally at last, if it be but held long and steadily enough on high to be seen of all"). He suffers terrible abuse, until at length the nation perceives he was in the right, and his enemies were wrong. But the abuse has taken its toll ("they had alienated his great spirit forever"), and so at the end of his second term he insists on resigning the office.

Prophetic utterances, the more oddly so when we recall that one of Wilson's inveterate enemies was his early rival in Washington scholarship, Senator Henry Cabot Lodge. It was young Lodge who once, while a magazine editor, turned down an article submitted by young Wilson, with the laconic notation "R.R.R."—received, rejected, returned. But of course there was nothing uncanny in these unconscious anticipations. When Woodrow Wilson wrote *George Washington* he had no idea that he himself might one day be president. He had only a hazily lofty notion of the scope and responsibilities of the office. What he did have was a burning though obscure ambition for statesmanlike fame. He employed the

[13] Donald Day, ed., *Woodrow Wilson's Own Story*, pp. 29–30.

metaphors of battle to describe his yearning, because he saw himself thwarted and challenged. In cheerful moments he felt irresistible; in not infrequent moments of depression he was conscious only that he would be resisted. Chronicling the career of George Washington, he unwittingly—as biographers usually do—disclosed his own buried hopes and fears. He revealed his strengths: energy, determination, integrity, intelligence, a kind of courtly charm. And he revealed something perhaps of his potential limitations: obstinacy, imperiousness, a disinclination to compromise, a fundamentally traditionalist outlook, a kind of glib superficiality. On balance his gifts were formidable. Among them, even with reservations, must be counted the stream of writings of his professorial years. Very few of his academic compeers managed to be so remarkably productive. But then Woodrow Wilson was no ordinary academic.

MARCUS CUNLIFFE

University of Sussex
Falmer, Brighton,
Sussex, England
July, 1968.

CONTENTS

GEORGE
WASHINGTON

CHAPTER I

IN WASHINGTON'S DAY

GEORGE WASHINGTON was bred a gentleman and a man of honor in the free school of Virginian society, with the generation that first learned what it meant to maintain English communities in America in safety and a self-respecting independence. He was born in a season of quiet peace, when the plot of colonial history was thickening noiselessly and almost without observation. He came to his first manhood upon the first stir of revolutionary events; caught in their movement,

he served a rough apprenticeship in arms at the thick of
the French and Indian war; the Revolution found him
a leader and veteran in affairs at forty-four; every turn
of fortune confirmed him in his executive habit of foresight and mastery; death spared him, stalwart and commanding, until, his rising career rounded and complete,
no man doubted him the first character of his age. "Virginia gave us this imperial man," and with him a companion race of statesmen and masters in affairs. It was
her natural gift, the times and her character being what
they were; and Washington's life showed the whole
process of breeding by which she conceived so great a
generosity in manliness and public spirit.

The English colonies in America lay very tranquil in
1732, the year in which Washington was born. It fell
in a season betweentimes, when affairs lingered, as if
awaiting a change. The difficulties and anxieties of
first settlement were long ago past and done with in all
the principal colonies. They had been hardening to
their "wilderness work," some of them, these hundred
years and more. England could now reckon quite six
hundred thousand subjects upon the long Atlantic sea-
board of the great continent which had lain remote and
undiscovered through so many busy ages, until daring
sailors hit upon it at last amidst the stir of the adventurous fifteenth century; and there was no longer
any thought that her colonists would draw back or
falter in what they had undertaken. They had grown
sedate even and self-poised, with somewhat of the air
of old communities, as they extended their settlements
upon the coasts and rivers and elaborated their means
of self - government amidst the still forests, and each
had already a bearing and character of its own. 'Twas

easy to distinguish the New-Englander from the man of the southern colonies; and the busy middle provinces that stretched back from the great bay at New York and from the waters of the spreading Delaware had also a breed of their own, like neither the men of the south nor the men of the northeast. Each region had bred for itself its characteristic communities, holding their own distinctive standards, knowing their own special purposes, living their own lives with a certain separateness and independence.

Virginia, the oldest of the colonies, was least to be distinguished by any private character of her own from the rural communities of England herself. Her population had come to her almost without selection throughout every stage of quick change and troubled fortune that England had seen during the fateful days since James Stuart became king; and Englishmen in Virginia were in no way radically distinguishable from Englishmen in England, except that they were provincials and frontiersmen. They had their own tasks and ways of life, indeed, living, as they did, within the old forests of a virgin continent, upon the confines of the world. But their tastes and temperament, spite of change and seclusion, they had in common with Englishmen at home. They gave leave to their opinions, too, with a like downright confidence and hardihood of belief, never doubting they knew how practical affairs should go. They had even kept the English character as they had received it, against the touch of time and social revolution, until Virginians seemed like elder Englishmen. England changed, but Virginia did not. There landed estates spread themselves with an ample acreage along the margins of the streams that everywhere threaded the virgin woodland; and the planter drew about him a body of dependants who knew no other master; to whom came, in their seclusion, none of that quick air of change that had so stirred in England throughout all her century of revolution. Some were his slaves, bound to him in perpetual subjection. Others were his tenants, and looked upon him as a sort of patron. In Maryland, where similar broad estates lay upon every shore, the law dubbed a great property here and there a "manor," and suffered it to boast its separate court baron and private jurisdiction. Virginian gentlemen enjoyed independence and authority without need of formal title.

There was but one centre of social life in Virginia: at Williamsburg, the village capital, where the Governor had his "palace," where stood the colonial college, where there were taverns and the town houses of sundry planters of the vicinage, and where there was much gay company and not a little formal ceremonial in the season. For the rest, the Old Dominion made shift to do without towns. There was no great mart to which all the trade of the colony was drawn. Ships came and went upon each broad river as upon a highway, taking and discharging freight at the private wharves of the several plantations. For every planter was his own merchant, shipping his tobacco to England, and importing thence in return his clothes, his tools, his household fittings, his knowledge of the London fashions and of the game of politics at home. His mechanics he found among his own slaves and dependants. Their "quarters" and the offices of his simple establishment showed almost like a village of themselves where they stood in irregular groups about his own square, broad-gabled house, with its airy hall and homelike living-rooms. He might have good plate upon his sideboard and on his table, palatable old wine in his cellar, and on the walls about him portraits of the stately men and dames from whom he took his blood and breeding. But there was little luxury in his life. Plain comfort and a homely abundance sufficed him. He was a gentleman, owned all he saw around him, exercised authority, and enjoyed consideration throughout the colony; but he was no prince. He lived always in the style of a provincial and a gentleman commoner, as his neighbors and friends did.

Slaves, dependants, and planters, however, did not by any means make up the tale of Virginia's population. She had been peopled out of the common stock of Englishmen, and contained her own variety. Most of the good land that lay upon the lower courses of the James, the York, the Rappahannock, and the Potomac rivers, and upon the bay on either hand, had been absorbed into the estates of the wealthier planters, who began to conceive themselves a sort of aristocracy; but not a few plain men owned their own smaller tracts within the broad stretches of country that lay back from the rivers or above their navigable depth. Upon the western front of the colony lived sturdy frontiersmen; and no man was so poor that he might not hope by thrift to hold his own with the best in the country. Few could own slaves in any number, for the negroes counted less than a third in a reckoning of the whole population. There were hired servants besides, and servants bound for a term of years by indenture; even criminals who could be had of the colony for private service; but most men must needs work their own plots of ground and devise a domestic economy without servants. A wholesome democratic spirit pervaded the colony, which made even the greater planters hesitate to give themselves airs. A few families that had thriven best and longest, and had built up great properties for themselves, did indeed lay claim, as royal governors found to their great displeasure, to a right to be heard before all others in the management of the government. But they could of course show no title but that of pride and long practice. 'Twas only their social weight in the parish vestries, in the Council, and in the House of Burgesses that gave them ascendency.

It was the same in church as in state. Virginia prided herself upon having maintained the Establishment without schism or sour dissent; but she had maintained it in a way all her own, with a democratic constitution and practice hardly to be found in the canons. Nominally the Governor had the right of presentation to all livings; but the vestries took care he should seldom exercise it, and, after they had had their own way for a century, claimed he had lost it by prescription. They chose and dismissed and ruled their ministers as they would. And the chief planters were nowhere greater figures than in the vestries of their own parishes, where so many neighborhood interests were passed upon—the care of the poor, the survey of estates, the correction of disorders, the tithe rates, and the maintenance of the church and minister. Sometimes the church building was itself the gift of the chief landowner of the parish; and the planters were always the chief rate-payers. Their leadership was natural and unchallenged. They enjoyed in their own neighborhood a sort of feudal pre-eminence, and the men about them easily returned in thought and estimation to that elder order of English life in which the chief proprietor of the country-side claimed as of course the homage of his neighbors. There were parishes, not a few, indeed, in which there was no such great planter to command consideration by a sort of social primacy. It was, after all, only here and there, and in the older parts of the colony, that affairs awaited the wish of privileged individuals. But it was the ascendency of the greater planters which most struck the imagination, and which gave to Virginia something of the same air and tone and turn of opinion that existed in England, with its veritable aristocracy, its lordly country gentlemen, its ancient distinctions of class and manners.

Those who took counsel in England concerning colonial affairs had constant occasion to mark the sharp contrast between the easy-going Virginians, who were no harder to govern than Englishmen everywhere, and the men of the northeastern colonies, with their dry reserve and their steadfast resolution not to be governed at all. These seemed unlike Englishmen elsewhere; a whit stiffer, shrewder, more self-contained and circumspect. They were, in fact, a peculiar people. Into New England had come a selected class, picked out of the general mass of Englishmen at home by test of creed. "God sifted the whole nation," one of their own preachers had told them, at election-time, in the far year 1668, "that he might send choice grain out into this wilderness." But the variety of the old life in England had been lost in the sifting. The Puritan, for all he was so strong and great a figure in his day, was but one man among a score in the quick and various English life. His single standard and manner of living, out of the many that strove for mastery in the old seats where the race was bred, had been transferred to New England ; and he had had separate and undisputed ascendency there to build new commonwealths as he would.   The Puritan Commonwealth in England had been the government of a minority. Cromwell had done his work of chastening with a might and fervor which he found, not in the nation, but in himself and in the stout men-at-arms and hardy reformers who stood with him while he purified England and brought upon all her foes a day of reckoning. The people had stood cowed and uneasy while he lived, and had broken into wild excess of joy at their release when he died. But in New England an entire community consented to the Puritan code and mastery with a hearty acquiescence. It was for this liberty they had come over sea.

And the thoughtful, strong-willed men who were their leaders had built, as they wished, a polity that should last.   Time wrought its deep changes in New England, as elsewhere, but the stamp set upon these Puritan settlements by the generation that founded them was not effaced. Trade made its characteristic mark upon them. Their merchants had presently their own fleets and markets. Their hardy people took more and more to the sea, lived the rough life of the ocean ways with a relish, beat in their small craft up and down the whole coast of the continent, drove bargains everywhere, and everywhere added a touch to their reputation as doughty sea-dogs and shrewd traders. The population that after a while came to New England did not stay to be sifted before attempting the voyage out of the Old World, and the quaint sedateness of the settlements began to be broken by a novel variety. New men beset the old order; a rough democracy began to make itself felt; and new elements waxed bold amidst the new conditions that time had wrought. The authority of the crown at last made a place of command for itself, despite every stubborn protest and astute evasion. It became necessary to be a trifle less observant of sect and creed, to cultivate, as far as might be, a temper of tolerance and moderation. But it was a slow change at best. The old order might be modified, but it could not so soon be broken. New England, through all her jurisdictions, remained a body of churches, as well as a body of towns, submissive to the doctrine and discipline of her learned clergy, keeping the old traditions distinct, indubitable, alike in her schools and her meeting-houses. Even in Rhode Island, where there had from the first been such diversity of creed and license of individual belief, there was little variety of type among the people, for all they counted themselves so free to be what they would. There was here a singular assortment, no doubt, of the units of the stock, but it was of the Puritan stuff, none the less, through all its variety.

New England, indeed, easily kept her character, for she lived apart. Her people mustered a full hundred thousand strong before the seventeenth century was out; her towns numbered many score, both upon the margins of the sea and within the forests; but she still lay within a very near frontier, pushed back only a short journey from the coast. Except where the towns of Connecticut ran in broken line close to the westward strait of Long Island Sound, a broad wilderness of untouched woodland, of thicketed hills and valleys that no white man yet had seen, stretched between them and Hudson's river, where New York's settlements lay upon the edge of a vast domain, reaching all the way to the great lakes and the western rivers. Not till 1725 did adventurous settlers dare go so far as the Berkshire Hills. "Our country," exclaimed Colonel Byrd, of Virginia, who had seen its wild interior, "has now been inhabited more than a hundred and thirty years, and still we hardly know anything of the Appalachian Mountains, which are nowhere above two hundred and fifty miles from the sea." A full century after the coming of the Pilgrims, New England, like Virginia, was still a frontier region, shut close about on every hand by thick forests beset by prowling bands of savages. She had as yet no intimate contact with the other colonies whose fortunes she was to share. Her simple life, quickened by adventure, but lacking the full pulse of old communities, kept, spite of slow change, to a single standard of conduct, made her one community from end to end, her people one people. She stood apart and compact, still soberly cultivating, as of old, a life and character all her own. Colonel Byrd noted how "New England improved much faster than Virginia," and was fain to think that "though these people may be ridiculed for some Pharisaical particularities in their worship and behavior, yet they were very useful subjects, as being frugal and industrious, giving no scandal or bad example." Public men in England, who had to face these "particularities in behavior," would hardly have agreed that the men of New England were good subjects, though they must have admitted their excellent example in thrift, and Virginia's need to imitate it.

This contrast between the northern and southern set

tlements was as old as their establishment, for Virginia
had from the first been resorted to by those who had
no other purpose than to better their fortunes, while
New England had been founded to be the home of a
creed and discipline ; but it was not until the Commonwealth was set up in England that the difference began
to be marked, and to give promise of becoming permanent. The English in Virginia, like the bulk of their
countrymen at home, had stood aghast at a king's death
upon the scaffold, and had spoken very hotly, in their
loyalty, of the men who had dared do the impious deed
of treason ; but when the *Guinea,* frigate, brought the
Commonwealth's commission into the river to demand
their submission, even Sir William Berkeley, the redoubtable Cavalier Governor, who had meant stubbornly to keep his province for the second Charles, saw
he must yield ; perceived there was too nice a balance
of parties in the colony to permit an execution of his
plans of resistance ; heard too many plain men in his
Council, and out of it, declare themselves very much of
a mind with the Puritans for the nonce in politics—
very willing to set up a democracy in Virginia which
should call itself a part of the Puritan state in England. But a great change had been wrought in Virginia while the Commonwealth lasted. When the Commonwealth's frigate came in at the capes she counted
scarcely fifteen thousand settlers upon her plantations,
but the next twenty years saw her transformed. By
1670 quite twenty-five thousand people were added to
the reckoning ; and of the new-comers a great multitude had left England as much because they hated the
Puritans as because they desired Virginia. They were
drawn out of that great majority at home to whom

Cromwell had not dared resort to get a new parliament in the stead of the one he had "purged." Many of them were of the hottest blood of the Cavaliers.

It was in these years Virginia got her character and received her leading gentry for the time to come—the years while the Commonwealth stood and royalists despaired, and the years immediately following the Restoration, when royalists took heart again and Englishmen turned with a new ardor to colonization as the times changed. Among the rest in the great migration came two brothers, John and Lawrence Washington, of a stock whose loyalty was as old as the Conquest. They came of a Norman family, the men of whose elder branch had for two hundred years helped the stout Bishops of Durham keep the border against the Scots; and in every branch of which men had sprung up to serve the king, the state, and the church with steadfastness and honor: dashing soldiers ready for the field at home or abroad, stout polemical priors, lawyers who knew the learning of their day and made their way to high posts in chancery, thrifty burghers, gallant courtiers, prosperous merchants—public-spirited gentlemen all. It was Colonel Henry Washington, cousin to the Virginian refugees, who had been with Rupert when he stormed Bristol, and who, with a handful of men, had made good an entrance into the town when all others were beaten back and baffled. It was he who had held Worcester for his master even after he knew Charles to be a prisoner in the hands of the parliamentary forces. "Procure his Majesty's commands for the disposal of this garrison," was all he would answer when Fairfax summoned him to surrender; "till then I shall make good the trust reposed in me. The

worst I know and fear not; if I had, the profession of
a soldier had not been begun." But it was an ill time
to revive the traditions of the knights of Durham;
loyalty only brought ruin. The Reverend Lawrence
Washington, uncle to the gallant colonel who was the
King's Governor at Worcester, had been cast out of his
living at Purleigh in 1643 by order of Parliament, upon
the false charge that he was a public tippler, oft drunk,
and loud to rail against the Parliament and its armies;
but really because, with all his race, he was a royalist,
and his living one of the best in Essex. It was his
sons who left off hoping to see things mend in England
and betook themselves to Virginia. His ruin had come
upon him while they were yet lads. He had been a
brilliant university scholar, fellow and lector of Brase-
nose, and rector of Oxford; but he could give his sons
neither a university career nor hope of fortune in the
humble parish pitying friends had found for him in an
obscure village of Essex; and when he was dead they
saw no reason why they should stay longer in England, where Cromwell was master.

John Washington, the oldest son of the unfortunate
rector, reached Virginia in 1656, having made his way
to the colony as "second man" to Edward Prescott,
merchant and ship-owner, in whose company he had
come; and his brother Lawrence, after passing to and
fro between England and the colony several times
upon errands of business, presently joined him in permanent residence upon the "northern neck" of rich
land that lay between the Rappahannock and the Potomac rivers. It was a region where every settlement
as yet was new. A few families had fixed themselves
upon it when Maryland drove Captain Clayborne and

his Virginian partisans forth from Kent Island in the years 1637 and 1638; and they had mustered numbers enough within a few years to send a representative to the House of Burgesses at Jamestown. But it was not till 1648 that the Assembly gave their lands a regular constitution as the County of Northumberland; for it was to this region the Indians had been driven by the encroachment of the settlements on the James and York, and for a while the Assembly had covenanted with the red men to keep it free from settlers. When once the ban was removed, however, in 1648, colonization set in apace—from the older counties of Virginia, from Maryland across the river and England over sea, from New England even, as if by a common impulse. In 1651 the Assembly found it necessary to create the two additional counties of Gloucester and Lancaster, and in 1653 still another, the County of Westmoreland, for the region's proper government, so quickly did it fill in; for the tide out of England already began to show its volume. The region was a natural seat of commerce, and merchants out of the trading ports of England particularly affected it. Rich land was abundant, and the Potomac ran strong and ample there, to carry the commerce alike of Virginia and Maryland to the bay, upon whose tributaries and inlets lay all the older settlements of both colonies. Lawrence Washington, though he still described himself, upon occasion, as "of Luton, County Bedford, merchant," found his chief profit where he made his home, with his brother John, in the new County of Westmoreland in Virginia. About them lived young men and old, come, like themselves, out of England, or drawn from the older settlements by the attractions of the goodly region, looking out, as it did, on either hand to a broad river and an easy trade. They felt it scarcely an expatriation to live there, so constantly did ships come and go between their wharves and the home ports at Bristol and London. It soon grew to be nothing singular to see well-to-do men go every year to England upon some errand of profit or pleasure.

It was with such a region and such stirring neighbors that the young Washingtons identified themselves while they were yet youths in their twenties; and there they prospered shrewdly with the rest. Prudent men and men of character readily accumulated estates in the untouched glades and forests of Westmoreland. The season of their coming, moreover, sadly as things seemed to go in 1656, turned out propitious. The Restoration opened a new era in the settlement of the country. Englishmen bestirred themselves to take actual possession of all the great coast-line they had so long claimed without occupying. "The Dutch had enjoyed New Netherland during the distractions of the reign of Charles I. without any other interruption" than the seizure of their post upon the Connecticut by the New-Englanders, and the aggressions alike of Swedes and English upon the Delaware; but the ministers of Charles II., though "for some time perplexed in what light to view them, whether as subjects or as aliens, determined at length that New Netherland ought in justice to be resumed," and the thing was presently accomplished in true sovereign fashion by force of arms. To the ducal province of New York, Penn presently added the thrifty Quaker colony which so promptly created a busy town and mart of trade at Philadelphia, and which pushed its rural settlements

back so speedily into the fertile lands that lay towards
the west. Then, while the new colonizing impulse still
ran strong, New Jersey, too, was added, with her limits
at one end upon the Hudson and the great bay at New
York, where she depended upon one rival for a port of
entry, and at the other upon the Delaware, where another rival presided over the trade of her southern
highway to the sea. To the southward straggling settlements upon Albemarle Sound grew slowly into the
colony of North Carolina; and still other settlements,
upon the rivers that lay towards Florida, throve so
bravely that Charleston presently boasted itself a substantial town, and South Carolina had risen to be a
considerable colony, prosperous, well ordered, and showing a quick life and individuality of her own.

A new migration had come out of England to the
colonies, and Englishmen looked with fresh confidence
to see their countrymen build an empire in America.
And yet perhaps not an empire of pure English blood.
New York was for long scarcely the less a Dutch province, for all she had changed owners, and saw Englishmen crowd in to control her trade.   There were Swedes
still upon the Delaware; and Pennsylvania mustered
among her colonists, besides a strange mixture out of
many nations — Germans, French, Dutch, Finns, and
English.   Even in Virginia, which so steadily kept its
English character, there were to be found groups of
French Huguenots and Germans who had been given
an ungrudging welcome; and South Carolina, though
strongly English too, had taken some of her best blood
out of France when Louis so generously gave the world
fifty thousand families of the finest breed of his kingdom by the revocation of the Edict of Nantes (1685).

The second quarter of the eighteenth century saw Scots-Irish enter Virginia and the middle colonies in hosts that for a time numbered ten thousand by the year. Pennsylvania alone, in the single year 1729, could reckon five thousand of these sturdy people who had come to multiply and strengthen her settlements. It was to the middle colonies that most foreigners came, and their coming gave to the towns and farms of that region a variety of tongues and customs, of manners and trades and ways of life and worship, to be found nowhere else. Boston, with all its trade and seafaring, had no touch of that cosmopolitan character which New York had taken on quite inevitably in the course of her varying fortunes, and which Philadelphia had assumed by choice; and rural Virginia scarcely felt amidst her scattered plantations the presence of the few families who lived by standards that were not English. The common feature of the new time, with its novel enterprises and its general immigration, was that the colonies everywhere, whether young or old, felt a keen stimulation and a new interest in affairs beyond their borders. A partial exchange of population began, a noticeable intercolonial migration. Whole congregations came out of New England to found towns in New Jersey, and individuals out of every colony ventured more freely than before to exchange one region for another, in order to coax health or fortune. Population was thus not a little compacted, while the colonies were drawn by insensible degrees to feel a certain community of interest and cultivate a certain community of opinion.

An expanding life, widened fields of enterprise and adventure, quickened hopes, and the fair prospects of a

growing empire everywhere heartened strong men in
the colonies to steady endeavor when the new century
opened—the scheming, calculating eighteenth century,
so unimpassioned and conventional at first, so tempest-
uous at last. The men of the colonies were not so
new as their continent in the ways of civilization. They
were Old World men put upon fresh coasts and a forest
frontier, to make the most of them, create markets,
build a new trade, become masters of vast resources as
yet untouched and incalculable ; and they did their work
for the most part with unmatched spirit and energy,
notwithstanding they were checked and hampered by
the statutes of the realm. The Navigation Acts forbade
the use of any but English ships in trade ; forbade all
trade, besides, which did not run direct to and from the
ports of England. The colonies must not pass England
by even in their trade with one another. What they
could not produce themselves they must bring straight
from England ; what they had to dispose of they must
send straight to England. If they would exchange
among themselves they must make England by the way,
so that English merchants should be their middlemen
and factors ; or else, if they must needs carry direct
from port to port of their own coasts, they must pay
such duties as they would have paid in English ports
had they actually gone the intermediate voyage to England preferred by the statutes. 'Twas the "usage of
other nations " besides England " to keep their plantation trade to themselves " in that day, as the Parliament
itself said and no man could deny, and 'twas the purpose
of such restrictions to maintain " a greater correspondence and kindness between " England and her subjects
in America, " keeping them in a firmer dependence,"

and at the same time "rendering them yet more bene-
ficial and advantageous" to English seamen, merchants,
wool-growers, and manufacturers; but it cost the colonists pride and convenience and profit to obey.

Some, who felt the harness of such law too smartly,
consoled themselves by inventing means to escape it.
The coast was long; was opened by many an unused
harbor, great and small; could not everywhere and always be watched by king's officers; was frequented by a
tolerant people, who had no very nice conscience about
withholding taxes from a sovereign whose messages and
commands came quickly over sea only when the wind held
fair for weeks together; and cargoes could be got both
out and in at small expense of secrecy and no expense at
all in duties. In short, smuggling was easy. 'Twas a
time of frequent wars, moreover, and privateering commissions were to be had for the asking; so that French
ships could be brought in with their lading, condemned,
and handsomely sold, without the trouble of paying
French prices or English port dues. Privateering, too,
was cousin-german to something still better; 'twas but
a sort of formal apprenticeship to piracy; and the quiet,
unused harbors of the coast showed many a place where
the regular profession might be set up. Veritable pirates
took the sea, hunted down what commerce they would
—English no less than French and Dutch and Spanish
—rendezvoused in lonely sounds, inlets, and rivers where
king's officers never came, and kept very respectable
company when they came at last to dispose of their
plunder at New York or Charleston, being men very
learned in subterfuges and very quick-fingered at brib-
ing. And then there was "the Red Sea trade," whose
merchants sent fleets to Madagascar in the season to ex-

change cargoes with rough men out of the Eastern seas,
of whom they courteously asked no questions. The
larger ports were full of sailors who waited to be engaged, not at regular wages, but "on the grand account"; and it took many weary years of hangman's
labor to bring enough pirates to the gallows to scotch
the ugly business. In 1717 it was reported in the colonies that there were quite fifteen hundred pirates on the
coast, full one-half of whom made their headquarters,
very brazenly, at New Providence in the Bahamas; and
there were merchants and mariners by the score who
had pangs of keen regret to see the breezy trade go
down, as the century drew on a decade or two, because
of the steady vigilance and stern endeavor of Governors
who had been straitly commanded to suppress it.

The Navigation Acts bred an irritation in the colonies
which grew with their growth and strengthened with
their consciousness of strength and capacity. Not because such restrictions were uncommon, but because the
colonies were forward and exacting. There was, indeed,
much to commend the legislation they resented. It at-
tracted the capital of English merchants to the American
trade, it went far towards securing English supremacy
on the seas, and it was strictly within the powers of
Parliament, as no man could deny. Parliament had an
undoubted right to regulate imperial interests, of this or
any other kind, even though it regulated them unreason-
ably. But colonies that reckoned their English population by the hundred thousand and lived by trade and
adventure would not long have brooked such a policy of
restraint had they had the leisure to fret over it. They
did not as yet have the leisure. The French stood men-
acingly at their western gates, through which the great

fur trade made its way; where the long rivers ran which threaded the central valleys of the continent; where the Mississippi stretched itself from north to south like a great body of dividing waters, flanking all the coast and its settlements—where alone a true mastery of the continent and its resources could be held. It would be time enough to reckon with Parliament touching the carrying trade when they had made good their title to what they were to trade withal.

The French had been a long time about their work, for they had done it like subjects, at the bidding of an ambitious king, rather than like free men striving as they pleased for themselves. But what they had done they had done systematically and with a fixed policy that did not vary, though ministers and even dynasties might come and go. The English had crowded to the coasts of the continent as they pleased, and had mustered their tens of thousands before the French reckoned more than a few hundreds. But the French had hit upon the mighty river St. Lawrence, whose waters came out of the great lakes and the heart of the continent; their posts were garrisons; what men they had they put forward, at each step of discovery, at some point of vantage upon lake or river, whence they were not easily dislodged. Their shrewd fur-traders and dauntless priests struck everywhere into the heart of the forests, leading forward both trade and conquest, until at last, through the country of the Illinois and out of far Lake Michigan, the streams had been found which ran down into the west to the flooding Mississippi. Colonists were sent to the mouth of the vast river, posts presently dotted its banks here and there throughout its length, trade passed up and down its spreading stream, and the English, their eyes at last caught by the stealthy movement, looked in a short space to see French settlements "running all along from our lakes by the back of Virginia and Carolina to the Bay of Mexico."

This was a business that touched the colonies to the quick. New York had her western frontiers upon the nearer lakes. Thence, time out of mind, had come the best furs to the markets at Albany, brought from tribe to tribe out of the farthest regions of the northwest. New England, with the French at her very doors, had to look constantly to her northern borders to keep them against the unquiet savage tribes the French every year stirred up against her. Virginia felt the French power among her savage neighbors too, the moment her people ventured across the Blue Ridge into the valley where many an ancient war-path ran; and beyond the Alleghanies she perceived she must stand in the very presence almost of the French themselves. English frontiersmen and traders, though they had no advancing military posts behind them, were none the less quick to go themselves deep into the shadowed wilderness, there to meet the French face to face in their own haunts. The Carolinas were hardly settled before their more adventurous spirits went straight into the far valley of the Tennessee, and made trade for themselves there against the coming of the French. Out of Virginia, too, and out of Pennsylvania, as well as out of New York, traders pressed towards the West, and fixed their lonely huts here and there along the wild banks of the Ohio. 'Twas diamond cut diamond when they met their French rivals in the wigwams of the Indian villages, and their canoes knew the waterways of the wilderness as well as any

man's. 'Twas they who learned at first hand what the
French were doing. They were like scouts sent out to
view the ground to be fought for.

This hazardous meeting of rival nations at the heart
of the continent meant many a deep change in the fortunes of the colonies. European politics straightway entered their counsels. Here was an end of their separateness and independence of England. Charles and
James and William all showed that they meant to be
veritable sovereigns, and had no thought but that the
colonists in America, like all other Englishmen, should
be their subjects; and here was their opportunity to be
masters upon an imperial scale and with an imperial excuse. In Europe, England beheld France her most formidable foe; she must look to it that Louis and his ministers take no advantage in America. The colonies, no
less than the Channel itself, were become the frontiers
of an empire—and there must be no trespass upon English soil by the French. The colonists must be rallied
to the common work, and, if used, they must be ruled
and consolidated.

As it turned out, the thing was quite impossible.
The colonies had too long been separate; their characters, their tempers, their interests, were too diverse and
distinct; they were unused to co-operate, and unwilling;
they were too slow to learn submission in anything.
The plan of grouping several of them under a single
governor was attempted, but they remained as separate
under that arrangement as under any other. Massachusetts would interest herself in nothing beyond her own
jurisdiction that did not immediately touch her safety
or advantage; New York cared little what the French
did, if only the Iroquois could be kept quiet and she

could get her furs in the season, and find a market for
them abroad or among the French themselves; Virginia
had no eye for any movement upon the frontiers that
did not menace her own fair valleys within the mountains with hostile occupation; the Carolinas were as yet
too young to be serviceable, and New Jersey too remote
from points of danger. Nowhere could either men or
supplies be had for use against the French except by the
vote of a colonial assembly. The law of the empire
might be what it would in the mouths of English
judges at home; it did not alter the practice of the colonies. The courts in England might say with what
emphasis they liked that Virginia, "being a conquered
country, their law is what the King pleases"; it was
none the less necessary for the King's Governor to
keep on terms with the people's representatives. "Our
government is so happily constituted," writes Colonel
Byrd to his friend in the Barbadoes, "that a governor
must first outwit us before he can oppress us. And if
ever he squeeze money out of us, he must first take care
to deserve it." Every colony held stoutly to a like
practice, with a like stubborn temper, which it was mere
folly to ignore. One and all they were even then "too
proud to submit, too strong to be forced, too enlightened
not to see all the consequences which must arise" should
they tamely consent to be ruled by royal command or
parliamentary enactment. Their obedience must be had
on their own terms, or else not had at all. Governors
saw this plainly enough, though the ministers at home
could not. Many a governor had his temper sadly
soured by the contentious obstinacy of the colonial assembly he was set to deal with. One or two died of sheer
exasperation. But the situation was not altered a whit.

When there is friction there must, sooner or later, be adjustment, if affairs are to go forward at all, and this contest between imperial system and colonial independence at last brought some things that had been vague to a very clear definition. 'Twas plain the colonies would not of themselves combine to meet and oust the French. They would supply neither men nor money, moreover. England must send her own armies to America, fight France there as she would have fought her in Europe, and pay the reckoning herself out of her own treasury, getting from the colonies, the while, only such wayward and niggardly aid as they chose to give. The colonies, meanwhile, might gather some of the fruits of experience; might learn how safe it was to be selfish, and how unsafe, if they hoped to prosper and be free; might perceive where their common interests lay, and their common power; might in some degree steady their lives and define their policy against the coming of more peaceful times. Two wars came and went which brought France and England to arms against each other in America, as in Europe, but they passed away without decisive incident in the New World, and there followed upon them thirty years of uneventful peace, during which affairs hung at a nice balance, and the colonies took counsel, each for itself, how they should prosper.

Virginia, meanwhile, had got the charter she was to keep. From the Potomac to the uncertain border of the Carolinas she had seen her counties fill with the men who were to decide her destiny. Her people, close upon a hundred thousand strong, had fallen into the order of life they were to maintain. They were no longer colonists merely, but citizens of a commonwealth of

which they began to be very proud, not least because
they saw a noble breed of public men spring out of
their own loins to lead them. Though they were scattered, they were not divided. There was, after all, no
real isolation for any man in Virginia, for all that he
lived so much apart and was a sort of lord within his
rustic barony. In that sunny land men were constantly
abroad, looking to their tobacco and the labor of all
kinds that must go forward, but would not unless they
looked to it, or else for the sheer pleasure of bestriding
a good horse, being quit of the house, and breathing
free in the genial air. Bridle-paths everywhere threaded
the forests; it was no great matter to ride from house
to house among one's neighbors; there were county-
court days, moreover, to draw the country-side together,
whether there was much business or little to be seen to.
Men did not thrive thereabouts by staying within doors,
but by being much about, knowing their neighbors, observing what ships came and went upon the rivers, and
what prices were got for the cargoes they carried away;
learning what the news was from Williamsburg and
London, what horses and cattle were to be had, and
what dogs, of what breeds. It was a country in which
news and opinions and friendships passed freely current;
where men knew each other with a rare leisurely intimacy, and enjoyed their easy, unforced intercourse
with a keen and lasting relish.

It was a country in which men kept their individuality very handsomely withal. If there was no town life,
there were no town manners either, no village conven-
tionalities to make all men of one carriage and pattern
and manner of living. Every head of a family was
head also of an establishment, and could live with a self-

respect and freedom which were subject to no man's private scrutiny. He had leave, in his independence, to be himself quite naturally, and did not need to justify his liberty by excuses. And yet he had responsibilities too, and a position which steadied and righted him almost in spite of himself. It required executive capacity to make his estate pay, and an upright way of life to maintain his standing. If he was sometimes loud and hectoring, or over-careless what he said or did, 'twas commonly because he was young or but half come into his senses; for his very business, of getting good crops of tobacco and keeping on dealing terms with his neighbors, demanded prudence and a conduct touched with consideration. He had to build his character very carefully by the plumb to keep it at an equilibrium, though he might decorate it, if it were but upright, as freely, as whimsically even, as he chose, with chance traits and self-pleasing tastes, with the full consent and tolerance of the neighborhood. He was his own man, might have his own opinions if he held them but courteously enough, might live his own life if he but lived it cleanly and without offence. 'Twas by their living rather than by their creed or their livelihood that men were assessed and esteemed.

It was not a life that bred students, though it was a life that begot thoughtfulness and leadership in affairs. Those who fell in the way of getting them had not a few books upon their shelves, because they thought every gentleman should have such means of knowing what the world had said and done before his day. But they read only upon occasion, when the weather darkened, or long evenings dragged because there were no guests in the house. Not much systematic education was possible where the population was so dispersed and separate. A few country schools undertook what was absolutely necessary, and gave instruction in such practical branches as every man must know something of who was to take part in the management of private and public business. For the rest, those who chose could get the languages from private tutors, when they were to be had, and then go over sea to read at the universities, or to Williamsburg when at last the colony had its own college of William and Mary. More youths went from the Northern Neck to England for their education, no doubt, than from any other part of Virginia. The counties there were somewhat closer than the rest to the sea, bred more merchants and travellers, kept up a more intimate correspondence both by travel and by letter with Bristol and London and all the old English homes. And even those who stayed in Virginia had most of them the tradition of refinement, spoke the mother tongue purely and with a proper relish, and maintained themselves somehow, with perhaps an added touch of simplicity that was their own, in the practices of a cultivated race.

No one in Virginia thought that " becoming a mere scholar " was " a desirable education for a gentleman." He ought to " become acquainted with men and things rather than books." Books must serve only to deepen and widen the knowledge he should get by observation and a free intercourse with those about him. When Virginians wrote, therefore, you might look to find them using, not studied phrases, but a style that smacked fresh of all the free elements of good talk—not like scholars or professed students, but like gentlemen of leisure and cultivated men of affairs—with a subtle, not unpleasing flavor of egotism, and the racy directness of speech, withal, that men may use who are sure of their position. Such was the writing of Robert Beverley, whose *History and Present State of Virginia,* published in London in 1705, spoke at first hand and authoritatively of affairs of which the world had heard hitherto only by uncertain report. He did not write the manly book because he had a pricking ambition to be an author, but because he loved Virginia, and wished to give such an account of her affairs as would justify his pride in her. He came of an ancient English family, whose ample means were scarcely more considerable in Virginia than they had been in Beverley, in Yorkshire. He had himself been carefully educated in England, and had learned to feel very much at home there; but the attractions of the old home did not wean him from his love of the new, where he had been born—that quiet land where men dealt with one another so frankly, where Nature was so genial in all her moods, and men so without pretence. Official occupations gave him occasion while yet a very young man to handle familiarly the records of the colony, the intimate letters of its daily life, and he took a proud man's pleasure in extracting from them, and from the traditions of those who still carried much of the simple history in their own recollections of a stirring life, a frank and genial story of what had been done and seen in Virginia. And so his book became "the living testimony of a proud and generous Virginian"—too proud to conceal his opinions or withhold censure where it was merited, too generous not to set down very handsomely whatever was admirable and of good report in the life of his people. His own manly character, speaking out everywhere, as it does, in lively phrase and candid meaning, is itself evidence of the wholesome native air he so praises in Virginia.

He thought himself justified in loving a country where "plantations, orchards, and gardens constantly afford fragrant and delightful walks. In their woods and fields they have an unknown variety of vegetables and other rarities of nature to discover and observe. They have hunting, fishing, and fowling, with which they entertain themselves in a thousand ways. Here is the most good nature and hospitality practised in the world, both towards friends and strangers; but the worst of it is this generosity is attended now and then with a little too much intemperance. The neighborhood is at much the same distance as in the country in England, but with this advantage, that all the better sort of people have been abroad and seen the world, by which means they are free from that stiffness and formality which discover more civility than kindness. And besides, the goodness of the roads and the fairness of the weather bring people oftener together."

Of a like quality of genuineness and good breeding is the writing of Colonel William Byrd, the accomplished master of Westover, who was of the same generation. He may well have been the liveliest man in Virginia, so piquant and irrepressible is the humor that runs through almost every sentence he ever wrote. It must be he wrote for pastime. He never took the pains to publish anything. His manuscripts lay buried a hundred years or more in the decent sepulture of private possession ere they were printed, but were even then as quick as when they were written. Beverley had often a grave smile for what he recorded, or a quiet sarcasm of tone in the

telling of it. "The militia are the only standing forces
in Virginia," he says, very demurely, and "they are
happy in the enjoyment of an everlasting peace." But
Colonel Byrd is very merry, like a man of sense, not
contriving the jest, but only letting it slip, revealing it;
looks very shrewdly into things, and very wisely, too,
but with an easy eye, a disengaged conscience, keeping
tally of the score like one who attends but is not too
deeply concerned. He was, in fact, very deeply engaged in all affairs of importance—no man more deeply
or earnestly ; but when he wrote 'twas not his chief
business to speak of that. He was too much of a gentleman and too much of a wit to make grave boast of
what he was doing.

No man born in Virginia had a greater property than
he, a house more luxuriously appointed, or a part to
play more princely ; and no man knew the value of
position and wealth and social consideration more ap-
preciatively. His breeding had greatly quickened his
perception of such things. He had had a long training
abroad, had kept very noble company alike in England
and on the Continent, had been called to the bar in the
Middle Temple and chosen a Fellow of the Royal
Society, and so had won his freedom of the world of
letters and of affairs. Yet he had returned to Virginia,
as all her sons did, with only an added zest to serve and
enjoy her. Many designs for her development throve
because of his interest and encouragement; he sought
her advantage jealously in her Council, as her agent in
England, as owner of great tracts of her fertile lands.
'Twas he who brought to her shores some of her best
settlers, gave her promise of veritable towns at Richmond and Petersburg, fought arbitrary power wherever

it showed itself in her government, and proved himself in every way "a true and worthy inheritor of the feelings and opinions of the old cavaliers of Virginia." But through all his busy life he carried himself like the handsome, fortunate man he was, with a touch of gayety, a gallant spirit of comradeship, a zest for good books, spirited men, and comely women—heartily, like a man who, along with honor, sought the right pleasures of the world.

Nothing daunted the spirits of this manly gentleman, not even rough work at the depths of the forest, upon the public business of determining the southern boundary-line of the colony, or upon the private business of seeing to his own distant properties in North Carolina. It gave him only the better chance to see the world; and he was never at a loss for something to do. There were stray books to be found even in the cabins of the remotest settlers; or, if not, there was the piquant literary gossip of those laughing times of Queen Anne, but just gone by, to rehearse and comment upon. Colonel Byrd was not at a loss to find interesting ways in which even a busy man might make shift to enjoy "the Carolina felicity of having nothing to do." A rough people lived upon that frontier in his day, who showed themselves very anxious to be put upon the southern side of the line; for, if taken into Virginia, "they must have submitted to some sort of order and government; whereas in North Carolina every one does what seems best in his own eyes." "They pay no tribute," he laughs, "either to God or to Cæsar." It would not be amiss, he thinks, were the clergy in Virginia, once in two or three years—not to make the thing burdensome —to "take a turn among these gentiles." " 'Twould

look a little apostolical," he argues, with the characteristic twinkle in his eye, " and they might hope to be re-
quited for it hereafter, if that be not thought too long
to tarry for their reward." A stray parson was to be
found once and again even at the depths of the forest—
on the Virginian side—though to find his humble quarters you must needs thread " a path as narrow as that
which leads to heaven, but much more dirty "; but a
stray parson was no great evangel. Colonel Byrd was
too sound a gentleman not to be a good churchman ; but
he accounted it no sin to see where the humor lurks
even in church. " Mr. Betty, the parson of the parish,
entertained us with a good, honest sermon," he chroni-
cles upon occasion ; " but whether he bought it, or borrowed it, would have been uncivil in us to inquire Be
that as it will, he is a decent man, with a double chin
that fits gracefully over his band. . . . When church was
done we refreshed our teacher with a glass of wine, and
then, receiving his blessing, took horse." 'Tis likely
Colonel Byrd would have found small amusement in
narrating the regular course of his life, his great errands
and permanent concerns of weighty business. That he
could as well leave to his biographer, should he chance
to have one. For himself, he chose to tell the unusual
things he had seen and heard and taken part in, and to
make merry as well as he might by the way.

The Virginian writers were not all country gentlemen. There were austere and stately scholars, too, like
the Reverend William Stith, who had held modest livings in more than one parish, had served the House of
Burgesses as chaplain, and the college, first as instructor
and then as president, until at length, having won " perfect leisure and retirement," he set himself in his last

days to straighten into order the confusion of early Virginian history. " Such a work," he reflected, " will be a noble and elegant entertainment for my vacant hours, which it is not in my power to employ more to my own satisfaction, or the use and benefit of my country." What with his scholarly love of documents set forth at length, however, his painstaking recital of details, and his roundabout, pedantic style, his story of the first seventeen years of the colony lingered through a whole volume; and his friends' laggard subscriptions to that single prolix volume discouraged him from undertaking another. There was neither art nor quick movement enough in such work, much as scholars have prized it since, to take the taste of a generation that lived its life on horseback and spiced it with rough sport and direct speech. They could read with more patience the plain, business - like sentences of the Reverend Hugh Jones's *Present State of Virginia*, and with more zest the downright, telling words in which the Reverend James Blair, "commissary" to the Bishop of London, spoke of their affairs.

James Blair, though born and bred in Scotland, educated at Edinburgh, and engaged as a minister at home till he was close upon thirty years of age, was as much a Virginian in his life and deeds as any man born in the Old Dominion. 'Twas he who had been the chief founder of the College of William and Mary, and who had served it as president through every vicissitude of fortune for fifty years. For fifty years he was a member, too, of the King's Council in the colony, and for fifty-eight the chief adviser of the mother Church in England concerning ecclesiastical affairs in Virginia. " Probably no other man in the colonial time did so much for the intellectual life of Virginia" as did this "sturdy and faithful" Scotsman. To the colonists, oftentimes, he seemed overbearing, dictatorial even, and, for all their " gentlemanly conformity to the Church of England," they did not mean to suffer any man to be set over them as bishop in Virginia; while to the royal governors he seemed sometimes a headstrong agitator and demagogue, so stoutly did he stand up for the liberties of the people among whom he had cast his lot. He was in all things a doughty Scot. He made very straight for the ends he deemed desirable; dealt frankly, honestly, fearlessly with all men alike; confident of being in the right even when he was in the wrong; dealing with all as he thought he ought to deal, " whether they liked it or not"; incapable of discouragement, as he was also incapable of dishonor ; a stalwart, formidable master of all work in church and college, piling up every day to his credit a great debt of gratitude from the colony, which honored him without quite liking him.

It was very noteworthy that masterful men of many kinds took an irresistible liking to Virginia, though they were but sent upon an errand to it. There was Alexander Spotswood, for example, who, after he had been twelve years Lieutenant-Governor in the stead of his lordship the Earl of Orkney, spent eighteen more good years, all he had left, upon the forty-odd thousand acres of land he had acquired in the fair colony, as a country gentleman, very busy developing the manufacture of iron, and as busy as there was any need to be as Postmaster-General of the colonies. He came of a sturdy race of gentlemen, had seen service along with Marlborough and my uncle Toby " with the army in Flanders," had gone much about the world upon many errands

and seen all manner of people, and then had found himself at last in Virginia when he was past forty. For all
its rough life, he liked the Old Dominion well enough
to adopt it as his home.   There was there, he said,
"less swearing, less profaneness, less drunkenness and
debauchery, less uncharitable feuds and animosities,
and less knavery and villany than in any part of the
world" where his lot had been.   Not all of his neighbors were gentlemen ; not very many could afford to
send their sons to England to be educated.   Men of all
sorts had crowded into Virginia : merchants and gentlemen not a few, but also commoner men a great many—
mariners, artisans, tailors, and men without settled trades
or handicrafts of any kind.   Spotswood had found it no
easy matter when he was Governor to deal patiently
with a House of Burgesses to which so many men of
"mean understandings" had been sent, and had allowed
himself to wax very sarcastic when he found how ignorant some of them were.   "I observe," he said, tartly,
"that the grand ruling party in your House has not
furnished chairmen of two of your standing committees
who can spell English or write common-sense, as the
grievances under their own handwriting will manifest."

'Twas not a country, either, where one could travel
much at ease, for one must ford the streams for lack
of bridges, and keep an eye sharply about him as he
travelled the rude forest roads when the wind was high
lest a rotten tree should fall upon him.   Nature was so
bountiful, yielded so easy a largess of food, that few men
took pains to be thrifty, and some parts of the colony
were little more advanced in the arts of life than North
Carolina, where, Colonel Byrd said, nothing was dear
"but law, physic, and strong drink."   No doubt the

average colonist in Virginia, when not sobered by important cares, was apt to be a fellow of coarse fibre, whose

> "addiction was to courses vain;
> His companies unlettered, rude, and shallow;
> His hours fill'd up with riots, banquets, sports;
> And never noted in him any study,
> Any retirement, any sequestration
> From open haunts and popularity."

But to many a scapegrace had come "reformation in a flood, with such a heady current, scouring faults," as to make a notable man of him. There were at least the traditions of culture in the colony, and enough men of education and refinement to leaven the mass. Life ran generously, even if roughly, upon the scattered plantations, and strong, thinking, high - bred men had somehow a mastery and leadership in it all which made them feel Virginia their home and field of honor.

Change of time and of affairs, the stir of growing life in Virginia as she ceased from being a mere colony and became a sturdy commonwealth, boasting her own breed of gentlemen, merchants, scholars, and statesmen, laid upon the Washingtons, as upon other men, a touch of transformation. Seventy-six years had gone by since John Washington came out of Bedfordshire and took up lands on Bridges' Creek in Westmoreland in Virginia, and still his children were to be found in the old seats he had chosen at the first. They had become thorough Virginians with the rest, woven into the close fibre of the new life. Westmoreland and all the counties that lay about it on the Northern Neck were strictly of a piece with the rest of Virginia, for all they had waited long to be settled. There the Washingtons had become country gentlemen of comfortable estate upon the accepted model. John had begotten Lawrence, and Lawrence had begotten Augustine. John had thriftily taken care to see his offspring put in a way to prosper at the very first. He had acquired a substantial property of his own where the land lay very fertile upon the banks of the Potomac, and he had, besides, by three marriages, made good a very close connection with several families that had thriven thereabouts before him. He had become a notable figure, indeed, among his neighbors ere he had been many years in the colony—a colonel in their militia, and their representative in the House of Burgesses; and they had not waited for his death to call the parish in which he lived Washington Parish. His sons and grandsons, though they slackened a little the pace he had set them in his energy at the outset, throve none the less substantially upon the estates he had left them, abated nothing of the dignity and worth they had inherited, lived simply, and kept their place of respect in the parish and state. Wars came and went without disturbing incident for them, as the French moved upon the borders by impulse of politics from over sea ; and then long peace set in, equally without incident, to stay a whole generation, while good farming went quietly forward, and politicians at home and in the colonies planned another move in their game. It was in the mid-season of this time of poise, preparation, and expectancy that George Washington was born, on the 22d of February, in the year 1732, " about ten in the morning," William Gooch, gentlest of Marlborough's captains, being Governor in Virginia. He came into the world at the plain but spacious homestead on Bridges' Creek, fourth son, fifth child, of Augustine Washington, and of the third generation from John Washington, son of the one-time rector of Purleigh. The homestead stood upon a green and gentle slope that fell away, at but a little distance, to the waters of the Potomac, and from it could be seen the broad reaches of the stream stretching wide to the Maryland shore beyond, and flooding with slow, full tide to the great bay below. The spot gave token of the quiet youth of the boy, of the years of grateful peace in which he was to learn the first lessons of life, ere war and the changing fortunes of his country hurried him to the field and to the council.

FAC-SIMILE OF THE ENTRY OF WASHINGTON'S BIRTH IN HIS MOTHER'S BIBLE

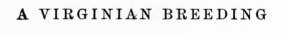

A VIRGINIAN BREEDING

GEORGE WASHINGTON was cast for his career by a very scant and homely training. Augustine Washington, his father, lacked neither the will nor the means to set him handsomely afoot, with as good a schooling, both in books and in affairs, as was to be had; he would have done all that a liberal and provident man should do to advance his boy in the world, had he lived to go with him through his youth. He owned land in four counties, more than five thousand acres all told, and lying upon both the rivers that refresh the fruitful Northern Neck; besides several plots of ground in the promising village of Fredericksburg, which lay opposite his lands upon the Rappahannock; and one-twelfth part of the stock of the Principio Iron Company, whose mines and furnaces in Maryland and Virginia yielded a better profit than any others in the two colonies. He had commanded a ship in his time, as so many of his neighbors had in that maritime province, carrying iron from the mines to England, and no doubt bringing convict laborers back upon his voyage home again. He himself raised the ore from the mines that lay upon his own land, close to the Potomac, and had it carried the easy six miles to the river. Matters were very well managed there, Colonel Byrd said, and no pains were spared to make the business profitable. Captain Washington had

represented his home parish of Truro, too, in the House
of Burgesses, where his athletic figure, his ruddy skin,
and frank gray eyes must have made him as conspicuous
as his constituents could have wished. He was a man
of the world, every inch, generous, hardy, independent.
He lived long enough, too, to see how stalwart and
capable and of how noble a spirit his young son was to
be, with how manly a bearing he was to carry himself in
the world ; and had loved him and made him his companion accordingly. But the end came for him before he
could see the lad out of boyhood. He died April 12,
1743, when he was but forty-nine years of age, and before George was twelve ; and in his will there was, of
course, for George only a younger son's portion. The
active gentleman had been twice married, and there were
seven children to be provided for. Two sons of the first
marriage survived. The bulk of the estate went, as
Virginian custom dictated, to Lawrence, the eldest son.
To Augustine, the second son, fell most of the rich lands
in Westmoreland. George, the eldest born of the second
marriage, left to the guardianship of his young mother,
shared with the four younger children the residue of the
estate. He was to inherit his father's farm upon the
Rappahannock, to possess, and to cultivate if he would,
when he should come of age ; but for the rest his fortunes were to make. He must get such serviceable
training as he could for a life of independent endeavor.
The two older brothers had been sent to England to get
their schooling and preparation for life, as their father
before them had been to get his—Lawrence to make
ready to take his father's place when the time should
come ; Augustine, it was at first planned, to fit himself
for the law. George could now look for nothing of the

kind. He must continue, as he had begun, to get such elementary and practical instruction as was to be had of schoolmasters in Virginia, and the young mother's care must stand him in the stead of a father's pilotage and oversight.

Fortunately Mary Washington was a wise and provident mother, a woman of too firm a character and too steadfast a courage to be dismayed by responsibility. She had seemed only a fair and beautiful girl when Augustine Washington married her, and there was a romantic story told of how that gallant Virginian sailor and gentleman had literally been thrown at her feet out of a carriage in the London streets by way of introduction—where she, too, was a visiting stranger out of Virginia. But she had shown a singular capacity for business when the romantic days of courtship were over. Lawrence Washington, too, though but five-and-twenty when his father died and left him head of the family, proved himself such an elder brother as it could but better and elevate a boy to have. For all he was so young, he had seen something of the world, and had already made notable friends. He had not returned home out of England until he was turned of twenty-one, and he had been back scarcely a twelvemonth before he was off again, to seek service in the war against Spain. The colonies had responded with an unwonted willingness and spirit in 1740 to the home government's call for troops to go against the Spaniard in the West Indies; and Lawrence Washington had sought and obtained a commission as captain in the Virginian regiment which had volunteered for the duty. He had seen those terrible days at Cartagena, with Vernon's fleet and Wentworth's army, when the deadly heat and blighting damps of the

tropics wrought a work of death which drove the English forth as no fire from the Spanish cannon could. He
had been one of that devoted force which threw itself
twelve hundred strong upon Fort San Lazaro, and came
away beaten with six hundred only. He had seen the
raw provincials out of the colonies carry themselves as gallantly as any veterans through all the fiery trial; had seen
the storm and the valor, the vacillation and the blunder-
ing, and the shame of all the rash affair; and had come
away the friend and admirer of the gallant Vernon, despite his headstrong folly and sad miscarriage. He had
reached home again, late in the year 1742, only to see
his father presently snatched away by a sudden illness,
and to find himself become head of the family in his
stead. All thought of further service away from home
was dismissed. He accepted a commission as major in
the colonial militia, and an appointment as adjutant-
general of the military district in which his lands lay ;
but he meant that for the future his duties should be
civil rather than military in the life he set himself to
live, and turned very quietly to the business and the
social duty of a proprietor among his neighbors in
Fairfax County, upon the broad estates to which he
gave the name Mount Vernon, in compliment to the
brave sailor whose friend he had become in the far, unhappy South.

Marriage was, of course, his first step towards domes-
tication, and the woman he chose brought him into new
connections which suited both his tastes and his training. Three months after his father's death he married
Anne Fairfax, daughter to William Fairfax, his neighbor. 'Twas William Fairfax's granduncle Thomas,
third Lord Fairfax, who had in that revolutionary year

1646 summoned Colonel Henry Washington to give into
his hands the city of Worcester, and who had got so sharp
an answer from the King's stout soldier. But the Fairfaxes had soon enough turned royalists again when they
saw whither the Parliament men would carry them. A
hundred healing years had gone by since those unhappy
days when the nation was arrayed against the King.
Anne Fairfax brought no alien tradition to the household of her young husband. Her father had served the
King, as her lover had—with more hardship than reward, as behooved a soldier—in Spain and in the Bahamas; and was now, when turned of fifty, agent here in
Virginia to his cousin Thomas, sixth Baron Fairfax, in
the management of his great estates, lying upon the
Northern Neck and in the fruitful valleys beyond.
William Fairfax had been but nine years in the colony,
but he was already a Virginian like his neighbors, and,
as collector of his Majesty's customs for the South Potomac and President of the King's Council, no small
figure in their affairs—a man who had seen the world
and knew how to bear himself in this part of it.

In 1746 Thomas, Lord Fairfax, himself came to Virginia—a man strayed out of the world of fashion at
fifty-five into the forests of a wild frontier. The better
part of his ancestral estates in Yorkshire had been sold
to satisfy the creditors of his spendthrift father. These
untilled stretches of land in the Old Dominion were now
become the chief part of his patrimony. 'Twas said,
too, that he had suffered a cruel misadventure in love at
the hands of a fair jilt in London, and so had become
the austere, eccentric bachelor he showed himself to be
in the free and quiet colony. A man of taste and culture, he had written with Addison and Steele for the

Spectator; a man of the world, he had acquired, for all his reserve, that easy touch and intimate mastery in dealing with men which come with the long practice of such men of fashion as are also men of sense. He brought with him to Virginia, though past fifty, the fresh vigor of a young man eager for the free pioneer life of such a province. He tarried but two years with his cousin, where the colony had settled to an ordered way of living. Then he built himself a roomy lodge, shadowed by spreading piazzas, and fitted with such simple appointments as sufficed for comfort at the depths of the forest, close upon seventy miles away, within the valley of the Shenandoah, where a hardy frontier people had but begun to gather. The great manor-house he had meant to build was never begun. The plain comforts of "Greenway Court" satisfied him more and more easily as the years passed, and the habits of a simple life grew increasingly pleasant and familiar, till thirty years and more had slipped away and he was dead, at ninety-one—broken-hearted, men said, because the King's government had fallen upon final defeat and was done with in America.

It was in the company of these men, and of those who naturally gathered about them in that hospitable country, that George Washington was bred. "A stranger had no more to do," says Beverley, "but to inquire upon the road where any gentleman or good housekeeper lived, and there he might depend upon being received with hospitality"; and 'twas certain many besides strangers would seek out the young major at Mount Vernon whom his neighbors had hastened to make their representative in the House of Burgesses, and the old soldier of the soldierly house of Fairfax who was President of the King's Council, and so next to the Governor himself. A boy who was much at Mount Vernon and at Mr. Fairfax's seat, Belvoir, might expect to see not a little that was worth seeing of the life of the colony. George was kept at school until he was close upon sixteen; but there was ample vacation-time for visiting. Mrs. Washington did not keep him at her apron-strings. He even lived, when it was necessary, with his brother Augustine, at the old home on Bridges' Creek, in order to be near the best school that was accessible, while the mother was far away on the farm that lay upon the Rappahannock. Mrs. Washington saw to it, nevertheless, that she should not lose sight of him altogether. When he was fourteen it was proposed that he should be sent to sea, as so many lads were, no doubt, from that maritime province; but the prudent mother preferred he should not leave Virginia, and the schooling went on as before—the schooling of books and manly sports. Every lad learned to ride—to ride colt or horse, regardless of training, gait, or temper —in that country, where no one went afoot except to catch his mount in the pasture. Every lad, black or white, bond or free, knew where to find and how to take the roving game in the forests. And young Washington, robust boy that he was, not to be daunted while that strong spirit sat in him which he got from his father and mother alike, took his apprenticeship on horseback and in the tangled woods with characteristic zest and ardor.

He was, above all things else, a capable, executive boy. He loved mastery, and he relished acquiring the most effective means of mastery in all practical affairs. His very exercise-books used at school gave proof of it.

They were filled, not only with the rules, formulæ, diagrams, and exercises of surveying, which he was taking special pains to learn, at the advice of his friends, but also with careful copies of legal and mercantile papers, bills of exchange, bills of sale, bonds, indentures, land warrants, leases, deeds, and wills, as if he meant to be a lawyer's or a merchant's clerk. It would seem that, passionate and full of warm blood as he was, he conned these things as he studied the use and structure of his fowling-piece, the bridle he used for his colts, his saddle-girth, and the best ways of mounting. He copied these forms of business as he might have copied Beverley's account of the way fox or 'possum or beaver was to be taken or the wild turkey trapped. The men he most admired—his elder brothers, Mr. Fairfax, and the gentlemen planters who were so much at their houses—were most of them sound men of business, who valued good surveying as much as they admired good horsemanship and skill in sport. They were their own merchants, and looked upon forms of business paper as quite as useful as ploughs and hogsheads. Careful exercise in such matters might well enough accompany practice in the equally formal minuet in Virginia. And so this boy learned to show in almost everything he did the careful precision of the perfect marksman.

In the autumn of 1747, when he was not yet quite sixteen, George quit his formal schooling, and presently joined his brother Lawrence at Mount Vernon, to seek counsel and companionship. Lawrence had conceived a strong affection for his manly younger brother. Himself a man of spirit and honor, he had a high-hearted man's liking for all that he saw that was indomitable and well-purposed in the lad, a generous man's tenderness in looking to the development of this thoroughbred boy; and he took him into his confidence as if he had been his own son. Not only upon his vacations now, but almost when he would, and as if he were already himself a man with the rest, he could live in the comradeship that obtained at Belvoir and Mount Vernon. Men of all sorts, it seemed, took pleasure in his company. Lads could be the companions of men in Virginia. Her outdoor life of journeyings, sport, adventure, put them, as it were, upon equal terms with their elders. where spirit, audacity, invention, prudence, manliness, resource, told for success and comradeship. Young men and old can be companions in arms, in sport, in woodcraft, and on the trail of the fox. 'Twas not an indoor life of conference, but an outdoor life of affairs in this rural colony. One man, indeed, gave at least a touch of another quality to the life Washington saw. This was Lord Fairfax, who had been almost two years in Virginia when the boy quit school, and who was now determined, as soon as might be, to take up his residence at his forest lodge within the Blue Ridge. George greatly struck his lordship's fancy, as he did that of all capable men, as a daring lad in the hunt and a sober lad in counsel; and, drawn into such companionship, he learned a great deal that no one else in Virginia could have taught him so well — the scrupulous deportment of a high-bred and honorable man of the world; the use of books by those who preferred affairs; the way in which strength may be rendered gracious, and independence made generous. A touch of Old World address was to be learned at Belvoir.

His association with Lord Fairfax, moreover, put him in the way of making his first earnings as a surveyor.

Fairfax had not come to America merely to get away from the world of fashion in London and bury himself in the wilderness. His chief motive was one which did him much more credit, and bespoke him a man and a true colonist. It was his purpose, he declared, to open up, settle, and cultivate the vast tracts of beautiful and fertile land he had inherited in Virginia, and he proved his sincerity by immediately setting about the business. It was necessary as a first step that he should have surveys made, in order that he might know how his lands lay, how bounded and disposed through the glades and upon the streams of the untrodden forests; and in young Washington he had a surveyor ready to his hand. The lad was but sixteen, indeed; was largely self-taught in surveying; and had had no business yet that made test of his quality. But surveyors were scarce, and boys were not tender at sixteen in that robust, out-of-door colony. Fairfax had an eye for capacity. He knew the athletic boy to be a fearless woodsman, with that odd, calm judgment looking forth at his steady gray eyes; perceived how seriously he took himself in all that he did, and how thorough he was at succeeding; and had no doubt he could run his lines through the thicketed forests as well as any man. At any rate, he commissioned him to undertake the task, and was not disappointed in the way he performed it. Within a very few weeks Washington conclusively showed his capacity. In March, 1748, with George Fairfax, William Fairfax's son, for company, he rode forth with his little band of assistants through the mountains to the wild country where his work lay, and within the month almost he was back again, with maps and figures which showed his lordship very clearly what lands he had upon the

sparkling Shenandoah and the swollen upper waters of
the Potomac. 'Twas all he wanted before making his
home where his estate lay in the wilderness. Before the
year was out he had established himself at Greenway
Court; huntsmen and tenants and guests had found
their way thither, and life was fairly begun upon the
rough rural barony.

It had been wild and even perilous work for the young
surveyor, but just out of school, to go in the wet spring-
time into that wilderness, when the rivers were swollen
and ugly with the rains and melting snows from off the
mountains, where there was scarcely a lodging to be
had except in the stray, comfortless cabins of the scattered settlers, or on the ground about a fire in the open
woods, and where a woodman's wits were needed to
come even tolerably off. But there was a strong relish
in such an experience for Washington, which did not
wear off with the novelty of it. There is an unmistakable note of boyish satisfaction in the tone in which he
speaks of it. " Since you received my letter in October
last," he writes to a young comrade, " I have not sleep'd
above three nights or four in a bed, but, after walking a
good deal all the day, I lay down before the fire upon a
little hay, straw, fodder, or bear-skin, whichever is to be
had, with man, wife, and children, like a parcel of dogs
and cats; and happy is he who gets the berth nearest
the fire. . . . I have never had my clothes off, but lay
and sleep in them, except the few nights I have lay'n
in Frederick Town." For three years he kept steadily
at the trying business, without loss either of health or
courage, now deep in the forests laboriously laying off
the rich bottom lands and swelling hill-sides of that
wild but goodly country between the mountains, now at

Greenway Court with his lordship, intent upon the busy life there,—following the hounds, consorting with huntsmen and Indians and traders, waiting upon the ladies who now and again visited the lodge; when other occupations failed, reading up and down in his lordship's copy of the *Spectator*, or in the historians who told the great English story. His first success in surveying brought him frequent employment in the valley. Settlers were steadily making their way thither, who must needs have their holdings clearly bounded and defined. Upon his lordship's recommendation and his own showing of what he knew and could do, he obtained appointment at the hands of the President and Master of William and Máry, the colony's careful agent in the matter, as official surveyor for Culpeper County, "took the usual oaths to his Majesty's person and government," and so got for his work the privilege of authoritative public record.

Competent surveyors were much in demand, and, when once he had been officially accredited in his profession, Washington had as much to do both upon new lands and old as even a young man's energy and liking for an independent income could reasonably demand. His home he made with his brother at Mount Vernon, where he was always so welcome; and he was as often as possible with his mother at her place upon the Rappahannock, to lend the efficient lady such assistance as she needed in the business of the estate she held for herself and her children. At odd intervals he studied tactics, practised the manual of arms, or took a turn at the broadsword with the old soldiers who so easily found excuses for visiting Major Washington at Mount Vernon. But, except when winter weather forbade him the fields, he was abroad, far and near, busy with his sur-

veying, and incidentally making trial of his neighbors
up and down all the country-side round about, as his
errands threw their open doors in his way. His pleasant bearing and his quiet satisfaction at being busy, his
manly, efficient ways, his evident self-respect, and his
frank enjoyment of life, the engaging mixture in him of
man and boy, must have become familiar to everybody
worth knowing throughout all the Northern Neck.

But three years put a term to his surveying. In 1751
he was called imperatively off, and had the whole course
of his life changed, by the illness of his brother. Lawrence Washington had never been robust; those long
months spent at the heart of the fiery South with Vernon's fever-stricken fleet had touched his sensitive constitution to the quick, and at last a fatal consumption
fastened upon him. Neither a trip to England nor the
waters of the warm springs at home brought him re-
cuperation, and in the autumn of 1751 his physician
ordered him to the Bahamas for the winter. George,
whom he so loved and trusted, went with him, to nurse
and cheer him. But even the gentle sea-air of the
islands wrought no cure of the stubborn malady. The
sterling, gifted, lovable gentleman, who had made his
quiet seat at Mount Vernon the home of so much that
was honorable and of good report, came back the next
summer to die in his prime, at thirty-four. George found
himself named executor in his brother's will, and looked
to of a sudden to guard all the interests of the young
widow and her little daughter in the management of a
large estate. That trip to the Bahamas had been his
last outing as a boy. He had enjoyed the novel journey
with a very keen and natural relish while it promised
his brother health. The radiant air of those summer

isles had touched him with a new pleasure, and the cordial hospitality of the homesick colonists had added the satisfaction of a good welcome. He had braved the small-pox in one household with true Virginian punctilio rather than refuse an invitation to dinner, had taken the infection, and had come home at last bearing some permanent marks of a three weeks' sharp illness upon him. But he had had entertainment enough to strike the balance handsomely against such inconveniences, had borne whatever came in his way very cheerily, with that wholesome strength of mind which made older men like him, and would have come off remembering nothing but the pleasure of the trip had his noble brother only found his health again. As it was, Lawrence's death put a final term to his youth. Five other executors were named in the will; but George, as it turned out, was to be looked to to carry the burden of administration, and gave full proof of the qualities that had made his brother trust him with so generous a confidence.

His brother's death, in truth, changed everything for him. He seemed of a sudden to stand as Lawrence's representative. Before they set out for the Bahamas Lawrence had transferred to him his place in the militia, obtaining for him, though he was but nineteen, a commission as major and district adjutant in his stead ; and after his return, in 1752, Lieutenant-Governor Dinwiddie, the crown's new representative in Virginia, added still further to his responsibilities as a soldier by reducing the military districts of the colony to four, and assigning to him one of the four, under a renewed commission as major and adjutant-general. His brother's will not only named him an executor, but also made him residuary legatee of the estate of Mount Vernon in case his child should die. He had to look to the discipline and accoutrement of the militia of eleven counties, aid his mother in her business, administer his brother's estate, and assume on all hands the duties and responsibilities of a man of affairs when he was but just turned of twenty.

The action of the colonial government in compacting the organization and discipline of the militia by reducing the number of military districts was significant of a sinister change in the posture of affairs beyond the borders. The movements of the French in the West had of late become more ominous than ever; 'twas possible the Virginian militia might any day see an end of that "everlasting peace" which good Mr. Beverley had smiled to see them complacently enjoy, and that the young major, who was now Adjutant-General of the Northern Division, might find duties abroad even more serious and responsible than his duties at home. Whoever should be commissioned to meet and deal with the French upon the western rivers would have to handle truly critical affairs, decisive of the fate of the continent, and it looked as if Virginia must undertake the fateful business. The northern borders, indeed, were sadly harried by the savage allies of the French; the brunt of the fighting hitherto had fallen upon the hardy militiamen of Massachusetts and Connecticut in the slow contest for English mastery upon the continent. But there was really nothing to be decided in that quarter. The French were not likely to attempt the mad task of driving out the thickly set English population, already established, hundreds of thousands strong, upon the eastern coasts. Their true lines of conquest ran within. Their strength lay in their command of the great watercourses which flanked the English colonies both north and west. 'Twas a long frontier to hold, that mazy line of lake and river that ran all the way from the Gulf of St. Lawrence to the wide mouths of the sluggish Mississippi. Throughout all the posts and settlements that lay upon it from end to end there were scarcely eighty thousand Frenchmen, while the English teemed upon the coasts more than a million strong. But the forces of New France could be handled like an army, while the English swarmed slowly westward, without discipline or direction, the headstrong subjects of a distant government they would not obey, the wayward constituents of a score of petty and jealous assemblies tardy at planning, clumsy at executing plans. They were still far away, too, from the mid-waters of the lakes and from the royal stream of the Mississippi itself, where lonely boats floated slowly down, with their cargoes of grain, meat, tallow, tobacco, oil, hides, and lead, out of the country of the Illinois, past the long, thin line of tiny isolated posts, to the growing village at New Orleans and the southern Gulf. But they were to be feared, none the less. If their tide once flowed in, the French well knew it could not be turned back again. It was not far away from the Ohio now ; and if once settlers out of Pennsylvania and Virginia gained a foothold in any numbers on that river, they would control one of the great highways that led to the main basins of the continent. It was imperative they should be effectually forestalled, and that at once.

The Marquis Duquesne, with his quick soldier blood, at last took the decisive step for France. He had hardly come to his colony, to serve his royal master as Governor upon the St. Lawrence, when he determined to occupy the upper waters of the Ohio, and block the western passes against the English with a line of military posts. The matter did not seem urgent to the doubting ministers at Versailles. " Be on your guard against new undertakings," said official letters out of France; " private interests are generally at the bottom of them." But Duquesne knew that it was no mere private interest of fur trader or speculator that was at stake now. The rivalry between the two nations had gone too far to make it possible to draw back. Military posts had already been established by the bold energy of the French at Niagara, the key to the western lakes, and at Crown Point upon Champlain, where lake and river struck straight towards the heart of the English trading settlements upon the Hudson. The English, accepting the challenge, had planted themselves at Oswego, upon the very lake route itself, and had made a port there to take the furs that came out of the West, and, though very sluggish in the business, showed purpose of aggressive movement everywhere that advantage offered. English settlers by the hundred were pressing towards the western mountains in Pennsylvania, and down into that " Virginian Arcady," the sweet valley of the Shenandoah: thrifty Germans, a few; hardy Scots-Irish, a great many—the blood most to be feared and checked. It was said that quite three hundred English traders passed the mountains every year into the region of the Ohio. Enterprising gentlemen in Virginia—Lawrence and Augustine Washington among the rest—had joined influential partners in London in the formation of an Ohio Company for the settlement of the western country and the absorption of the western trade; had sent out men who knew the region to make interest with the Indians and fix upon points of vantage for trading-posts and settlements; had already set out upon the business by erecting storehouses at Will's Creek, in the heart of the Alleghanies, and, farther westward still, upon Redstone Creek, a branch of the Monongahela itself.

It was high time to act; and Duquesne, having no colonial assembly to hamper him, acted very promptly. When spring came, 1753, he sent fifteen hundred men into Lake Erie, to Presque Isle, where a fort of squared logs was built, and a road cut through the forests to a little river whose waters, when at the flood, would carry boats direct to the Alleghany and the great waterway of the Ohio itself. An English lieutenant at Oswego had descried the multitudinous fleet of canoes upon Ontario carrying this levy to its place of landing in the lake beyond, and a vagrant Frenchman had told him plainly what it was. It was an army of six thousand men, he boasted, going to the Ohio, " to cause all the English to quit those parts." It was plain to every English Governor in the colonies who had his eyes open that the French would not stop with planting a fort upon an obscure branch of the Alleghany, but that they would indeed press forward to take possession of the Ohio, drive every English trader forth, draw all the native tribes to their interest by force or favor, and close alike the western lands and the western trade in very earnest against all the King's subjects.

Governor Dinwiddie was among the first to see the danger and the need for action, as, in truth, was very natural. In office and out, his study had been the colonial trade, and he had been merchant and official now a long time. He was one of the twenty stockholders of the Ohio Company, and had come to his governorship in Virginia with his eye upon the western country. He had but to look about him to perceive that Virginia would very likely be obliged to meet the crisis unaided, if, indeed, he could induce even her to meet it. Governor Hamilton, of Pennsylvania, also saw how critically affairs stood, it is true, and what ought to be done. His agents had met and acted with the agents of the Ohio Company already in seeking Indian alliances and fixing upon points of vantage beyond the Alleghanies. But the Pennsylvania Assembly could by no argument or device be induced to vote money or measures in the business. The placid Quaker traders were as stubborn as the stolid German farmers. They opposed warlike action on principle. The Germans opposed it because they could not for the life of them see the necessity of parting with their money to send troops upon so remote an errand. Dinwiddie did not wait or parley. He acted first, and consulted his legislature afterwards. It was in his Scots blood to take the business very strenuously, and in his trader's blood to take it very anxiously. He had kept himself advised from the first of the movements of the French. Their vanguard had scarcely reached Presque Isle ere he despatched letters to England apprising the government of the danger. Answer had come very promptly, too, authorizing him to build forts upon the Ohio, if he could get the money from the Burgesses; and meantime, should the French trespass further, "to require of them peaceably to depart." If they would not desist for a warning, said his Majesty, "we do hereby strictly charge and command you to drive them off by force of arms."

Even to send a warning to the French was no easy matter when the King's letter came and the chill autumn rains were at hand. The mountain streams, already swollen, presently to be full of ice, would be very dangerous for men and horses, and the forests were likely enough to teem with hostile savages, now the French were there. A proper messenger was found and despatched, nevertheless — young Major George Washington, of the Northern District. The errand lay in his quarter; his three years of surveying at the heart of the wilderness had made him an experienced woodsman and hardy traveller, had tested his pluck and made proof of his character; he was well known upon the frontier, and his friends were very influential, and very cordial in recommending him for this or any other manly service that called for steadiness, hardihood, and resource. Dinwiddie had been a correspondent of Lawrence Washington's ever since the presidency of the Ohio Company had fallen to the young Virginian upon the death of his neighbor Thomas Lee, writing to him upon terms of intimacy. He knew the stock of which George, the younger brother, came, and the interests in which he might be expected to embark with ardor; he could feel that he took small risk in selecting such an agent. Knowing him, too, thus through his family and like a friend, he did not hesitate in writing to Governor Hamilton, of Pennsylvania, to speak of this youth of twenty-one as "a person of distinction."

Washington performed his errand as Dinwiddie must have expected he would. He received his commission and the Governor's letter to the French commandant on the last day of October, and set out the same day for the mountains. Jacob Vanbraam, the Dutch soldier of fortune who had been his fencing-master at Mount Vernon, accompanied him as interpreter, and Christopher

Gist, the hardy, self-reliant frontier trader, whom the
Ohio Company had employed to make interest for them
among the Indians of the far region upon the western
rivers which he knew so well, was engaged to act as his
guide and counsellor ; and with a few servants and pack-
horses he struck straight into the forests in the middle
of bleak November. It was the 11th of December before the jaded party rode, in the cold dusk, into the
drenched and miry clearing where the dreary little fort
stood that held the French commander. Through two
hundred and fifty miles and more of forest they had
dragged themselves over swollen rivers, amidst an almost
ceaseless fall of rain or snow, with not always an Indian
trail, even, or the beaten track of the bison, to open the
forest growth for their flagging horses, and on the
watch always against savage treachery. It had become
plain enough before they reached their destination what
answer they should get from the French. Sixty miles
nearer home than these lonely headquarters of the French
commander at Fort Le Bœuf they had come upon an
outpost where the French colors were to be seen flying
from a house from which an English trader had been
driven out, and the French officers there had uttered
brutally frank avowal of their purpose in that wilderness
as they sat at wine with the alert and temperate young
Virginian. "It was their absolute design," they said,
"to take possession of the Ohio, and, by G—, they
would do it. . . . They were sensible the English
could raise two men for their one, yet they knew their
motions were too slow and dilatory to prevent any undertaking of theirs." The commandant at Fort Le
Bœuf received the wayworn ambassador very courteously, and even graciously—a thoughtful elderly man,

Washington noted him, "with much the air of a soldier"
—but would make no profession even that he would
consider the English summons to withdraw; and the
little party of Englishmen presently turned back amidst
the winter's storms to carry through the frozen wilderness a letter which boasted the French lawful masters
of all the continent beyond the Alleghanies. When
Washington reached Williamsburg, in the middle of
January, 1754, untouched by even the fearful fatigues
and anxieties of that daring journey, he had accomplished nothing but the establishment of his own character in the eyes of the men who were to meet the crisis
now at hand. He had been at infinite pains, at every
stage of the dreary adventure, to win and hold the confidence of the Indians who were accounted friends of
the English, and had displayed an older man's patience,
address, and fortitude in meeting all their subtle shifts;
and he had borne hardships that tried even the doughty
Gist. When the horses gave out, he had left them to
come by easier stages, while he made his way afoot,
with only a single companion, across the weary leagues
that lay upon his homeward way. Gist, his comrade in
the hazard, had been solicitously "unwilling he should
undertake such a travel, who had never been used to
walking before this time," but the imperative young
commander would not be stayed, and the journey was
made, spite of sore feet and frosts and exhausting weariness. He at least knew what the French were about,
with what strongholds and forces, and could afford to
await orders what to do next.

COLONEL WASHINGTON

DINWIDDIE had not been idle while Washington went his perilous errand. He had gotten the Burgesses together by the 1st of November, before Washington had left the back settlements to cross the wilderness, and would have gotten a liberal grant of money from them had they not fallen in their debates upon the question of the new fee charged, since his coming, for every grant out of the public lands of the colony, and insisted that it should be done away with. "Subjects," they said, very stubbornly, "cannot be deprived of the least part of their property without their consent;" and such a fee, they thought, was too like a tax to be endured. They would withhold the grant, they declared, unless the fee was abolished, notwithstanding they saw plainly enough in how critical a case things stood in the West; and the testy Governor very indignantly sent them home again. He ordered a draft of two hundred men from the militia, nevertheless, with the purpose of assigning the command to Washington and seeing what might be done upon the Ohio, without vote of Assembly. A hard-headed Scotsman past sixty could not be expected to wait upon a body of wrangling and factious provincials for leave to perform his duty in a crisis, and, inasmuch as the object was to save their own lands, and perhaps their own persons, from the French, could hardly be blamed for proposing in his anger that they be taxed for the purpose by act of Parliament. " A Governor," he exclaimed, " is really to be pitied in the discharge of his duty to his King and country in having to do with such obstinate, self-conceited people!" Some money he advanced out of his own pocket. When Washington came back from his fruitless mission, Dinwiddie ordered his journal printed and copies sent to all the colonial Governors. " As it was thought advisable by his Honour the Governor to have the following account of my proceedings to and from the French on Ohio committed to print," said the modest young major, " I think I can do no less than apologize, in some measure, for the numberless imperfections of it." But it was a very manly recital of noteworthy things, and touched the imagination and fears of every thoughtful man who read it quite as near the quick as the urgent and repeated letters of the troubled Dinwiddie.

Virginia, it turned out, was, after all, more forward than her neighbors when it came to action. The Pennsylvania Assembly very coolly declared they doubted his Majesty's claim to the lands on the Ohio, and the Assembly in New York followed suit. " It appears," they said, in high judicial tone, " that the French have built a fort at a place called French Creek, at a considerable distance from the river Ohio, which may, but does not by any evidence or information appear to us to be, an invasion of any of his Majesty's colonies." The Governors of the other colonies whose safety was most directly menaced by the movements of the French in the West were thus even less able to act than Dinwiddie. For the Virginian Burgesses, though they would not yield the point of the fee upon land grants, did not mean to leave Major Washington in the lurch, and before an expedition could be got afoot had come together again to vote a sum of money. It would be possible with the sum they appropriated to put three or four hundred men into the field; and as spring drew on, raw volunteers began to gather in some numbers at Alexandria—a ragged regiment, made up for the most part of idle and shiftless men, who did not always have shoes, or even shirts, of their own to wear; anxious to get their eightpence a day, but not anxious to work or submit to discipline. 'Twas astonishing how steady and how spirited they showed themselves when once they had shaken their lethargy off and were on the march or face to face with the enemy. A body of backwoodsmen had been hurried forward in February, ere spring had opened, to make a clearing and set to work upon a fort at the forks of the Ohio; but it was the 2d of April before men enough could be collected at Alexandria to begin the main movement towards the frontier, and by that time it was too late to checkmate the French. The little force sent forward to begin fortifications had set about their task very sluggishly and without skill, and their commander had turned back again with some of his men to rejoin the forces behind him before the petty works he should have stayed to finish were well begun. When, therefore, on the 17th of April, the river suddenly filled with canoes bearing an army of more than five hundred Frenchmen, who put cannon ashore, and summoned the forty men who held the place to surrender or be blown into the water, there was no choice but to comply. The young ensign who commanded the little garrison urged a truce till he could communicate with his superiors, but the French commander would brook

no delay. The boy might either take his men off free
and unhurt, or else fight and face sheer destruction ; and
the nearest succor was a little force of one hundred and
fifty men under Colonel Washington, who had not yet
topped the Alleghanies in their painful work of cutting
a way through the forests for their field-pieces and
wagons.

The Governor's plans had been altered by the Assembly's vote of money and the additional levy of men
which it made possible. Colonel Joshua Fry, whom
Dinwiddie deemed "a man of good sense, and one of
our best mathematicians," had been given the command
in chief, and Washington had been named his second in
command, with the rank of lieutenant-colonel. " Dear
George," wrote Mr. Corbin, of the Governor's Council,
" I enclose you your commission. God prosper you
with it !" and the brunt of the work in fact fell upon the
younger man. But three hundred volunteers could be
gotten together ; and, all too late, half of the raw levy
were sent forward under Washington to find or make a
way for wagons and ordnance to the Ohio. The last
days of May were almost at hand before they had
crossed the main ridge of the Alleghanies, so inexperi-
enced were they in the rough labor of cutting a road
through the close-set growth and over the sharp slopes
of the mountains, and so ill equipped ; and by that time
it was already too late by a full month and more to
forestall the French, who had only to follow the open
highway of the Alleghany to bring what force they
would to the key of the West at the forks of the Ohio.
As the spring advanced, the French force upon the river
grew from five to fourteen hundred men, and work was
pushed rapidly forward upon fortifications such as the

little band of Englishmen they had ousted had not thought of attempting—a veritable fort, albeit of a rude frontier pattern, which its builders called Duquesne, in honor of their Governor. Washington could hit upon no watercourse that would afford him quick transport; 'twould have been folly, besides, to take his handful of ragged provincials into the presence of an intrenched army. He was fain to go into camp at Great Meadows, just across the ridge of the mountains, and there await his Colonel with supplies and an additional handful of men.

It was "a charming field for an encounter," the young commander thought, but it was to be hoped the enemy would not find their way to it in too great numbers. An "Independent Company" of provincials in the King's pay joined him out of South Carolina, whence they had been sent forward by express orders from England; and the rest of the Virginia volunteers at last came up to join their comrades at the Meadows—without good Colonel Fry, the doughty mathematician, who had sickened and died on the way—so that there were presently more than three hundred men at the camp, and Washington was now their commander-in-chief. The officers of the Independent Company from South Carolina, holding their commissions from the King, would not, indeed, take their orders from Washington, with his colonial commission merely; and, what was worse, their men would not work; but there was no doubt they would fight with proper dignity and spirit for his Majesty, their royal master. The first blood had already been drawn, on the 28th of May, before reinforcements had arrived, when Washington had but just come to camp. Upon the morning of that day Washington, with forty men, guided by friendly Indians, had come upon a party of some thirty Frenchmen where they lurked deep within the thickets of the dripping forest, and, with thrust of bayonet when the wet guns failed, had brought them to a surrender within fifteen minutes of the first surprise. No one in the Virginian camp doubted that there was war already, or dreamed of awaiting the action of diplomats and cabinets over sea. The French had driven an English garrison from the forks of the Ohio with threats of force, which would certainly have been executed had there been need. These men hidden in the thickets at Great Meadows would have it, when the fight was over, that they had come as messengers merely to bear a peaceful summons ; but did it need thirty odd armed men to bear a message ? Why had they lurked for five days so stealthily in the forest ; and why had they sent runners back post-haste to Fort Duquesne to obtain support for their diplomacy ? Washington might regret that young M. Jumonville, their commander, had lost his life in the encounter, but he had no doubt he had done right to order his men to fire when he saw the French spring for their arms at the first surprise.

Now, at any rate, war was unquestionably begun. That sudden volley fired in the wet woods at the heart of the lonely Alleghanies had set the final struggle ablaze. It was now either French or English in America : it could no longer be both. Jumonville with his thirty Frenchmen was followed ere many weeks were out by Coulon de Villiers with seven hundred—some of them come all the way from Montreal at news of what had happened to France's lurking ambassadors in the far-away mountains of Virginia. On the 3d of July they closed to an encounter at "Fort Necessity," Washington's rude intrenchments upon the Great Meadows. There were three hundred and fifty Englishmen with him able to fight, spite of sickness and short rations; and as the enemy began to show themselves at the edges of the neighboring woods through the damp mists of that dreary morning, Washington drew his little force up outside their works upon the open meadow. He "thought the French would come up to him in open field," laughed a wily Indian, who gave him counsel freely, but no aid in the fight; but Villiers had no mind to meet the gallant young Virginian in that manly fashion. Once, indeed, they rushed to his trenches, but, finding hot reception there, kept their distance afterwards. Villiers brought them after that only "as near as possible without uselessly exposing the lives of the King's subjects," and poured his fire in from the cover of the woods. For nine hours the unequal fight dragged on, the French and their Indians hardly showing themselves outside the shelter of the forest, the English crouching knee - deep in water in their rude trenches, while the rain poured incessantly, reducing their breastworks to a mass of slimy mud, and filling all the air with a chill and pallid mist. Day insensibly darkened into night in such an air, and it was eight o'clock when the firing ceased and the French asked a parley. Their men were tired of the dreary fight, their Indian allies threatened to leave them when morning should come, and they were willing the English should withdraw, if they would, without further hurt or molestation. The terms they offered seemed very acceptable to Washington's officers as the interpreter read them out, standing there in the drenching downpour and the black night.

"It rained so hard we could hardly keep the candle lighted to read them by," said an officer; but there was really no choice what to do. More than fifty men lay dead or wounded in the flooded camp; the ammunition was all but spent; the French strength had hardly been touched in the fight, and might at any moment be increased. Capitulation was inevitable, and Washington did not hesitate.

The next morning saw his wretched force making their way back again along the rude road they had cut through the forests. They had neither horses nor wagons to carry their baggage. What they could they burned; and then set out, sore stricken in heart and body, their wounded comrades and their scant store of food slung upon their backs, and dragged themselves very wearily all the fifty miles to the settlements at home. Two of the King's Independent Companies from New York ought to have joined them long ago, but had gotten no farther than Alexandria when the fatal day came at the Great Meadows. North Carolina had despatched three hundred and fifty of her militiamen, under an experienced officer, to aid them, but they also came too late. It had been expected that Maryland would raise two hundred and fifty men, and Pennsylvania had at last voted money, to be spent instead of blood, for she would levy no men; but no succor had come from any quarter when it should. The English were driven in, and all their plans were worse than undone.

It was a bitter trial for the young Virginian commander to have his first campaign end so disastrously— to be worsted in a petty fight, and driven back hopelessly outdone. No one he cared for in Virginia blamed him. His ragged troops had borne themselves like men

in the fight; his own gallantry no man could doubt.
The House of Burgesses thanked him and voted money
to his men. But it had been a rough apprenticeship, and
Washington felt to the quick the lessons it had taught
him. The discouraging work of recruiting at Alexandria, the ragged idlers to be governed there, the fruitless drilling of listless and insolent men, the two months'
work with axe and spade cutting a way through the
forests, the whole disheartening work of making ready
for the fight, of seeking the enemy, and of choosing a
field of encounter, he had borne as a stalwart young
man can while his digestion holds good. He had at
least himself done everything that was possible, and it
had been no small relief to him to write plain-spoken
letters to the men who were supposed to be helping him
in Williamsburg, telling them exactly how things were
going and who was to blame—letters which showed
both how efficient and how proud he was. He had
even shown a sort of boyish zest in the affair when it
came to actual fighting with Jumonville and his scouts
hidden in the forest. He had pressed to the thick of
that hot and sudden skirmish, and had taken the French
volleys with a lad's relish of the danger. " I heard the
bullets whistle," he wrote his brother, "and believe me
there is something charming in the sound." But after
he had stood a day in the flooded trenches of his wretched
" fort " at Great Meadows, and fought till evening in
the open with an enemy he could not see, he knew that
he had been taught a lesson ; that he was very young
at this terrible business of fighting ; and that something
more must be learned than could be read in the books
at Mount Vernon. He kept a cheerful front in the
dreary retreat, heartening his men bravely by word and

example of steadfastness; but it was a sore blow to his
pride and his hopes, and he must only have winced
without protest could he have heard how Horace Walpole called him a " brave braggart " for his rodomontade
about the music of deadly missiles.

He had no thought, however, of quitting his duty because his first campaign had miscarried. When he had
made his report at Williamsburg he rejoined his demoralized regiment at Alexandria, where it lay but an hour's
ride from Mount Vernon, and set about executing his
orders to recruit once more, as if the business were only
just begun. Captain Innes, who had brought three hundred and fifty men from North Carolina too late to be
of assistance at the Meadows, and who had had the chagrin of seeing them take themselves off home again because there was no money forthcoming to pay them what
had been promised, remained at Will's Creek, amidst
the back settlements, to command the King's provincials
from South Carolina who had been with Washington at
the Meadows, and the two Independent Companies from
New York, who had lingered so long on the way; and to
build there a rough fortification, to be named Fort Cumberland, in honor of the far-away Duke who was commander-in-chief in England. Dinwiddie, having such
hot Scots blood in him as could brook no delays, and
having been bred no soldier or frontiersman, but a merchant and man of business, would have had Washington's recruiting despatched at once, like a bill of goods,
and a new force sent hot-foot to the Ohio again to catch
the French while they were at ease over their victory and
slackly upon their guard at Duquesne. When he was
flatly told it was impossible, he turned to other plans,
equally ill considered, though no doubt equally well

meant. By October he had obtained of the Assembly twenty thousand pounds, and from the government at home ten thousand more in good specie, such as was scarce in the colony—for the sharp stir of actual fighting had had its effect alike upon King and Burgesses—and had ordered the formation and equipment of ten full companies for the frontier. But the new orders contained a sad civilian blunder. The ten companies should all be Independent Companies; there should be no officer higher than a captain amongst them. This, the good Scotsman thought, would accommodate all disputes about rank and precedence, such as had come near to making trouble between Washington and Captain Mackay, of the Independent Company from South Carolina, while they waited for the French at Great Meadows.

Washington at once resigned, indignant to be so dealt with. Not only would he be reduced to a captaincy under such an arrangement, but every petty officer would outrank him who could show the King's commission. It was no tradition of his class to submit to degradation of rank thus by indirection and without fault committed, and his pride and sense of personal dignity, for all he was so young, were as high-strung as any man's in Virginia. He had shown his quality in such matters already, six months ago, while he lay in camp in the wilderness on his way towards the Ohio. The Burgesses had appointed a committee of their own to spend the money they had voted to put his expedition afoot in the spring, lest Dinwiddie should think, were they to give him the spending of it, that they had relented in the matter of the fees; and these gentlemen, in their careful parsimony, had cut the officers of the already straitened little force down to such pay and food as Washington deemed unworthy a

gentleman's acceptance. He would not resign his commission there at the head of his men upon the march, but
he asked to be considered a volunteer without pay, that
he might be quit of the humiliation of being stinted like
a beggar. Now that it was autumn, however, and wars
stood still, he could resign without reproach, and he did
so very promptly, in spite of protests and earnest solicitations from many quarters. " I am concerned to find
Colonel Washington's conduct so imprudent," wrote
Thomas Penn. But the high - spirited young officer
deemed it no imprudence to insist upon a just consideration of his rank and services, and quietly withdrew to
Mount Vernon, to go thence to his mother at the " ferry
farm" upon the Rappahannock, and see again all the
fields and friends he loved so well.

It was a very brief respite. He had been scarcely five
months out of harness when he found himself again in
camp, his plans and hopes once more turned towards
the far wilderness where the French lay. He had set a
great war ablaze that day he led his forty men into the
thicket and bade them fire upon M. Jumonville and his
scouts lurking there ; and he could not, loving the deep
business as he did, keep himself aloof from it when he
saw how it was to be finished. Horace Walpole might
laugh lightly at the affair, but French and English statesmen alike — even Newcastle, England's Prime-Minister,
as busy about nothing as an old woman, and as thoroughly ignorant of affairs as a young man — knew that something must be done, politics hanging at so doubtful a balance between them, now that Frederick of Prussia had
driven France, Austria, and Russia into league against
him. The French Minister in London and the British
Minister in Paris vowed their governments still loved

and trusted one another, and there was no declaration of war.   But in the spring of 1755 eighteen French ships of war put to sea from Brest and Rochefort, carrying six battalions and a new Governor to Canada, and as many ships got away under press of sail from English ports to intercept and destroy them.   Transports carrying two English regiments had sailed for Virginia in January, and by the 20th of February had reached the Chesapeake.   The French ships got safely in at the St. Lawrence despite pursuit, losing but two of their fleet, which had the ill luck to be found by the English befogged and bewildered off the coast.   The colonies were to see fighting on a new scale.

The English ministers, with whom just then all things went either by favor or by accident, had made a sorry blunder in the choice of a commander.   Major-General Edward Braddock, whom they had commissioned to take the two regiments out and act as commander-in-chief in America, was a brave man, a veteran soldier, bred in a thorough school of action, a man quick with energy and indomitable in resolution ; but every quality he had un-fitted him to learn.   Self-confident, brutal, headstrong, "a very Iroquois in disposition," he would take neither check nor suggestion.   But energy, resolution, good soldiers, and a proper equipment might of themselves suffice to do much in the crisis that had come, whether wisdom held the reins or not ; and it gave the Old Dominion a thrill of quickened hope and purpose to see Keppel's transports in the Potomac and Braddock's red-coats ashore at Alexandria.

The transports, as they made their way slowly up the river, passed beneath the very windows of Mount Vernon, to put the troops ashore only eight miles beyond.

Washington had left off being soldier for Dinwiddie, but he had resigned only to avoid an intolerable indignity, not to shun service, and he made no pretence of indifference when he saw the redcoats come to camp at Alexandria. Again and again was he early in the saddle to see the stir and order of the troops, make the acquaintance of the officers, and learn, if he might, what it was that fitted his Majesty's regulars for their stern business. The self-confident gentlemen who wore his Majesty's uniform and carried his Majesty's commissions in their pockets had scant regard, most of them, for the raw folk of the colony, who had never been in London or seen the set array of battle.   They were not a little impatient that they must recruit among such a people.   The transports had brought but a thousand men — two half-regiments of five hundred each, whose colonels had instructions to add two hundred men apiece to their force in the colony.   Six companies of "rangers," too, the colonists were to furnish, and one company of light horse, besides carpenters and teamsters.   By all these General Braddock's officers set small store, deeming it likely they must depend, not upon the provincials, but upon themselves for success.   They were at small pains to conceal their hearty contempt for the people they had come to help.

But with Washington it was a different matter. There was that in his proud eyes and gentleman's bearing that marked him a man to be made friends with and respected.   A good comrade he proved, without pretence or bravado, but an ill man to scorn, as he went his way among them, lithe and alert, full six feet in his boots, with that strong gait as of a backwoodsman, and that haughty carriage as of a man born to have his will.

He won their liking, and even their admiration, as a fellow of their own pride and purpose. General Braddock, knowing he desired to make the campaign if he might do so without sacrifice of self-respect, promptly invited him to go as a member of his staff, where there could be no question of rank, asking him, besides, to name any young gentlemen of his acquaintance he chose for several vacant ensigncies in the two regiments. The letter of invitation, written by Captain Orme, aide-de-camp, was couched in terms of unaffected cordiality. Washington very gladly accepted, in a letter that had just a touch of the young provincial in it, so elaborate and over-long was its explanation of its writer's delicate position and self-respecting motives, but with so much more of the proud gentleman and resolute man that the smile with which Captain Orme must have read it could have nothing of disrelish in it. The young aide-de-camp and all the other members of the General's military "family" found its author, at any rate, a man after their own hearts when it came to terms of intimacy among them.

By mid-April the commander-in-chief had brought five Governors together at Alexandria, in obedience to his call for an immediate conference—William Shirley, of Massachusetts, the stout-hearted old lawyer, every inch "a gentleman and politician," who had of a sudden turned soldier to face the French, for all he was past sixty; James De Lancey, of New York, astute man of the people; the brave and energetic Horatio Sharpe, of Maryland; Robert Hunter Morris, fresh from the latest wrangles with the headstrong Quakers and Germans of Pennsylvania; and Robert Dinwiddie, the busy merchant Governor of the Old Dominion, whose urgent let-

ters to the government at home had brought Braddock
and his regiments to the Potomac. Plans were promptly agreed upon. New York and New England, seeing
war come on apace, were astir no less than Virginia,
and in active correspondence with the ministers in London. Two regiments had already been raised and taken
into the King's pay; the militia of all the threatened
colonies were afoot; in all quarters action was expected
and instant war. Governor Shirley, the council agreed,
should strike at once at Niagara with the King's new
provincial regiments, in the hope to cut the enemy's
connections with their western posts; Colonel William
Johnson, the cool-headed trader and borderer, who had
lived and thriven so long in the forests where the dreaded Mohawks had their strength, should lead a levy from
New England, New York, and New Jersey to an attack
upon Crown Point, where for twenty-four years the
French had held Champlain; and Lieutenant-Colonel
Monckton, of the King's regulars, must take a similar
force against Beauséjour in Acadia, while General Braddock struck straight into the western wilderness to take
Duquesne. 'Twere best to be prompt in every part of
the hazardous business, and Braddock turned from the
conference to push his own expedition forward at once.
"After taking Fort Duquesne," he said to Franklin, "I
am to proceed to Niagara; and after having taken that,
to Frontenac, if the season will allow time; and I suppose it will, for Duquesne can hardly detain me above
three or four days; and then I can see nothing that can
obstruct my march to Niagara." "To be sure, sir," quietly replied the sagacious Franklin; "if you arrive well
before Duquesne with these fine troops, so well provided
with artillery, the fort . . . can probably make but a

short resistance." But there was the trouble. 'Twould
have been better, no doubt, had a route through Pennsylvania been chosen, where cultivated farms already
stretched well into the West, with their own roads and
grain and cattle and wagons to serve an army with; but
the Virginia route had been selected (by intrigue of gentlemen interested in the Ohio Company, it was hinted),
and must needs be made the best of. There was there,
at the least, the rough track Washington's men had cut
to the Great Meadows. This must be widened and lev-
elled for an army with its cumbrous train of artillery,
and its endless procession of wagons laden with baggage
and provisions. To take two thousand men through
the dense forests with all the military trappings and
supplies of a European army would be to put, it might
be, four miles of its rough trail between van and rear of
the struggling line, and it would be a clumsy enemy, as
fighting went in the woods, who could not cut such a
force into pieces—"like thread," as Franklin said.

The thing was to be attempted, nevertheless, with
stubborn British resolution. It was the 19th of May
before all the forces intended for the march were finally
collected at Fort Cumberland, twenty-two hundred men
in all—fourteen hundred regulars, now the recruits were
in; nearly five hundred Virginians, horse and foot; two
Independent Companies from New York; and a small
force of sailors from the transports to rig tackle for the
ordnance when there was need on the rough way. And
it was the 10th of June when the advance began,
straight into that "realm of forests ancient as the
world" that lay without limit upon all the western
ways. It was a thing of infinite difficulty to get that
lumbering train through the tangled wilderness, and it

kept the temper of the truculent Braddock very hot to
see how it played havoc with every principle and practice of campaigning he had ever heard of. He charged
the colonists with an utter want alike of honor and of
honesty to have kept him so long awaiting the transpor-
tation and supplies they had promised, and to have done
so little to end with, and so drew Washington into
"frequent disputes, maintained with warmth on both
sides"; but the difficulties of the march presently
wrought a certain forest change upon him, and disposed
him to take counsel of his young Virginian aide—the
only man in all his company who could speak out of
knowledge in that wild country. On the 19th, at
Washington's advice, he took twelve hundred men and
pressed forward with a lightened train to a quicker advance, leaving Colonel Dunbar to bring up the rest of
the troops with the baggage. Even this lightened force
halted "to level every mole-hill, and to erect bridges over
every brook," as Washington chafed to see, and " were
four days in getting twelve miles"; but the pace was
better than before, and brought them at last almost to
their destination.

On the 9th of July, at mid-day, they waded the
shallow Monongahela, but eight miles from Duquesne,
making a brave show as the sun struck upon their
serried ranks, their bright uniforms, their fluttering
banners, and their glittering arms, and went straight
into the rough and shadowed forest path that led to the
French post. Upon a sudden there came a man bound-
ing along the path to meet them, wearing the gorget of
a French officer, and the forest behind him swarmed
with a great host of but half-discovered men. Upon
signal given, these spread themselves to the right and

left within the shelter of the forest, and from their covert poured a deadly fire upon Braddock's advancing
lines. With good British pluck the steady regulars
formed their accustomed ranks, crying, " God save the
King !" to give grace to the volleys they sent back into
the forest ; the ordnance was brought up and swung to
its work ; all the force pressed forward to take what
place it could in the fight; but where was the use ?
Washington besought General Braddock to scatter his
men too, and meet the enemy under cover as they came,
but he would not listen. They must stand in ranks, as
they were bidden, and take the fire of their hidden foes
like men, without breach of discipline. When they
would have broken in spite of him, in their panic at
being slaughtered there in the open glade without sight
of the enemy, Braddock beat them back with his sword,
and bitterly cursed them for cowards. He would have
kept the Virginians, too, back from the covert if he
could, when he saw them seek to close with the attacking party in true forest fashion. As it was, they were
as often shot down by the terror-stricken regulars behind them as by their right foes in front. They alone
made any head in the fight; but who could tell in such
a place how the battle fared ? No one could count
the enemy where they sprang from covert to covert.
They were, in fact, near a thousand strong at the first
meeting in the way—more than six hundred Indians, a
motley host gathered from far and near at the summons
of the French, sevenscore Canadian rangers, seventy odd
regulars from the fort, and thirty or forty French officers, come out of sheer eagerness to have a hand in the
daring game. Contrecœur could not spare more Frenchmen from his little garrison, his connections at the lakes

being threatened, and he sorely straitened for men and
stores.   He was staking everything, as it was, upon this
encounter on the way.   If the English should shake the
savages off, as he deemed they would, he must no doubt
withdraw as he could ere the lines of siege were closed
about him.   He never dreamed of such largess of good
fortune as came pouring in upon him.   The English
were not only checked, but beaten.   They had never
seen business like this.   'Twas a pitiful, shameful
slaughter—men shot like beasts in a pen there where
they cowered close in their scarlet ranks.   Their first
blazing volleys had sent the craven Canadians scamper-
ing back the way they had come; Beaujeu, who led the
attack, was killed almost at the first onset; but the gallant youngsters who led the motley array wavered never
an instant, and readily held the Indians to their easy
work.   Washington did all that furious energy and reckless courage could to keep the order of battle his commander had so madly chosen, to hold the regulars to
their blind work and hearten the Virginians to stay the
threatened rout, driving his horse everywhere into the
thick of the murderous firing, and crying upon all alike
to keep to it steadily like men.   He had but yesterday
rejoined the advance, having for almost two weeks lain
stricken with a fever in Dunbar's camp.   He could
hardly sit his cushioned saddle for weakness when the
fight began; but when the blaze of the battle burst, his
eagerness was suddenly like that of one possessed, and
his immunity from harm like that of one charmed.
Thrice a horse was shot under him, many bullets cut his
clothing, but he went without a wound.   A like mad
energy drove Braddock storming up and down the
breaking lines; but he was mortally stricken at last,

and Washington alone remained to exercise such control as was possible when the inevitable rout came.

It was impossible to hold the ground in such fashion. The stubborn Braddock himself had ordered a retreat ere the fatal bullet found him. Sixty-three out of the eighty-six officers of his force were killed or disabled; less than five hundred men out of all the thirteen hundred who had but just now passed so gallantly through the ford remained unhurt; the deadly slaughter must have gone on to utter destruction. Retreat was inevitable—'twas blessed good fortune that it was still possible. When once it began it was headlong, reckless, frenzied. The men ran wildly, blindly, as if hunted by demons whom no man might hope to resist — haunted by the frightful cries, maddened by the searching and secret fire of their foes, now coming hot upon their heels. Wounded comrades, military stores, baggage, their very arms, they left upon the ground, abandoned. Far into the night they ran madly on, in frantic search for the camp of the rear division, crying, as they ran, for help; they even passed the camp, in their uncontrollable terror of pursuit, and went desperately on towards the settlements. Washington and the few officers and provincials who scorned the terror found the utmost difficulty in bringing off their stricken General, where he lay wishing to die. Upon the fourth day after the battle he died, loathing the sight of a redcoat, they said, and murmuring praises of " the blues," the once despised Virginians. They buried his body in the road, that the army wagons might pass over the place and obliterate every trace of a grave their savage enemies might rejoice to find and desecrate.

He had lived to reach Dunbar's camp, but not to see

the end of the shameful rout.   The terror mastered the
rear-guard too.   They destroyed their artillery, burned
their wagons and stores, emptied their powder into the
streams, and themselves broke into a disordered, fever-
ish retreat which was a mere flight, their craven commander shamefully acquiescing.   He would not even
hold or rally them at Fort Cumberland, but went on,
as if upon a hurried errand, all the way to Philadelphia, leaving the fort, and all the frontier with it,
"to be defended by invalids and a few Virginians."
" I acknowledge," cried Dinwiddie, " I was not brought
up to arms; but I think common - sense would have
prevailed not to leave the frontier exposed after having opened a road over the mountains to the Ohio,
by which the enemy can the more easily invade us.
The whole conduct of Colonel Dunbar seems to be
monstrous."   And so, indeed, it was.   But the colonies
at large had little time to think of it.   Governor Shirley had gone against Niagara only to find the French
ready for him at every point, now that they had read
Braddock's papers, taken at Duquesne, and to come back
again without doing anything.   Beauséjour had been
taken in Acadia, but it lay apart from the main field of
struggle.   Johnson beat the French off at Lake George
when they attacked him, and took Dieskau, their commander; but he contented himself with that, and left
Crown Point untouched.   There were other frontiers
besides those of Virginia and Pennsylvania to be looked
to and guarded.   For three long years did the fortunes
of the English settlements go steadily from danger to
desperation, as the French and their savage allies advanced from victory to victory.   In 1756 Oswego was
taken; in 1757, Fort William Henry.   Commander suc-

ceeded commander among the English, only to add blunder to blunder, failure to failure. And all the while it
fell to Washington, Virginia's chief stay in her desperate
trouble, to stand steadfastly to the hopeless work of
keeping three hundred and fifty miles of frontier with
a few hundred men against prowling bands of savages, masters of the craft of swift and secret attack,
"dexterous at skulking," in a country "mountainous
and full of swamps and hollow ways covered with
woods."

For twenty years now settlers had been coming
steadily into this wilderness that lay up and down upon
the nearer slopes of the great mountains—Germans,
Scots-Irish, a hardy breed. Their settlements lay scattered far and near among the foot-hills and valleys.
Their men were valiant and stout-hearted, quick with
the rifle, hard as flint when they were once afoot to re-
venge themselves for murdered wives and children and
comrades. But how could they, scattered as they were,
meet these covert sallies in the dead of night—a sudden
rush of men with torches, the keen knife, the quick rifle?
The country filled with fugitives, for whom Washington's militiamen could find neither food nor shelter.
"The supplicating tears of the women, and moving petitions of the men," cried the young commander, "melt
me into such deadly sorrow that I solemnly declare, if
I know my own mind, I could offer myself a willing
sacrifice to the butchering enemy, provided that would
contribute to the people's ease. . . . I would be a willing offering to savage fury, and die by inches to save a
people." It was a comfort to know, at the least, that
he was trusted and believed in. The Burgesses had
thanked him under the very stroke of Braddock's defeat,

in terms which could not be doubted sincere. In the
very thick of his deep troubles, when he would have
guarded the helpless people of the border, but could not,
Colonel Fairfax could send him word from Williamsburg, " Your good health and fortune are the toast at
every table." " Our Colonel," wrote a young comrade
in arms, " is an example of fortitude in either danger or
hardships, and by his easy, polite behavior has gained
not only the regard but affection of both officers and
soldiers." But it took all the steadiness that had been
born or bred in him to endure the strain of the disheartening task, from which he could not in honor
break away. His plans, he complained, were " to-day
approved, to-morrow condemned." He was bidden do
what was impossible. It would require fewer men to
go against Duquesne again and remove the cause of
danger than to prevent the effects while the cause remained. Many of his officers were careless and inefficient, many of his men mutinous. " Your Honor will,
I hope, excuse my hanging instead of shooting them,"
he wrote to the Governor; " it conveyed much more
terror to others, and it was for example' sake that we
did it." It was a test as of fire for a young colonel in
his twenties.

But a single light lies upon the picture. Early in
1756, ere the summer's terror had come upon the border, and while he could be spared, he took horse and
made his way to Boston to see Governor Shirley, now
acting as commander-in-chief in the colonies, and from
him at first hand obtain settlement of that teasing question of rank that had already driven the young officer
once from the service. He went very bravely dight in
proper uniform of buff and blue, a white-and-scarlet

cloak upon his shoulders, the sword at his side knotted
with red and gold, his horse's fittings engraved with the
Washington arms, and trimmed in the best style of the
London saddlers. With him rode two aides in their
uniforms, and two servants in their white-and-scarlet
livery. Curious folk who looked upon the celebrated
young officer upon the road saw him fare upon his way
with all the pride of a Virginian gentleman, a handsome man, and an admirable horseman—a very gallant
figure, no one could deny. Everywhere he was fêted
as he went; everywhere he showed himself the earnest,
high-strung, achieving youth he was. In New York he
fell into a new ambush, from which he did not come off
without a wound. His friend Beverly Robinson must
needs have Miss Mary Philipse at his house there, a
beauty and an heiress, and Washington came away
from her with a sharp rigor at his heart. But he could
not leave that desolate frontier at home unprotected to
stay for a siege upon a lady's heart; he had recovered
from such wounds before, had before that left pleasure
for duty; and in proper season was back at his post,
with papers from Shirley which left no doubt who
should command in Virginia.

At last, in 1758, the end came, when William Pitt
thrust smaller men aside and became Prime-Minister in
England. Amherst took Louisbourg, Wolfe came to
Quebec, and General Forbes, that stout and steady soldier, was sent to Virginia to go again against Duquesne.
The advance was slow to exasperation in the view of
every ardent man like Washington, and cautious almost
to timidity; but the very delay redounded to its success
at last. 'Twas November before Duquesne was reached.
The Indians gathered there, seeing winter come on, had

not waited to meet them; and the French by that time
knew themselves in danger of being cut off by the English operations in the North. When Forbes's forces,
therefore, at last entered those fatal woods again, where
Braddock's slaughtered men had lain to rot, the French
had withdrawn; nothing remained but to enter the
smoking ruins of their abandoned fort, hoist the King's
flag, and re-name the post Fort Pitt; and Washington
turned homeward again to seek the rest he so much
needed. It had been almost a bloodless campaign, but
such danger as it had brought Washington had shared
to the utmost. The French had not taken themselves
off without at least one trial of the English strength.
While yet Forbes lay within the mountains a large detachment had come from Duquesne to test and recon-
noitre his force. Colonel Mercer, of the Virginian line,
had been ordered forward with a party to meet them.
He stayed so long, and the noise of the firing came
back with so doubtful a meaning to the anxious ears at
the camp, that Washington hastened with volunteers'to
his relief. In the dusk the two bodies of Englishmen
met, mistook each other for enemies, exchanged a deadly fire, and were checked only because Washington,
rushing between their lines, even while their pieces
blazed, cried his hot commands to stop, and struck up
the smoking muzzles with his sword. 'Twas through
no prudence of his he was not shot.

For a long time his friends had felt a deep uneasiness
about his health. They had very earnestly besought
him not to attempt a new campaign. "You will in all
probability bring on a relapse," George Mason had
warned him, "and render yourself incapable of serving
the public at a time when there may be the utmost oc-

casion. There is nothing more certain than that a gentleman of your station owes the care of his health and his life not only to himself and his friends, but to his country." But he had deemed the nearest duty the most imperative; and it was only after that duty was disposed of that he had turned from the field to seek home and new pleasures along with new duties. The winter brought news from Quebec of the fall of the French power in America, which made rest and home and pleasure the more grateful and full of zest.

MOUNT VERNON DAYS

CHAPTER IV

On a May day in 1758, as he spurred upon the way to
Williamsburg, under orders from the frontier, Washington rode straight upon an adventure he had not looked
for. He was within a few hours' ride of the little capital; old plantations lay close upon the way; neighborly
homes began to multiply; and so striking a horseman,
riding uniformed and attended, could not thereabouts
go far unrecognized. He was waylaid and haled to dinner, despite excuses and protests of public business calling for despatch. There was a charming woman to be
seen at the house, his friend told him, if a good dinner
was not argument enough—and his business could not
spoil for an hour's stay in agreeable company. And so,
of a sudden, under constraint of Virginian hospitality,
he was hurried into the presence of the gracious young
matron who was at once, and as if of right, to make his
heart safe against further quest or adventure. Martha
Custis was but six-and-twenty. To the charm of youth
and beauty were added that touch of quiet sweetness
and that winning grace of self-possession which come to
a woman wived in her girlhood, and widowed before
age or care has checked the first full tide of life. At
seventeen she had married Daniel Parke Custis, a man
more than twenty years her senior; but eight years of
quiet love and duty as wife and mother had only made

her youth the more gracious in that rural land of leisure
and good neighborhood; and a year's widowhood had
been but a suitable preparation for perceiving the charm
of this stately young soldier who now came riding her
way upon the public business. His age was her own;
all the land knew him and loved him for gallantry and
brave capacity; he carried himself like a prince—and
he forgot his errand to linger in her company. Dinner
was soon over, and his horses at the door; there was
the drilled and dutiful Bishop, trained servant that he
was, leading his restless and impatient charge back and
forth within sight of the windows and of the terrace
where his young Colonel tarried, absorbed and forget-
ful; man and beast alike had been in the service of the
unhappy Braddock, and might seem to walk there lively
memorials of duty done and undertaken. But dusk
came; the horses were put up; and the next morning
was well advanced before the abstracted young officer
got at last to his saddle, and spurred on belated to
Williamsburg. His business concerned the preparations
then afoot for General Forbes's advance upon Duquesne.
"I came here at this critical juncture," said Washington
to the President of the Council, " by the express order
of Sir John St. Clair, to represent in the fullest manner the posture of our affairs at Winchester"—lack
of clothes, arms, and equipage, lack of money, lack of
wise regulations touching rank and discipline. General
Forbes had been in Philadelphia a month already,
awaiting the formation of his army in Virginia; Sir
John St. Clair, his quartermaster-general, had come into
the province to see that proper plans were made and
executed; it was necessary that matters should be
pressed forward very diligently and at once; and Wash-

ington, when once at the seat of government, was not
slack to urge and superintend official action.   But, the
troublesome business once in proper course, he turned
back to seek Mrs. Custis again, this time at her own
home, ere he went the long distance of the frontier.
The onset was made with a soldier's promptness and
audacity.   He returned to his post, after a delay too
slight to deserve any reasonable man's remark, and yet
with a pledge given and taken which made him look
forward to the end of the campaign with a new longing
as to the winning of a real home and an unwonted hap-
piness.

This was not his first adventure in love, but it was his
last, and gave him a quiet joy which stood him in stead
a whole lifetime.   No young Virginian could live twenty-
six years amidst fair women in that hale and sociable
colony without being touched again and again by the
quick passion ; and this man had the blood of a lover
beyond his fellows.   Despite the shyness of a raw lad
who lived much in the open, he had relished the company of lively women from the first, meeting their gay
sallies sometimes with a look from his frank blue eyes
that revealed more than he knew.   Love had first found
him out in earnest six years ago, when he was but just
turned of twenty ; and it had taken all the long while
since to forget his repulse at the hands of a fair young
beauty in that day of passion.   Mary Phillipse had but
taken his fancy for a moment, because he could not pass
such a woman by and deem himself still a true Virginian.   It was more serious that he had been much in the
company, these last years, of a fair neighbor of the
vivacious house of Cary, whose wit and beauty had
haunted him in the very thick of campaigns upon the

frontier, and who still mastered his heart now and again, with a sort of imperious charm, in the midst of this very happy season when he knew Martha Custis his veritable heart's mistress for the future. It may well have made him glad of misadventures in the past to know his heart safe now.

The campaign dragged painfully, far into the drear autumn. December had come before the captured post on the Ohio could be left to the keeping of Colonel Mercer and a little garrison of provincials. But when at last he was free again there was no reason why Washington should wait longer to be happy, and he was married to Martha Custis on the 6th of January, 1759. The sun shone very bright that day, and there was the fine glitter of gold, the brave show of resplendent uniforms, in the little church where the marriage was solemnized. Officers of his Majesty's service crowded there, in their gold lace and scarlet coats, to see their comrade wedded; the new Governor, Francis Fauquier, himself came, clad as befitted his rank; and the bridegroom took the sun not less gallantly than the rest, as he rode, in blue and silver and scarlet, beside the coach and six that bore his bride homeward amidst the thronging friends of the country - side. The young soldier's love of a gallant array and a becoming ceremony was satisfied to the full, and he must have rejoiced to be so brave a horseman on such a day. For three months of deep content he lived with his bride at her own residence, the White House, by York River side, where their troth had been plighted, forgetting the fatigues of the frontier, and learning gratefully the new life of quiet love and homely duty.

These peaceful, healing months gone by, he turned

once more to public business. Six months before his
marriage he had been chosen a member of the House of
Burgesses for Frederick County—the county which had
been his scene of adventure in the old days of surveying
in the wilderness, and in which ever since Braddock's
fatal rout he had maintained his headquarters striving
to keep the border against the savages. Small wonder
that he led the poll taken there in Winchester, where
through so many seasons men had seen him bear himself like a capable man and a gallant, indomitable soldier. 'Twas no unwelcome duty, either, to take his
young wife to Williamsburg in "the season," when all
Virginia was in town in the persons of the Burgesses
and the country gentry come to enjoy the festivities
and join in the business then sure to be afoot. The
young soldier was unused to assemblies, however, and
suffered a keen embarrassment to find himself for a
space too conspicuous amidst the novel parliamentary
scene. He had hardly taken his seat when the gracious
and stately Robinson, Speaker of the House and Treas-
urer of the colony these twenty years, rose, at the bidding of the Burgesses, to thank him for the services of
which all were speaking. This sudden praise, spoken
with generous warmth there in a public place, was more
than Washington knew how to meet. He got to his
feet when Mr. Speaker was done, but he could not utter
a syllable. He stood there, instead, hot with blushes,
stammering, all a-tremble from head to foot. "Sit
down, Mr. Washington," cried the Speaker; "your
modesty is equal to your valor, and that surpasses the
power of any language that I possess."

Again and again, as the years passed, Washington returned at each session to Williamsburg to take his place

in the Assembly; and with custom came familiarity and the ease and firmness he at first had lacked upon the floor. His life broadened about him; all the uses of peace contributed to give him facility and knowledge and a wide comradeship in affairs. Along with quiet days as a citizen, a neighbor, and a country gentleman, came maturity and the wise lessons of a various experience. No man in Virginia lived more or with a greater zest henceforth than Colonel Washington. His marriage brought him great increase of wealth, as well as increase of responsibility. Mr. Custis had left many thousand acres of land, and forty-five thousand pounds sterling in money, a substantial fortune to the young wife and the two little children who survived him; and Washington had become, by special decree of the Governor and Council in General Court, trustee and manager of the whole. It needed capacity and knowledge and patience of no mean order to get good farming out of slaves, and profitable prices out of London merchants; to find prompt and trustworthy ship-masters by whom to send out cargoes, and induce correspondents over sea to ship the perishable goods sent in return by the right vessels, bound to the nearest river; and the bigger your estate the more difficult its proper conduct and economy, the more disastrous in scale the effects of mismanagement. No doubt the addition of Mrs. Custis's handsome property to his own broad and fertile acres at Mount Vernon made Colonel Washington one of the wealthiest men in Virginia. But Virginian wealth was not to be counted till crops were harvested and got to market. The current price of tobacco might leave you with or without a balance to your credit in London, your only clearing-house, as it chanced. Your principal purchases, too,

must be made over sea and through factors. Both what
you sold and what you bought must take the hazards of
the sea voyage, the whims of sea captains, the chances of
a foreign market. To be farmer and merchant at once,
manage your own negroes and your own overseers, and
conduct an international correspondence; to keep the run
of prices current, duties, port dues, and commissions, and
know the fluctuating rates of exchange; to understand
and meet all changes, whether in merchants or in markets, three thousand miles away, required an amount of
information, an alertness, a steady attention to detail, a
sagacity in farming and a shrewdness in trade, such as
made a great property a burden to idle or inefficient
men. But Washington took pains to succeed. He had
a great zest for business. The practical genius which
had shone in him almost prematurely as a boy now
grew heartily in him as a man of fortune. Messrs.
Robert Cary & Company, his factors in London, must
soon have learned to recognize his letters, in the mere
handling, by their bulk. No detail escaped him when
once he had gotten into the swing of the work.
They must be as punctilious as he was, they found, in
seeing to every part of the trade and accounting with
which he intrusted them, or else look to lose his lucra-
tive patronage. He was not many years in learning
how to make the best tobacco in Virginia, and to get it
recognized as such in England. Barrels of flour marked
" George Washington, Mount Vernon," were ere long
suffered to pass the inspectors at the ports of the British West Indies without scrutiny. It was worth while
to serve so efficient a man to his satisfaction ; worth
while or not, he would not be served otherwise.

He had emerged, as it were, after a tense and troubled

youth, upon a peaceful tract of time, where his powers
could stretch and form themselves without strain or
hurry. He had robust health, to which he gave leave
in unstinted work, athletic strength, and an insatiable
relish for being much afoot and in the open, which he
satisfied with early rounds of superintendence in the
fields where the men were at their tasks, with many a
tireless ride after the hounds, or steadfast wait at the
haunts of the deer; a planning will that craved some
practical achievement every day, which he indulged by
finding tasks of betterment about the estate and keeping his men at them with unflagging discipline; a huge
capacity for being useful and for understanding how to
be so, which he suffered his neighbors, his parish, his
county, the colony itself, to employ when there was
need. To a young man, bred these ten years in the forests and in the struggle of warfare upon a far frontier,
it had been intolerable to live tamely, without executive
tasks big and various enough to keep his energy from
rust. The clerical side of business he had learned very
thoroughly in camp, as well as the exceeding stir and
strain of individual effort—the incessant letter writing
necessary to keep promised performance afoot, the reckoning of men and of stores, the nice calculations of time
and ways and means; the scrutiny of individual men,
too, which is so critical a part of management, and the
slow organization of effort : he had been in a fine school
for these things all his youth, and would have thought
shame to himself not to have learned temperance, sagacity, thrift, and patience wherewith to use his energy.
His happy marriage did him the service to keep him
from restlessness. His love took his allegiance, and
held him to his home as to a post of honor and reward.

He had never before had leave to be tender with children, or show with what a devotion he could preside over a household all his own. His home got strong hold upon him. His estates gave him scope of command and a life of action. 'Twas no wonder he kept his factors busy, and shipped goods authenticated by the brand.

The soldierly young planter gave those who knew him best, as well as those who met him but to pass, the impression of a singular restraint and self-command, which lent a peculiar dignity and charm to his speech and carriage. They deemed him deeply passionate, and yet could never remember to have seen him in a passion. The impression was often a wholesome check upon strangers, and even upon friends and neighbors, who would have sought to impose upon him. No doubt he had given way to bursts of passion often enough in camp and upon the march, when inefficiency, disobedience, or cowardice angered him hotly and of a sudden. There were stories to be heard of men who had reason to remember how terrible he could be in his wrath. But he had learned, in the very heat and discipline of such scenes, how he must curb and guard himself against surprise, and it was no doubt trials of command made in his youth that had given him the fine self-poise men noted in him now. He had been bred in a strict school of manners at Belvoir and Greenway Court, and here at his own Mount Vernon in the old days, and the place must have seemed to him full of the traditions of whatsoever was just and honest and lovely and of good report as he looked back to the time of his gentle brother. It was still dangerous to cross or thwart him, indeed. Poachers might look to be caught and

soundly thrashed by the master himself if he chanced
their way. Negligent overseers might expect sharp
penalties, and unfaithful contractors a strict accounting,
if necessary work went wrong by their fault. He was
exacting almost to the point of harshness in every matter of just right or authority. But he was open and
wholesome as the day, and reasonable to the point of
pity in every affair of humanity, through it all. Now
it was " my rascally overseer, Hardwick," in his diary,
when certain mares were sent home " scarce able to
highlone, much less to assist in the business of the
plantations"; but not a month later it was " my worthy
overseer, Hardwick, lying in Winchester of a broken
leg." It was not in his way to add anything to the
penalties of nature.

A quiet simplicity of life and a genuine love of real
sport rid him of morbid humors. All up and down the
English world, while the eighteenth century lasted, gentlemen were commonly to be found drunk after dinner
—outside New England, where the efficient Puritan
Church had fastened so singular a discipline in manners
upon a whole society—and Virginian gentlemen had a
reputation for deep drinking which they had been at
some pains to deserve. A rural society craves excitement, and can get it very simply by such practices.
There is always leisure to sleep afterwards, even
though your dinner come in the middle of the day; and
there is good reason you should be thirsty if you have
been since daybreak in the saddle. To ride hard and to
drink hard seemed to go together in Virginia as inevitably as the rhymes in a song; and 'twas famous hard
riding after the fox over the rough fields and through
the dense thickets. If Washington drank only small

beer or cider and a couple of glasses of Madeira at dinner, it was no doubt because he had found his quick
blood tonic enough, and had set himself a hard regimen
as a soldier. He did not scruple to supply drink enough
for the thirstiest gathering when he presented himself
to the voters of the country-side as a candidate for the
House of Burgesses. " A hogshead and a barrel of
punch, thirty - five gallons of wine, forty- three gallons
of strong cider, and dinner for his friends," was what
he cheerfully paid for at his first election, and the poll
footed but a few hundred votes all told. Mount Vernon
saw as much company and as constant merriment and
good cheer as any house in Virginia ; and the master
was no martinet to his guests, even though they came
upon professional errands. " Doctor Laurie came here,
I may add drunk," says his quiet diary, without comment, though the doctor had come upon summons to attend Mrs. Washington, and was next morning suffered
to use his lancet for her relief. No doubt a good fellow when sober, and not to be lightly chidden when
drunk, like many a gallant horseman and gentleman
who joined the meet of the country-side at the hospitable place to follow the hounds when the hunting was
good. There was fox-hunting winter and summer, in
season and out, but the sport was best in the frosty
days of January and February, when the year was
young and the gentlemen of the country round gathered
at Belvoir or Gunston Hall or Mount Vernon two or
three times a week to warm their blood in the hale
sport, and dine together afterwards—a cordial company
of neighbors, with as many topics of good talk as foxes
to run to cover. The hunt went fastest and most incessantly when Lord Fairfax came down from his lodge

in the Valley and joined them for days together in the
field and at the table.

Washington loved horses and dogs with the heartiest
sportsman of them all.   He had a great gusto for stalk-
ing deer with George Mason on the broad forested
tracts round Gunston Hall, and liked often to take gun
or rod after lesser game when the days fell dull; but
best of all he loved a horse's back, and the hard ride for
hours together after the dogs and a crafty quarry—a
horse it put a man to his points to ride, a country
where the running was only for those who dared.   His
own mounts could nowhere be bettered in Virginia.
There was full blood of Araby in his noble Magnolia,
and as good hunting blood as was to be found in the
colony in his Blueskin and Ajax, Valiant and Chink-
ling.   His hounds he bred " so flew'd, so sanded," so
matched in speed and habit, that they kept always tune
and pace together in the field.   " A cry more tuneable
was never holla'd to, nor cheered with horn," than theirs
when they were let " spend their mouths " till echo replied " as if another chase were in the skies."   'Twas
first to the stables for him always in the morning, and
then to the kennels.

It had been hard and anxious work to get his affairs
into prosperous shape again when the war was over,
and those long, hopeless summers on the stricken frontier.   Stock, buildings, fences — everything had to be
renewed, refitted, repaired.   For the first two or three
years there were even provisions to buy, so slow was the
place to support itself once more.   Not only all his own
ready money, but all he got by his marriage too, and
more besides, was swallowed up, and he found himself
in debt before matters were finally set to rights and

profitable crops made and marketed. But, the thing once done, affairs cleared and became easy as if of their own accord in the business of the estate. The men he had to deal with presently knew their master: the young planter had matured his plans and his discipline. Henceforth his affairs were well in hand, and he could take his wholesome pleasures both handsomely and with a free heart. There was little that was debonair about the disciplined and masterful young soldier. He had taken Pallas's gift: " Self-reverence, self-knowledge, self-control, these three alone lead life to sovereign power. And because right is right, to follow right were wisdom in the scorn of consequence." But he took heed of his life very genially, and was matured by pleasure no less than by duty done. He loved a game of cards in almost any company, and paid his stakes upon the rubber like every other well-conducted man of his century. He did not find Annapolis, or even Philadelphia, too far away to be visited for the pleasure of seeing a good horse-race or enjoying a round of balls and evenings at the theatre, to shake the rustic dulness off of a too constant stay at home. Mrs. Washington enjoyed such outings, such little flings into the simple world of provincial fashion, as much as he did ; and they could not sit waiting all the year for the short season at Williamsburg.

A young man at once so handsome, so famous, and so punctilious in point of dress as Colonel Washington could not but make a notable figure in any society. " I want neither lace nor embroidery," was the order he sent to London. " Plain clothes, with a gold or silver button (if worn in genteel dress), are all I desire. My stature is six feet ; otherwise rather slender than corpulent." But he was careful the material, the color, and

the fit should be of the best and most tasteful, and that
very elegant stuffs should be provided from over sea
for Mrs. Washington and her children, and very substantial for the servants who were to be in attendance
upon the household — a livery of white and scarlet.
'Twas a point of pride with Virginians to know how to
dress, both well and in the fashion; and the master of
Mount Vernon would have deemed it an impropriety to
be less careful than his neighbors, less well dressed than
his station and fortune warranted. He watched the
tradesmen sharply. " 'Tis a custom, I have some reason
to believe, with many shopkeepers and tradesmen in
London," he wrote bluntly to the Messrs. Cary, " when
they know goods are bespoken for exportation, to palm
sometimes old, and sometimes very slight and indifferent, goods upon us, taking care at the same time to advance the price," and he wished them informed that
their distant customers would not be so duped.

He longed once and again to be quit of the narrow
life of the colony, and stretch himself for a little upon
the broader English stage at home. " But I am tied by
the leg," he told his friends there, "and must set inclination aside. My indulging myself in a trip to England depends upon so many contingencies, which, in all
probability, may never occur, that I dare not even think
of such a gratification." But the disappointment bred
no real discontent. There could be no better air or
company to come to maturity in than were to be had
there in Virginia, if a young man were poised and master of himself. " We have few things here striking to
European travellers (except our abundant woods)," he
professed, when he wrote to his kinsman Richard Washington in England; " but little variety, a welcome recep-

tion among a few friends, and the open and prevalent
hospitality of the country "; but it was a land that bred
men, and men of affairs, in no common fashion.

Especially now, after the quickening of pulses that
had come with the French war, and its sweep of continental, even of international, forces across the colonial
stage, hitherto set only for petty and sectional affairs.
The colonies had grown self-conscious and restless as
the plot thickened and thrust them forward to a rôle
of consequence in the empire such as they had never
thought to play, and the events which succeeded hurried
them to a quick maturity. It was a season a young
man was sure to ripen in, and there was good company.
The House of Burgesses was very quiet the year Washington first took his place in it and stood abashed to
hear himself praised ; but before Mr. Robinson, its already veteran Speaker, was dead, a notable change had
set in. Within five years, before the country on the St.
Lawrence and the lakes was well out of the hands of
the French, the Parliament in England had entered
upon measures of government which seemed meant of
deliberate purpose to set the colonies agog, and every
body of counsellors in America stood between anger
and amazement to see their people in danger to be so
put upon.

The threat and pressure of the French power upon
the frontiers had made the colonies thoughtful always,
so long as it lasted, of their dependence upon England
for succor and defence should there come a time of
need. Once and again — often enough to keep them
sensible how they must stand or fall, succeed or fail,
with the power at home — their own raw levies had
taken part with the King's troops out of England in

some clumsy stroke or other against a French strong-
hold in the North or a Spanish fortress in the South ;
and now at last they had gone with English troops into
the field in a national cause. Provincials and redcoats
had joined for a final grapple with the French, to settle
once and for all who should be owners and masters on
the coveted continent. The issue had been decisive.
By the summer of 1760 Washington could write his
kinsman in England that the French were so thoroughly
drubbed and humbled that there remained little to do
to reduce Canada from end to end to the British power.
But the very thoroughness of the success wrought a
revolution in the relations of the colonies to the mother-
country. It rid them of their sense of dependence.
English regiments had mustered their thousands, no
doubt, upon the battle-fields of the war in order that
the colonies might be free to possess the continent, and
it was hard to see how the thing could have been accomplished without them. But it had been accomplished, and would not need to be done again. Moreover, it had shown the colonial militia how strong they
were even in the presence of regulars. They had almost
everywhere borne an equal part in the fighting, and,
rank and file, they had felt with a keen resentment the
open contempt for their rude equipment and rustic discipline which too many arrogant officers and insolent
men among the regulars had shown. They knew that
they had proved themselves the equals of any man in
the King's pay in the fighting, and they had come out
of the hot business confident that henceforth, at any
rate, they could dispense with English troops and take
care of themselves. They had lost both their fear of
the French and their awe of the English.

THE HEAT OF POLITICS

'Twas hardly an opportune time for statesmen in London to make a new and larger place for England's authority in America, and yet that was what they immediately attempted. Save Chatham and Burke and a few discerning men who had neither place nor power, there was no longer any one in England who knew, though it were never so vaguely, the real temper and character of the colonists. 'Twas matter of common knowledge and comment, it is true, that the men of Massachusetts were beyond all reason impatient of command or restraint, affecting an independence which was hardly to be distinguished from contumacy and insubordination ; but what ground was there to suppose that a like haughty and ungovernable spirit lurked in the loyal and quiet South, or among the prudent traders and phlegmatic farmers who were making the middle colonies so rich, and so regardful of themselves in every point of gain or interest ? Statesmen of an elder generation had had a sure instinct what must be the feeling of Englishmen in America, and had, with " a wise and salutary neglect," suffered them to take their own way in every matter of self-government. Though ministry after ministry had asserted a rigorous and exacting supremacy for the mother-country in every affair of commerce, and had determined as they pleased what

the colonies should be suffered to manufacture, and how
they should be allowed to trade—with what merchants,
in what commodities, in what bottoms, within what
limits — they had nevertheless withheld their hands
hitherto from all direct exercise of authority in the
handling of the internal affairs of the several settlements, had given them leave always to originate their
own legislation and their own measures of finance, until
self-government had become with them a thing as if of
immemorial privilege.   Sir William Keith, sometime
Governor of Pennsylvania, had suggested to Sir Robert
Walpole that he should raise revenue from the colonies.
"What!" exclaimed that shrewd master of men.   " I
have Old England set against me, and do you think I
will have New England likewise?"

But men had come into authority in England now
who lacked this stout sagacity, and every element of
sound discretion.   English arms and English money,
they could say, had swept the French power from
America in order that the colonies might no longer suffer menace or rivalry.   A great debt had been piled up
in the process.   Should not the colonies, who had reaped
the chief benefit, bear part of the cost?   They had
themselves incurred burdensome debts, no doubt, in the
struggle, and their assemblies would very likely profess
themselves willing to vote what they could should his
Majesty call upon them and press them.   But an adequate and orderly system of taxation could not be
wrought out by the separate measures of a dozen petty
legislatures; 'twere best the taxation should be direct
and by Parliament, whose authority, surely, no man
outside turbulent Boston would be mad enough seriously
to question or resist.   It would, in any event, be whole-

some, now the colonies were likely to grow lusty as kingdoms in their roomy continent, to assert a mother's power to use and restrain—a power by no means lost because too long unexercised and neglected. It was with such wisdom the first step was taken. In March, 1764, Parliament voted it "just and necessary that a revenue be raised in America," passed an act meant to secure duties on wines and sugars, and took measures to increase the efficiency of the revenue service in America.

George Grenville was Prime - Minister. He lacked neither official capacity nor acquaintance with affairs. He thought it just the colonists should pay their quota into the national treasury, seeing they were so served by the national power; and he declared that in the next session of Parliament he should propose certain direct taxes in addition to the indirect already in force. He saw no sufficient reason to doubt that the colonies would acquiesce, if not without protest, at least without tumult or dangerous resistance. It was a sad blunder. Virginia resented threat and execution alike in such a matter as deeply as did litigious Massachusetts. A long generation ago, in the quiet year 1732, when bluff Sir Robert was Prime-Minister, there had been an incident which Governor Keith, maybe, had forgotten. The ministry had demanded of Massachusetts that she should establish a fixed salary for her governors by a standing grant; but she had refused, and the ministers had receded. The affair had not been lost upon the other colonies. That sturdy onetime royal Governor, Alexander Spotswood, in Virginia, had noted it very particularly, and spoken of it very bluntly, diligent servant of the crown as he was, to Colonel William Byrd, when he came his way on his "progress to the mines."

He declared "that if the Assembly in New England would stand bluff, he did not see how they could be forced to raise money against their will, for if they should direct it to be done by act of Parliament, which they have threatened to do (though it be against the right of Englishmen to be taxed but by their representatives), yet they would find it no easy matter to put such an act in execution." No observing man could so much as travel in Virginia without finding very promptly what it was that gave point and poignancy to such an opinion. That quiet gentleman the Rev. Andrew Burnaby, Vicar of Greenwich, was in Virginia in 1759, and saw plainly enough how matters stood. "The public or political character of the Virginians," he said, "corresponds with their private one; they are haughty and jealous of their liberties, impatient of restraint, and can scarcely bear the thought of being controlled by any superior power. Many of them consider the colonies as independent states, not connected with Great Britain otherwise than by having the same common King and being bound to her with natural affection." Not only so, but "they think it a hardship not to have an unlimited trade to every part of the world." All this, and more, Grenville might have learned by the simple pains of inquiry. One had but to open his eyes and look to see how imperious a race had been bred in the almost feudal South; and, for all they had never heard revolutionary talk thence, ministers ought to have dreaded the leisure men had there to think, the provocation to be proud, the necessity to be masterful and individual, quite as much as they had ever dreaded the stubborn temper and the quick capacity for united action they had once and again seen excited in New England.

It was not necessary to try new laws to see what the colonies would do if provoked. The difficulty already encountered in enforcing the laws of trade was object-lesson enough; and the trouble in that matter had grown acute but yesterday. For long, indeed, no one in the colonies questioned the right of Parliament to regulate their trade; but it was notorious that the laws actually enacted in that matter had gone smoothly off in America only because they were not seriously enforced. "The trade hither is engrossed by the Saints of New England," laughed Colonel Byrd, "who carry off a great deal of tobacco without troubling themselves with paying that impertinent duty of a penny a pound." The Acts of Trade practically forbade direct commerce with foreign countries or their dependencies, especially in foreign bottoms; but ships from France, Spain, and the Canary Isles came and went very freely, notwithstanding, in colonial ports; for royal officials liked to enjoy a comfortable peace and the esteem of their neighbors, and very genially winked at such trangressions. Cargoes without number were sent to the Dutch and Spanish West Indies every year, and as many brought thence, which were undoubtedly forfeit under the navigation laws Parliament had been at such pains to elaborate and enforce; and privateering as well as smuggling had for long afforded the doughty seamen of Boston, Salem, Charleston, and New York a genteel career of profit. Things had come to such a pass that where business went briskly the people of the colonial ports demanded as of right "a full freedom of illegal trade," and broke sometimes into riot when it was denied them. The Boston *News Letter* had been known very courteously to mourn the death of a worthy collector of his Majesty's customs because, " with much humanity," he had been used to take "pleasure in directing masters of vessels how they ought to avoid the breach of the Acts of Trade." Sea captains grew accustomed to very confidential relations with owners and consignees, and knew very well, without official counsel, how to take the advice "not to declare at the Custom-house"; and things went very easily and cordially with all parties to the understanding.

In 1761 that understanding was of a sudden rudely broken and the trouble began, which Grenville had the folly to add to. The Board of Trade determined to collect the duties on sugar, molasses, and rum, so long and so systematically evaded in the trade between New England and the West Indies, at whatever cost of suit and scrutiny, and directed their agents in Boston to demand "writs of assistance" from the courts, giving them leave to enter what premises they would in search of smuggled goods. There were instant exasperation and resistance. General search - warrants, opening every man's door to the officers of the law, with or without just and explicit ground of suspicion against him, no English subject anywhere would submit to; and yet these writs authorized nothing less. Issued under a questionable extension to America of an exceptional power of the Court of Exchequer, they violated every precedent of the common law, no less than every principle of prudent administration; and the excitement which they provoked was at once deep and ominous. Sharp resistance was made in the courts, and no officer ever ventured to serve one of the obnoxious writs. Such challenge of the process was uttered by colonial counsel upon trial of the right, moreover, that ministers would be without

excuse should they ignore the warning, so explicit and
so eloquent of revolutionary purpose. It was James
Otis who uttered it. He had but the other day carried
the royal commission in his pocket as Advocate-General
in his Majesty's Court of Admiralty ; but he would not
have scrupled, even as his Majesty's servant, he said, to
oppose the exercise of a power which had already cost
one King his head and another his throne. To oppose
in such a case was to defend the very constitution under
which the King wore his crown. That constitution secured to Englishmen everywhere the rights of freemen ;
the colonists had, besides, the plain guarantees of their
own charters ; if constitution and charter failed, or were
gainsaid, the principles of natural reason sufficed for defence against measures so arrogant and so futile. No
lawyer could justify these extraordinary writs ; no King
with an army at his back could ever force them to execution.

Protest not only, but defiance, rang very clear in these
fearless words ; and ministers must avow themselves
very ignorant should they pretend they did not know
how Mr. Otis had kindled fire from one end of the colonies to the other. But Grenville was resolute to take
all risks and push his policy. He did not flinch from
the enforcement of the measures of 1764, and in the session of 1765 calmly fulfilled his promise of further taxation. He proposed that the colonists should be required
to use revenue stamps upon all their commercial paper,
legal documents, pamphlets, and newspapers ; and that,
at once as a general measure of convenience and a salutary exhibition of authority, his Majesty's troops stationed in the plantations should be billeted on the people. Parliament readily acquiesced. It was thus Gren-

ville purposed "defraying the expenses of defending, protecting, and securing" the colonies; but he came near losing them instead. The act was passed in March; it was not to go into effect until November; but the colonists did not keep him waiting until November for their protests. It was the voice of a veritable tempest that presently came over sea to the ear of the startled minister. And it was not the General Court of turbulent Massachusetts, but the House of Burgesses of loyal Virginia that first spoke the general indignation. Already in the autumn of 1764, upon the mere threat of what was to come, that House had spoken very urgently against the measures proposed, in a memorial to King and Parliament, which, amidst every proper phrase of loyalty and affection, had plainly declared it the opinion of his Majesty's subjects in Virginia that such acts would be in flat violation of their undoubted rights and liberties; and the committee by which that memorial was drawn up had contained almost every man of chief consequence in the counsels of the colony, the King's Attorney-General himself not excepted. But it was one thing to protest against measures to come and quite another to oppose their execution when enacted into laws. The one was constitutional agitation; the other, flat rebellion—little less. It was very ominous to read the words of the extraordinary resolutions passed by the Burgesses on the 30th of May, 1765, after the Stamp Act had become law, and note the tone of restrained passion that ran through them. They declared that from the first the settlers of " his Majesty's colony and dominion " of Virginia had possessed and enjoyed all the privileges, franchises, and immunities at any time enjoyed by the people of Great Britain itself; and that this, their freedom, had been explicitly secured to them by their charters, "to all intents and purposes as if they had been abiding and born within the realm of England"; "that the taxation of the people by themselves or by persons chosen by themselves to represent them" was "a distinguishing characteristic of British freedom, without which the ancient constitution" of the realm itself could not subsist; "and that his Majesty's liege people of this most ancient colony" had "uninterruptedly enjoyed the right of being thus governed by their assemblies in the article of their taxes and internal police," had never forfeited or relinquished it, and had seen it "constantly recognized by the Kings and people of Great Britain."

Spoken as it was in protest against actual legislation already adopted by Parliament in direct despite of all such privileges and immunities, this declaration of rights seemed to lack its conclusion. The constitutional rights of Virginians had been invaded. What then? *Resolved*, therefore, "that his Majesty's liege people, the inhabitants of this colony, are not bound to yield obedience to any law or ordinance whatever designed to impose any taxation whatsoever upon them, other than the laws or ordinances of the General Assembly aforesaid," and "that any person who shall, by speaking or writing, assert or maintain" the contrary "shall be deemed an enemy of his Majesty's colony." Such had been the uncompromising conclusion drawn by the mover of the resolutions. What other conclusion could any man draw if he deemed the colonists men, and proud men at that? But the Burgesses would not go so far or be so explicit. They feared to speak treason; they were content to protest of their rights, and let the issue bring conclusions to light. It had been hot fighting to get even that much said. The men hitherto accepted always as leaders in the House had wished to hold it back from rash and heated action, and there had been bitter debates before even those significant premises for a revolutionary conclusion had been forced to adoption. Old leaders and new, young men and old alike, had willingly united in the memorial of 1764; but now that the Stamp Act was law, conservative members shrank from doing what must look so like a flat defiance of Parliament. Only young men would have had the audacity to urge such action; only very extraordinary young men would have had the capacity to induce the House to take it. But such young men were at hand, their leader as veritable a democrat as had ever taken the floor in that assembly.

Patrick Henry was not of the aristocracy of the colony. Good Scots blood ran in his veins, quickened by the lively strain of an old Welsh stock. His father came of a race of scholars, and, good churchman though he was, knew his Livy and his Horace better than his Bible. His mother came of a vivacious line of easy-going wits and talkers, which but a touch more of steadiness and energy might any day have made famous. His father had served his county of Hanover very capably and acceptably as surveyor, colonel, magistrate, and his uncle had been beloved as the faithful pastor of quiet parishes. But they had been no long time in the colony; they lived back from the tide-water counties where the real aristocracy had its strength and supremacy; they were of that middle class of yeomen-gentlemen who love liberty but do not affect rank. " A vigorous aristocracy favors the growth of personal eminence even in those

who are not of it, but only near it," and these plain men
of the middle counties were the more excellent and individual in the cultivation of their powers by reason of
the contact. But there was a touch of rusticity, a neglect of polish, a rough candor of speech, about them
which set them apart and distinguished them sharply
enough when they came into the presence of the courtly
and formal gentlemen who practised the manners of
London in the river counties. Patrick Henry, at any
rate, must have seemed a very rustic figure to the Burgesses when he first came to take his seat amongst them
on a May day in 1765. He was known, indeed, to
many. This was the man, they must have known, who
had won so strange a verdict from a jury two years ago
in the celebrated parsons' case at Hanover court-house,
against the law and the evidence. But his careless
dress and manner, his loose, ungainly figure, his listless,
absent bearing, must have set many a courtly member
staring. For such men as Washington, indeed, there
can have been nothing either strange or unattractive in
the rough exterior and unstudied ways of the new member. Punctilious though he was himself in every point
of dress and bearing, Washington's life had most of it
been spent with men who looked thus, and yet were
stuff of true courage and rich capacity within. The
manner of a man could count as no test of quality with
him. His experience had covered the whole variety of
Virginian life. He was an aristocrat by taste, not by
principle. And Patrick Henry had, in fact, come to the
same growth as he in essential quality and principle,
though by another way. Henry's life had been wilful,
capricious, a bit haphazard, Washington's all the while
subject to discipline; but both men had touched and

seen the whole energy of the commonwealth, knew its hope, could divine its destiny. There was but one Virginia, and they were her children. It could not take long to bring them to an understanding and comradeship in affairs.

It was characteristic of the new member that he should step at once and unhesitatingly to a place of leadership when debate of the Stamp Act stirred the House, and that he should instantly sweep the majority into his following with a charm and dash of eloquence that came like a revelation upon the quiet assembly. He was but twenty-nine years old, but he had spent all his life in learning how the world went, and by what manner of speech it was moved and governed. He had roamed the woods with no thought but for sport, or a quiet hour with a book or his fancy in the shade of the trees. He had kept a country store, and let gossip and talk of affairs of colony and country - side take precedence of business. Finally he had turned with a permanent relish to the law, and had set himself to plead causes for his neighbors in a way that made judges stare and juries surrender at discretion. In everything he had seemed to read the passions of men. Books no less than men, the chance company of an old author no less than the constant talk of the neighborly land he lived in, seemed to fill him with the quick principles of the people and polity to which he belonged, and to lend him as inevitably every living phrase in which to utter them. The universal sympathy and insight which made his pleasantry so engaging to men of every stamp rendered his power no less than terrible when he turned to play upon their passions. He was not conscious of any audacity when he sprang to his feet upon the in-

stant he saw the House resolved into committee to consider the Stamp Act. It was of the ardor of his nature
to speak when conviction moved him strongly, without
thought of propriety or precedence; and it was like him
to stand there absorbed, reading his resolutions from a
fly-leaf torn from an old law-book.

It seemed no doubt a precious piece of audacity in
the eyes of the prescriptive leaders of the House to hear
this almost unknown man propose his high recital of
Virginia's liberties and his express defiance of Parliament—in tones which rang no less clear and confident
upon the clause which declared "his Majesty's liege
people" of the colony in no way bound to yield obedience, than in the utterance of the accepted matter of
his premises. Debate flamed up at once, hot, even passionate. The astounding, moving eloquence of the
young advocate, his instant hold upon the House, the
directness with which he purposed and executed action
in so grave a matter, stirred the pulses of his opponents
and his followers with an equal power, and roused those
who would have checked him to a vehemence as great
as his own. The old leaders of the House, with whom
he now stood face to face in this critical business, were
the more formidable because of the strong reason of
their position. No one could justly doubt that they
wished to see the Old Dominion keep and vindicate her
liberty, but they deemed it folly to be thus intemperately
beforehand with the issue. Almost to a man they were
sprung of families who had come to Virginia with the
great migration that had brought the Washingtons, in
the evil day when so many were fleeing England to be
quit of the Puritan tyranny—royalists all, and touched
to the quick with the sentiment of loyalty. 'Twas now

a long time since Cromwell's day, indeed ; generations
had passed, and a deep passion for Virginia had been
added to that old reverence for the wearer of the crown
in England. But these men prided themselves still upon
their loyalty ; made it a point of honor to show themselves no agitators, but constitutional statesmen. It
made them grave and deeply anxious to see the privileges that were most dear to them thus violated and
denied, but it did not make them hasty to quarrel with
the Parliament of the realm. They had intended opposition, but they feared to throw their cause away by
defiance. 'Twas as little wise as dignified to flout thus
at the sovereign power before all means had been ex-
hausted to win it to forbearance.

It was not the least part of the difficulty to face the
veteran Speaker, John Robinson, so old in affairs, so
stately in his age, so gravely courteous, and yet with
such a threat of good manners against those who should
make breach of the decorous traditions of the place.
But the men chiefly to be feared were on the floor.
There was Richard Bland, "wary, old, experienced,"
with "something of the look," a Virginian wit said,
"of old musty parchments, which he handleth and
studieth much," author of a "treatise against the Quakers on water-baptism"; with none of the gifts of an
orator, but a veritable antiquarian in law and the pre-
cedents of public business, a very formidable man in
counsel. Quiet men trusted him, and thought his prudence very wise. George Wythe was no less learned,
and no less influential. Men knew him a man of letters,
bringing the knowledge of many wise books to the
practice of affairs, and set great store by his sincerity, as
artless as it was human, and sweetened with good feel-

ing. It made Randolph and Pendleton and Nicholas,
the elder orators of the House, seem the more redoubtable that they should have such men as these at their
elbows to prompt and steady them. And yet they would
have been formidable enough of themselves. Edmund
Pendleton had not, indeed, the blood or the breeding
that gave his colleagues prestige. He had won his way
to leadership by his own steady genius for affairs. He
read nothing but law-books, knew nothing but business,
cared for nothing but to make practical test of his
powers. But he took all his life and purpose with such
a zest, made every stroke with so serene a self-possession, was so quick to see and act upon every advantage
in his business of debate, and was withal so transparent,
bore himself with such a grace and charm of manner,
was so obviously right-minded and upright, that it meant
a great deal to the House to hear him intervene in its
discussions with his melodious voice, his cool, distinct,
effective elocution. Robert Carter Nicholas added to
like talents for business and debate a reverent piety, a
title to be loved and trusted without question, which no
man ever thought to gainsay. And Peyton Randolph,
with his "knowledge, temper, experience, judgment, integrity" as of a true Roman spirit, was a sort of prince
among the rest. No man could doubt he wished Virginia to have her liberties. He had gone over sea to
speak for her in Dinwiddie's day, though he was the
King's attorney, and had lost his office for his boldness.
But there were traditions of loyalty and service in his
breeding which no man might rightly ignore. His
father before him had won knighthood and the royal
favor by long and honorable service as his Majesty's
attorney in the colony. Pride and loyalty had gone

hand in hand in the annals of a proud race, and had
won for the Randolphs a prestige which made it impossible Sir John's son should very long be kept from the
office he had so honorably inherited. And so Peyton
Randolph was now once again the King's attorney. It
was not as the King's officer, however, but as an experienced Parliamentary tactician, a trained debater, a
sound man of affairs, that he had set himself to check
Henry in his revolutionary courses.

Henry found himself, in truth, passionately set upon.
Even threats were uttered, and abuse such as proud
men find ill to bear. They cried "Treason! treason!"
upon him when he dared declare the King would do
well to look to the fate of Cæsar and Charles the First
for profitable examples. But he was not daunted a
whit. "If this be treason, make the most of it," was
his defiance to them. One ally who might have stood
with him, had he known, was absent. Richard Henry
Lee would have brought to his support a name as ancient and as honorable as any in the colony, and an
eloquence scarcely less than his own. But, as it was,
he was left almost alone, and won his battle with no
other aid than very plain men could lend by vote and
homely utterance. The vote was very close, but enough.
Randolph flung out of the House, muttering in his heat
that he "would have given five hundred guineas for a
single vote." Henry, taking the triumph very simply,
as was his wont, and knowing his work for the session
done, quietly made his way homeward that very day,
striding unconcernedly down Duke of Gloucester Street,
chatting with a friend, his legs clad in buckskin as if
for the frontier, his saddle-bags and the reins of his lean
nag slung carelessly over his arm.

The Assembly had adopted Henry's declaration of rights, not his resolution of disobedience, and had softened a little the language he would have used ; but its action seemed seditious enough to Fauquier, the Governor, and he promptly dissolved them. It did little good to send Virginians home, however, if the object was to check agitation. The whole manner of their life bred thought and concert of action. Where men have leave to be individual, live separately and with a proud self-respect, and yet are much at each other's tables, often in vestry council together, constantly coming and going, talking and planning throughout all the country-side, accustomed to form their opinions in league, and yet express each man his own with a dash and flavor of independence; where there is the leisure te reflect, the habit of joint efforts in business, the spirit to be social, and abundant opportunity to be frank withal, if you will — you may look to see public views form themselves very confidently, and as easily without assemblies as with them. Washington had taken no part in the stormy scenes of the House, but had sat calmly apart rather, concerned and thoughtful. He was not easily caught by the excitement of a sudden agitation. He had the soldier's steady habit of self-possession in the presence of a crisis, and his own way of holding things at arm's-length for scrutiny — "like a bishop at his prayers," a wag said. He had a soldier's loyalty, too, and slowness at rebellion. His thought, no doubt, was with the conservatives, whatever may have been the light that sprang into his quiet eye when Henry's voice rang out so like a clarion, calling Virginia to her standard; and he went home, upon the dissolution, to join and aid his neighbors in the slow discussion which must shape affairs to an issue.

"The Virginia Resolutions" had run like a flame through the colonies—not as the Burgesses had adopted them, but as Henry had drawn them, with their express threat of disobedience. Nor was that all. October, 1765, saw delegates from nine colonies come together in New York, at the call of Massachusetts, to take counsel what should be done. Every one knew that Virginia, North Carolina, and Georgia, the only colonies absent from the "congress," would have sent delegates too had their Governors not prevented them by the dissolution of their Assemblies before they could act on the call. A deep excitement and concern had spread everywhere throughout the settlements. Not only did the impending enforcement of the act engross "the conversation of the speculative part of the colonists," as Washington wrote to Francis Dandridge in London; it promised to engross also the energies of very active, and it might be very violent, men in many quarters, and it began to grow evident that some part of government itself would be brought to a standstill by its processes. "Our courts of judicature," declared Washington, "must inevitably be shut up; for it is impossible (or next of kin to it), under our present circumstances, that the act of Parliament can be complied with . . .; and if a stop be put to our judicial proceedings, I fancy the merchants of Great Britain trading to the colonies will not be among the last to wish for a repeal of it." The congress at New York drew up nothing less than a bill of rights and immunities, and sent resolutions over sea which arrested the attention of the world. The Virginian Assembly despatched like papers for itself; and Richard

Henry Lee, when he had assisted to draw its memorials, hastened home to form in his own Cavalier county a "Westmoreland Association," whose members (four Washingtons among the rest) bound themselves by a solemn covenant to "exert every faculty to prevent the execution of the said Stamp Act in any instance whatsoever within this colony." The ministry could not stand the pressure. They gave way to Lord Rockingham, and the act was repealed.

Meanwhile Washington, his calm temper unshaken, was slowly coming to a clear vision of affairs in all their significance. Fox-hunting did not cease. He was much in the saddle and at table with the Fairfaxes, whom nothing could shake from their allegiance, and who looked with sad forebodings upon the temper the colony was in. It was proper they should speak so if they deemed it just, and Washington had no intolerance for what they urged. But George Mason, the neighbor whom he most trusted, was of a very different mind, and strengthened and confirmed him in other counsels. Mason was six years his senior; a man, too, cast by nature to understand men and events, how they must go and how be guided. They conferred constantly, at every turn of their intimate life, in the field or in the library, mounted or afoot in the forests, and came very deliberately and soberly to their statesman's view. Randolph and Pendleton and Wythe and Bland had themselves turned, after the first hesitation, to act with ardent men like Lee in framing the memorials to King, Lords, and Commons which were to go from the Burgesses along with the resolutions of the Stamp Act Congress in New York; and Washington, who had never hesitated, but had only gone slowly and with his

eyes open, with that self-poise men had found so striking in him from the first, came steadily with the rest to
the at last common purpose of resolute opposition. The
repeal of the act came to all like a great deliverance.

Governor Fauquier had deemed it his duty to dissolve
the Assembly upon the passage of Henry's resolutions,
but he had acted without passion in the matter, and had
kept the respect of the men he dealt with. He was not
a man, indeed, to take public business very seriously,
having been bred a man of fashion and a courtier rather
than a master of affairs. He loved gay company and
the deep excitement of the gaming-table, not the round
of official routine. Affable, generous, elegant, a scholar
and real lover of letters, he vastly preferred the talk of
vivacious women and accomplished men to the business
of the General Court, and was a man to be liked rather
than consulted. Washington, always admitted to the
intimacy of official circles at Williamsburg, very likely
relished the gallant Fauquier better than the too officious
Dinwiddie. It was, unhappily, no portent to see a man
still devoted to dissipation at sixty-two, even though he
were Governor of one of his Majesty's colonies and a
trusted servant of the crown ; and Fauquier's gifts as a
man of wit and of instructed tastes made his companionship no less acceptable to Washington than to the other
men of discernment who frequented the ballrooms and
receptions, ate formal dinners, and played quiet games
of cards during the brief season at the little capital. It
did not seriously disturb life there that the Governor
upheld the power of Parliament to tax, while the Burgesses strenuously opposed it. Washington, for one,
did not hesitate on that account to be seen often in
friendly talk with the Governor, or to accept frequent

invitations to the "palace." He was of the temper which has so distinguished the nobler sort of English-men in politics: he might regard opposition as a public duty, but he never made it a ground of personal feeling or private spite. In a sense, indeed, he had long been regarded as belonging to official circles in the colony, more intimately than any other man who did not hold office. He had been put forward by the Fairfaxes in his youth; men in the Council and at the head of af-fairs had been his sponsors and friends from the first; he had been always, like his brother before him, a mem-ber of one of the chief groups in the colony for influence and a confidential connection with the public business. It was even understood that he was himself destined for the Council, when it should be possible to put him in it without seeming to give too great a preponderance to the Fairfax interest, already so much regarded in its make-up.

The first flurry of differing views and conflicting pur-poses among the Virginian leaders had passed off. The judgment of high-spirited men everywhere sustained Henry — gave him unmistakable authentication as a leader; put all public men in the way of understanding their constituents. Some were bold and some were timid, but all were animated by the same hope and pur-pose, and few were yet intemperate. "Sensible of the importance of unanimity among our constituents," said Jefferson afterwards, looking back to that time when he was young and in the first flush of his radical senti-ments, "although we often wished to have gone faster, we slackened our pace, that our less ardent colleagues might keep up with us; and they, on their part, differ-ing nothing from us in principle, quickened their gait

somewhat beyond that which their prudence might of
itself have advised." Patrick Henry was received to
the place he had earned; and although the older leaders
resumed that sway in counsel to which their tried skill
and varied experience in affairs fairly entitled them,
there was no longer any jealous exclusion of new men.
Henry's fame crept through the colonies as the man
who had first spoken the mind not of Virginians only,
but of all just men, with regard to the liberties of Englishmen in America. Before a year was out Richard
Bland himself, parchment man and conservative that he
was, had written and published a pamphlet entitled "An
Inquiry into the Rights of the British Colonies," which
said nothing less than that in all that concerned her
internal affairs Virginia was "a distinct, independent
state," though "united with the parent state by the
closest league and amity, and under the same allegiance." A colony "treated with injury and violence,"
he exclaimed, "is become an alien." When antiquari-
ans and lawyers, fresh from poring upon old documents,
spoke thus, there were surely signs of the times.

   The government at home kept colonial sentiment very
busy. Even Lord Rockingham's government, with
Burke to admonish it, coupled its repeal of the stamp
duties with a "declaratory act" which sought to quiet
controversy by giving the lie direct to every argument
urged against its authority in the colonies. "Parliament
has power to bind the colonies in all cases whatsoever,"
was its round assertion :—"a resolution for England's
right to do what the Treasury pleased with three mill-
ions of freemen," cried Chatham. Though Rockingham's government would not act on that right, its suc-
cessors would without scruple; and they were soon

about it, for Rockingham's ministry retained office
scarcely a twelvemonth. Grenville was, indeed, discredited; but Grafton and Townshend were as bad, as
stubborn in temper, as reckless in policy. The year 1767
saw taxes proposed and enacted on glass, paper, painters'
colors, and tea imported into the colonies, with a purpose to pay fixed salaries to the crown's officers in the
colonies out of the proceeds; and the contested ground
was all to go over again. To show their temper, the
new ministers suspended the legislative powers of the
Colonial Assembly in New York for refusing to make
provision for troops quartered upon the colony. To
complete their fiscal arrangements they presently created
a custom-house and board of revenue commissioners for
America. It was an ominous year, and set opinion forward not a little in the colonies.

The House of Burgesses broke, at its next session
(1768), into fresh protests and remonstrances, and there
was no one to restrain or rebuke it. Fauquier was dead,
and gone to his reckoning; the reins of government were
in the hands of gentle John Blair, President of the
Council, a Virginian every inch, and with never a
thought of checking his fellow-colonists in the expression of their just opinions. The autumn brought Lord
Botetourt, the new Governor - General, who came in
showy state, and with genial display of courtly manners and good feeling; but his arrival made little difference. The Burgesses smiled to see him come to open
their session of 1769 with pageant of coach and six,
brave display of royal insignia, and the manner of a
sovereign meeting Parliament; and turned from him almost in contempt to denounce once more the course of
the ministers, argue again the rights of America, de-

clare they would draw the colonies together in concerted opposition, and call upon the other colonies to concur
with them alike in their principles and in their purpose.
Botetourt came hot foot to dissolve them; but they
only shifted their place of meeting, gathered again at
the private house of Mr. Anthony Hay, and there resolved no longer to import the things which Parliament
had taxed in despite of them.   George Mason had drawn
the resolutions, at Washington's request, and Washington himself presented them.

Mason's thought had hastened very far along the path
of opposition under the whip of England's policy; and
Washington's quite as far.   The government had not
only sent troops to Boston and dissolved every Assembly that protested, but had advised the King to press
prosecutions for treason in the colonies, and, should
there be deemed sufficient ground, transport the accused
to England to be tried by special commission.   It was
this last measure that had provoked the Burgesses to
their hottest outburst.   " At a time when our lordly
masters in Great Britain will be satisfied with nothing
less than the deprivation of American freedom," wrote
Washington to Mason, with a sudden burst of passion,
" it seems highly necessary that something should be
done to avert the stroke, and maintain the liberty which
we have derived from our ancestors. . . . That no man
should scruple, or hesitate a moment, to use a-ms in defence of so valuable a blessing, on which all the good
and evil of life depends, is clearly my opinion.   Yet
a-ms, I would beg leave to add, should be the last resource."   Addresses to the throne and remonstrances to
Parliament had failed: it remained to try "starving
their trades and manufactures," to see if that at last

would arrest their attention. No doubt even that would
prove of little avail; but it was at least peaceable and
worth the trial. The next month, accordingly, he got
unhesitatingly to his feet in the private meeting of the
Burgesses at Mr. Hay's and moved George Mason's
resolutions; nor did he forget to subscribe his quota to
the fund which was to defray the expenses of the " association " there formed.

The next evening he attended the "Queen's Birth-
Night" at the palace with the same naturalness of de-
meanor and frankness of dealing towards the Governor
as before. Botetourt was not all show and gallantry,
but was a genuine man at bottom. He had come to
Virginia thinking the colonists a pleasure-loving people
who could be taken by display and cajoled by hospitality: he had been told they were such in London. But
he knew his mistake almost as soon as he had made it;
and was prompt, even while he upheld prerogative, to
do what he could to deal with them in a liberal and
manly spirit. He had acquiesced very heartily at the
outset of his administration in a decision of the Council
that writs of assistance could not legally be issued in
Virginia,—for the process had been tried there too. He
made such representations with regard to the state of
the colony to the ministers at home as were both just
and wise; was assured in reply that the ministers were
willing to make every necessary concession; pledged
his word in Virginia that there should be a substantial
change of policy; and died the sooner (October 15,
1770) because the government would not, after all, redeem his promises. "Your Governor is becoming very
popular, as we are told here," wrote Arthur Lee to his
brother, from London, "and I have the worst proof of

it in the increased orders for fineries from the ladies."
Virginians did not find it easy to break an immemorial
habit in order to starve the English trades and manufactures; and it was more than once necessary to urge
and renew the non-importation agreements alike among
the Burgesses and merchants at Williamsburg and by
means of local associations throughout the colony. But
Washington was punctilious to observe to the letter the
agreements he had himself proposed. Again and again
he bade his mercantile agents in London assist him to
guard against any inadvertent breach of them : not to
send him the articles Parliament had picked out for
taxation in the colonies.

Life still continued to go, it is true, with something
of the old sumptuousness at Mount Vernon. It was in
June, 1768, that Colonel Washington ordered a new
chariot, "made in the newest taste, handsome, genteel,
and light, to be made of the best seasoned wood, and by
a celebrated workman," which was to cost him, fittings
and all, £133. For all he grew uneasy lest the colonies'
disagreement with England should come at last to a
conflict of arms, he pushed his private interests with no
abatement of thoroughness or self-possession, as if there
were no fear but that things would long enough stand
as they were. He had not run surveyor's lines for Lord
Fairfax, or assisted to drive the French from the Ohio,
without seeing what fair lands lay upon the western
rivers awaiting an owner; and, though there was still
doubt how titles were to be established in that wilderness, he took care, through the good offices of an old
comrade in arms, at least to be quietly beforehand with
other claimants in setting up such titles as might be
where the land lay richest and most accessible. " A

silent management" was what he advised, "snugly carried on under the guise of hunting other game," lest
there should be a premature rush thither that would set
rival interests a-clashing. A strange mixture of the
shrewdness of the speculator and the honesty of the
gentleman — claims pushed with privacy, but without
trickery or chicane—ran through his letters to Captain
Crawford, and drew as canny replies from the frontiered
soldier. Business gave way often to sport and pleasure,
too, as of old, when politics fell dull between sessions.
Now it was the hunt; then a gunning party in the
woods; and again a day or two aboard his schooner,
dropping down the river, and drawing the seine for
sheepsheads upon the bar at Cedar Point. Even politics was mixed with diversion. He must needs give a
ball at Alexandria on the evening of his election to the
House which was to meet Lord Botetourt, no less than
on other like occasions, of whatever kind the business of
the Assembly was likely to be. He did not lose his passion for fine horse-flesh, either, at the thickest of the
plot. In 1770 he was with Governor Eden, of North
Carolina, at the Jockey Club races in Philadelphia, no
doubt relieved by the news that all but the tea tax had
been repealed. The next year it was the races in Annapolis that claimed him; and in 1773 Jacky Custis
held him again at Philadelphia on the same errand. It
was wholesome to be thus calmly in pursuit of diversion
in the intervals of trying business. It bespoke a hearty
life and a fine balance in the man.

There was one matter to which Washington felt it his
bounden duty as a soldier and a man of honor to devote
his time and energies, whether politics pressed or not.
A grant of two hundred thousand acres of the western

lands had been promised by the government of the colony to those who enlisted for the war against the French and Indians in 1754; but nothing had ever been done to fulfil the promise, and Washington undertook to act as agent for his comrades in the business. In the autumn of 1770, accordingly, he turned away for a space from the deepening trouble in the east to plunge once more into the western ways and search out proper tracts for the grant along the reaches of the Ohio. 'Twas a two-months journey, for he did not stop till he had gone close upon three hundred miles beyond Fort Pitt. And when he was home again no one in the government who could lend a hand in the matter got any peace from the stirring, thorough man until the business was put finally into shape. There was a tidy profit in the grant for himself; for his own share was large, and he providently bought, besides, the shares of others who were unwilling to spend or co-operate in the matter. But there were months upon months of weary, unrequited service for his comrades, too, given with hearty diligence and without grudging. Their portions were as well placed as his own, they were to find, when it came to the survey. He came off from the business very rich in western lands — buying the Great Meadows, among the rest, for memory's sake — but richer still in the gratitude and admiration of the men for whom he had labored.

Meanwhile events darkened ominously. A new administration had been formed in England under Lord North, and had begun its government by repealing all the taxes of 1769 except that on tea. But it was Parliament's right to tax them that the colonists were fighting, not the taxes themselves, and one tax was as

hateful as a hundred. The year had been marked in
sinister fashion, moreover, by a broil between townsmen
and troops in the streets of Boston, in which arms had
been used and men slain, and in the heated imaginations
of the colonists the affair had taken on the ugly aspect
of a massacre. The year 1771 went quietly enough for
Virginians. Botetourt was dead, and that good merchant of York, William Nelson, President of the Council, sat in the place of authority throughout the year.
Although the whole country refused the taxed tea, the
attention of the ministers, as it happened, was fixed
chiefly upon Massachusetts, where trade centred at a
growing port and opposition had a local habitation. In
Virginia there was no place to send troops to, unless
the whole country were occupied, and so long as Mr.
Nelson was acting Governor, Colonel Washington could
go without preoccupation to the races, and gentlemen
everywhere follow their own devices in the quiet counties. There was rioting — rebellion, even — in North
Carolina, so uneasily did affairs go there; but Governor
Tryon was a soldier as well as a despot, and did not
need to trouble his neighbors about that. It was not
until the first months of 1772 that Virginians began to
read plain signs of change in the face of their new Governor, John Murray, Earl Dunmore — a dark and distant man, who seemed to the Virginians to come like a
satrap to his province, who brought a soldier with him
for secretary and confidential adviser, set up a fixed
etiquette to be observed by all who would approach
him, spoke abruptly and without courtesy, displayed in
all things an arbitrary temper, and took more interest,
it presently appeared, in acquiring tracts of western
land than in conducting the government of the colony.

The year of his coming was marked by the secret destruction of the revenue - schooner *Gaspé* in Rhode Island, and by many significant flaws of temper here and there throughout the colonies; and 1773 saw affairs at last come to a crisis.

Dunmore had summoned the Burgesses to meet him upon his first coming, but had liked their proud temper as little as they liked his, and was careful not to call them together again till March, 1773, though he had promised to convene them earlier. There was instant trouble. In view of the affair of the *Gaspé*, Parliament had again resolved upon the trial of malcontents in England, and the Burgesses were hot at seeing the sentiments of the colonies so flouted. Conservative men would still have waited to try events, but their fellow-members of quicker pulse were diligent to disappoint them. Leadership fell to those who were bold enough to take it; and Patrick Henry, Richard Henry Lee, Dabney Carr, and Thomas Jefferson, radicals all, drew together, a self-constituted committee of guidance. Evening after evening they met in a private room at the Raleigh, with now and again one or two other like spirits called into counsel, to consult what should be done. Richard Henry Lee proposed that the colonies should be invited to join Virginia in appointing committees of correspondence, through which to devise steady concert of action, and that Virginia's committee, to be appointed at once, should be instructed to look into the character of the new court of trial lately established in Rhode Island. Dabney Carr was directed to move the resolutions, and the eloquence of Lee and Henry won for them an instant and hearty acceptance. Dunmore promptly dissolved the Assembly, and Wash-

ington was free to set out for New York to place Jacky
Custis at King's College, lingering on the way in Philadelphia to see the races, and pick up the talk of the
hour during half a dozen evenings at the rooms of the
Jockey Club, at the balls and assemblies of the gay
town, and at the hospitable tables of his friends.

The opening of the year had found Washington in a
very genial humor, his letters touched with pleasantry
and gossip. "Our celebrated fortune, Miss French,
whom half the world was in pursuit of," he wrote, in
February, to Colonel Bassett, "bestowed her hand on
Wednesday last, being her birthday (you perceive, I
think myself under a necessity of accounting for the
choice), on Mr. Ben Dulany, who is to take her to Maryland. . . . . Mentioning of one wedding puts me in mind
of another"—and so through the news of Miss More,
"remarkable for a very frizzled head and good singing,"
and the rest of the neighborhood talk. But the year
turned out a very sad one for him. He had been scarcely ten days back from New York when Patsy Custis,
whom he loved as his own daughter, died. It called
forth all the latent Christian faith of the thoughtful,
steadfast man to withstand the shock. And Master
Jack Custis, the girl's wayward brother, gave him little
but anxiety. He would not study, for all Washington
was so solicitous he should have the liberalizing outlook
of books, and be made "fit for more useful purposes
than horse-racer," and though he was but twenty, could
hardly be induced to see the year out at college before
getting married.

It was no doubt very well that public affairs of the
first consequence called Washington's mind imperatively
off from these private anxieties, which could not but be

dwarfed in the presence of transactions which threatened to shake the continent. As the year drew on, the government in England undertook to force cargoes of the East India Company's tea into the ports. When all resisted, and Boston, more forward even than the rest, threw three hundred and forty odd chests of tea into the harbor, acts passed Parliament giving dangerous increase of power to the Governor of Massachusetts, and directing that Boston port be closed to all commerce on and after the first day of June; and it became evident that vigorous action must be taken in response. The Burgesses in Virginia (May, 1774) resolved that June 1st should be set apart as a day of fasting and prayer—prayer that civil war might be averted and the people of America united in a common cause. Again Dunmore dissolved them; but they gathered in the long room of the Raleigh tavern, and there resolved to urge a congress of all the colonies, and to call a convention for Virginia to meet at that place on the first day of August to take action for the colony. They showed no spleen towards the Governor. Washington dined with him the very day of the dissolution, spent the evening at the palace, even rode out with him to his farm on the following morning and breakfasted there; and the Burgesses did not fail to give the ball they had planned in honor of Lady Dunmore and her daughters on the evening of the day they had held their meeting in the "Appolo room" at the Raleigh. But there were fasting and prayer on the 1st of June; the convention met on the first day of August; very outspoken resolutions were adopted; and Peyton Randolph, Richard Henry Lee, Patrick Henry, Richard Bland, Edmund Pendleton, George Washington, and Benjamin Harrison were

directed to attend the congress of the colonies appointed
to meet in Philadelphia on the fifth day of September.
When the time came for the journey, Henry and Pendleton joined Washington at Mount Vernon. It must
have been with many grave thoughts that the three
companions got to horse and turned to ride through the
long August day towards the north.

PILOTING A REVOLUTION

In the congress of 1774 the leaders of Virginia were for the first time brought into face-to-face conference with the men of the other colonies. In 1765 Fauquier had dissolved the Burgesses with such sharp despatch, upon the passage of Mr. Henry's resolutions, that they were all gone home before the call for a congress to act upon the stamp duties could reach them. But in 1774 they were not to be so cheated. They had themselves issued the call for a congress this time, and dissolution could not drive them home. Their leaders could at least linger at the Raleigh and concert means to have their way, House or no House. A convention took the place of the Assembly; and seven leading members of the House were sent to Philadelphia, with as full authority to speak and act for the colony as if the Burgesses themselves had commissioned them. Mr. Harrison declared in Philadelphia that "he would have come on foot rather than not come"; and quiet Richard Bland, that "he would have gone if it had been to Jericho." Colonel Harrison struck his new colleagues from the North as a bit rough in his free Southern speech and manner; and Mr. Bland seemed to them "a plain, sensible man," such as would be more given to study than to agitation. If such men, artless and steady as any downright country gentleman of old

England, held so high a fancy for the business of the
congress, it was easy to conclude what the hastier,
younger men would be likely to plan and do; and
the Massachusetts delegates found themselves greatly
heartened.

John Adams, Thomas Cushing, Samuel Adams, and
Robert Treat Paine were the representatives of Massachusetts. It was their people who had most provoked
Parliament to be high - handed and aggressive. The
struggle with the ministry at home had taken shape in
Boston. It had come to actual riot there. All the
continent and all England had seen how stubborn was
the temper, how incorrigible the spirit of resistance, in
that old seat of the Puritan power, always hard set and
proud in its self-willed resolution to be independent;
and all eyes were turned now upon Cushing and Paine
and this " brace of Adamses," who had come, it was
thought, to hurry the congress into radical courses.
Kindness, applause, hospitality, "studied and expensive
respect," had attended them at every stage of their long
ride from Boston to Philadelphia. The country was
much stirred by the prospect of a general " congress of
committees" at Philadelphia; and the delegates from
Massachusetts were greeted as they passed even more
generously than the rest, because their people had been
the first to suffer in this bad business; because their
chief port at Boston was closed, and red-coated sentries
were on their streets. It behooved the Massachusetts
men, however, not to suffer themselves to be misled.
Many looked upon them askance; some distrusted them
heartily. Their own hot-headed mob had provoked the
"massacre," of which they made so much. They had
wantonly destroyed private property when they threw

the tea into their harbor to show the government their
spirit. There had been more than a touch of violence,
more than a little turbulence, and a vast deal of radical
and revolutionary talk in all that they had done; and
the colonies were full yet of men who had no tolerance
for anything that transgressed, were it never so little,
the moderate limits of constitutional agitation. "There
is an opinion which does in some degree obtain in the
other colonies that the Massachusetts gentlemen, and
especially of the town of Boston, do affect to dictate
and take the lead in continental measures; that we are
apt, from an inward vanity and self-conceit, to assume
big and haughty airs," said Joseph Hawley, who, for
all he had grown old as a quiet Massachusetts lawyer
among his neighbors, had kept his shrewd eyes abroad.
"It is highly probable," he told John Adams, with a
wholesome bluntness, "that you will meet gentlemen
from several of the other colonies fully equal to yourselves or any of you in their knowledge of Great Britain, the colonies, law, history, government, commerce.
. . . By what we from time to time see in the public
papers, and what our Assembly and committees have
received from the Assemblies and committees of the
more southern colonies, we must be satisfied that they
have men of as much sense and literature as any we
can, or ever could, boast of." It was mere counsel of
prudence that they should play their part in the congress with modesty and discretion.

Not Cushing and Paine, but the Adamses, carried the
strength of the Massachusetts delegation; and it was
Samuel Adams, rather than John, who was just now
the effective master in the great Bay Colony—"master
of puppets," his enemies called him.   Hale, bluff, adroit,

plain, a man of the people, he had grown old in the
business of agitation. Fifty-two years he had lived,
planning always for others, never for himself. He had
"never looked forward in his life," he frankly said;
"never planned, laid a scheme, or framed a design of
laying up anything for himself or others after him";
had let all his private business go neglected, and lived
upon the petty salary of a small public office, the indulgence of fortune, and the good offices of the friends and
neighbors who loved him. He was in Philadelphia now
wearing the plain suit and spending the modest purse
with which his friends and partisans had fitted him out
—the very impersonation of the revolution men were
beginning so to fear. No man had ever daunted him;
neither could any corrupt him. He was possessed with
the instinct of agitation: led the people, not the leaders;
cared not for place, but only for power; showed a mastery of means, a self-containment, a capacity for timely
and telling speech, that marked him a statesman, though
he loved the rough ways of a people's government, and
preferred the fierce democracy of the town meeting to
the sober dignity of senates. Like an eagle in his high
building and strength of audacious flight, but in instinct
and habit a bird of the storm. Not over-nice what he
did, not too scrupulous what he devised, he was yet not
selfish, loved the principles he had given his life to, and
spent himself without limit to see them triumph.

John Adams, his cousin, was of a very different mould:
a younger man by thirteen years; no man of the people,
but with a taste rather for the exclusive claims of education and breeding; self-regardful; a thought too calculating; too quick-witted to be patient with dull men,
too self-conscious to be at ease with great ones; and yet

public-spirited withal, and generous in action if not in judgment; of great powers, if only he could manage to use them without jealousy. Samuel Adams thought only of his end, not of himself; seldom spoke of himself, indeed; seemed a sort of subtle engine for the people's business. John Adams thought of himself always, and yet mastered himself to play a great part with the nobility of a man of genius, if not with the grace of a man of modesty and self-forgetful devotion. For the time he could even hold back with his wily cousin, resign leadership in the congress to Virginia, and act in all things the wise part of those who follow.

It was a circumstance full of peril that the delegates of the several colonies should at such a juncture be strangers to one another, and provincials all, nowhere bred to continental affairs. Only since the passage of the Stamp Act had they taken any thought for each other. There was no assurance that even the best leaders of a colony could rise to the statesman's view and concert measures to insure the peace of an empire. Rising lawyers like John Adams, brusque planters like Colonel Harrison, well-to-do merchants like Thomas Mifflin, might bring all honesty and good intention to the task and yet miserably fail. A provincial law practice, the easy ascendency of a provincial country gentleman, the narrow round of provincial trade, might afford capable men opportunity to become enlightened citizens, but hardly fitted them to be statesmen. The real first business of the delegates was to become acquainted, and to learn how to live in the foreign parts to which most of them had come. There was a continual round of entertainment in the hospitable town, therefore, a universal exchange of courtesies, a rush of visiting and dining, a flow of excellent wine, a rich abundance of good cheer, such as for a while made the occasion seem one of festivity rather than of anxious counsel.   Many of the delegates had come to town a week or more before the date set for the congress, and had settled to an acquaintance before it was time to effect an organization; but the gentlemen from Maryland and Virginia, more familiar with the journey, arrived almost upon the day.   They made an instant impression upon their new colleagues. John Adams promptly declared them " the most spirited and consistent of any," and deemed Mr. Lee particularly "a masterly man."   Joseph Hawley's prediction was fulfilled.   "The Virginia and indeed all the Southern delegates appear like men of importance," said Silas Deane; "I never met, nor scarcely had an idea of meeting, with men of such firmness, sensibility, spirit, and thorough knowledge of the interests of America."   Mr. Lynch of South Carolina, though he wore " the manufacture of this country," and was in all things "plain, sensible, above ceremony," seemed to Mr. Deane to carry with him " more force in his very appearance than most powdered folks in their conversation."

The high bearing and capacity of the Southern delegates came upon the New England men like a great surprise: where they had expected to see rustic squires they found men of elegance and learning.   But there was, in fact, no good reason to wonder at the natural leadership of these men.   Their life had bred them more liberally than others.   It required a much more various capacity and knowledge of the world to administer a great property and live the life of a local magnate in the South than sufficed to put a man at the front of trade or of legal practice in Boston or New York or Philadelphia.

The Southern colonies, besides, had lived more in sympathy with the life of the empire than had their Northern neighbors. Their life had depended directly upon that of England hitherto, and had partaken of it with a constant zest. They had no rival trade; they had wanted no rival government. The general air of the wide empire had blown in all ordinary seasons through their affairs, and they had cultivated none of that shrewd antagonism towards the home government which had so sharpened the wits and narrowed the political interests of the best men in New England. They had read law because they were men of business, without caring too much about its niceties or meaning to practise it in litigation. They had read their English history without feeling that they were separate from it. Their passion for freedom was born not of local feeling so much as of personal pride and the spirit of those who love old practices and the just exemptions of an ancient constitution. It was the life they had lived, and the conceptions of personal dignity and immemorial privilege that had gone always with it, that gave them so striking an air of mastery. It was not simply because the Massachusetts delegates kept themselves prudently in the background and the rest yielded to her pretensions that Virginia was accorded primacy in the congress: it was also because her representatives were men to whom power naturally fell, and because she had won so honorable a place of leadership already in the common affairs of the continent.

Colonel Washington, striking and forceable man though he was, did not figure as a leader among the Virginian delegates. Peyton Randolph was elected president of the congress; Richard Henry Lee and Patrick Henry stood forth as the Virginian leaders on the

floor.   "If you speak of solid information and sound
judgment, Colonel Washington is unquestionably the
greatest man on that floor," was Henry's confident and
generous verdict ; but Washington was no politician,
and did not stand in exactly the same class with the
rest.   He had headed committees and presided over
popular meetings among his own neighbors in Fairfax,
and had been prompt to join them in speaking with
high spirit against the course of the ministry in England.   He had been forward in urging and punctiliously
careful in practising non-importation.   He had declared
Gage's conduct in Boston "more becoming a Turkish
bashaw than an English governor."   But he was a man
of action rather than of parliaments.   " I will raise one
thousand men, enlist them at my own expense, and
march myself at their head for the relief of Boston,"
had been his impetuous utterance in the Virginian convention — "the most eloquent speech that ever was
made," Mr. Lynch declared.   "I have heard he said,"
reported an admiring Philadelphian—" I have heard he
said he wished to God the liberties of America were to
be determined by a single combat between himself and
George !"   But his fellow Virginians understood him
better.   They had chosen him for force and sobriety ;
not as an orator, but as the first soldier and one of the
first characters of the commonwealth ; and he had made
the impression they expected.   He had not been put upon
their committee of correspondence, or been appointed
with Nicholas and Pendleton and Lee and Henry to
draw resolutions and remonstrances ; but when it came
to choosing those who should represent the Old Dominion in the congress, but two names stood before
his in the vote.   Peyton Randolph, 104; Richard Henry

Lee, 100; George Washington, 98; Patrick Henry, 89; Richard Bland, 79; Benjamin Harrison, 66; Edmund Pendleton, 62—such had been the preference of the convention. The Northern delegates admired his "easy, soldier-like air and gesture" and his modest and "cool but determined" style and accent when he spoke; and wondered to see him look scarce forty, when they recalled how his name had gone through the colonies twenty years ago, when he had met the French so gallantly at Great Meadows, and with Braddock at the forks of the Ohio.

The Massachusetts delegates had reason to admire his manly openness, too, and straightforward candor. An old comrade in arms whom he esteemed—a Virginian now in regular commission, and stationed with the troops in Boston—had written him very damaging things about the "patriot" leaders of the beset town; of their "tyrannical oppression over one another," and "their fixed aim at total independence," and had charged them roundly with being no better than demagogues and rebels. Washington went at once to the men accused, to learn from their own lips their principles and intentions, taking Richard Henry Lee and discreet Dr. Shippen along with him as his sponsors and witnesses. "Spent the evening at home with Colonel Lee, Colonel Washington, and Dr. Shippen, who came in to consult us," was John Adams's entry in his diary for September 28th. No doubt Samuel Adams found the interview a trying one, and winced a little under the examination of the calm and steady soldier, going so straight to the point, for all his Virginian ceremony. There had been many outward signs of the demagogue in Adams's career. He had been consciously and deliberately planning and scheming for independence ever since 1768, and had made public avowal of his purpose no longer ago than last year. It must have taxed even his adroit powers to convince these frank Virginians that his purpose was not rebellion, but liberty; that he venerated what they venerated, and wished only what they wished. But the truth somehow lay open before the evening was gone. There was frank cordiality in the parting: Washington was convinced of their genuineness and sobriety. "Though you are led to believe by venal men," he replied to Captain Mackenzie, " that the people of Massachusetts are rebellious, setting up for independency, and what not, give me leave, my good friend, to tell you that you are abused, grossly abused. This I advance with a degree of confidence and boldness which may claim your belief, having better opportunities for knowing the real sentiments of the people you are among, from the leaders of them, in opposition to the present measures of the administration, than you have from those whose business it is not to disclose truths, but to misrepresent facts in order to justify as much as possible to the world their own conduct."

The Massachusetts men had come to a better understanding of the game—began to see how cautiously it must be played, how slowly and how wisely. It was a critical business, this of drawing all the colonies into a common congress, as if to create a directing body for the continent, without constitution or warrant. The establishment of committees of correspondence had seemed little short of seditious, for it was notorious the committees were formed to concert action against the government at home; but this "congress of committees" was an even more serious matter. Would the

colonies venture a continental organization to defy Parliament ?   Dangerous differences of opinion were blown
hot between neighbors by such measures.   Some of the
best men in America were opposed to the course which
was now evidently to be taken.   So long as it was
merely a matter of protest by the colonies severally,
they had no criticism to make — except perhaps that
Mr. Otis and Mr. Henry had held unnecessarily high
language, and had been bold and defiant beyond measure ; but when they saw how the opposition gathered
head, hastened from protest to concerted resistance, put
popular conventions into the place of lawful legislative
assemblies, and advanced at length to a continental organization, they deemed it high time to bestir themselves, vindicate their loyalty to his Majesty's government, and avert a revolution.   They were not men to
be trifled with.   Had they been able to unite upon active measures, had they advanced from defence to aggressive action, they might have rendered themselves
formidable beyond possibility of defeat.   Everywhere
men of substance and of influence were to be found by
the score who were opposed to a revolutionary agitation, such as this that now seemed to be gathering head.
Even in Massachusetts men who bore the best and the
oldest names of the commonwealth were of this number; in New York and Pennsylvania, at the very heart
of the continent, they could, it was believed, boast a
majority, as well as to the far southward, in the low
country of South Carolina and Georgia.   No one, they
declared, but designing politicians and men without
property, those who had much to gain and nothing to
lose by the upsetting of law and ordered government,
wished to see this contest with the ministry pushed to

extremes. They wished no less than others to see the colonies keep their lawful and chartered liberties, but the thing must be accomplished soberly, and without loss of things equally dear—of honor, and the maintenance of an unbroken English Empire.

The nice balance of parties was disclosed in the congress itself. The Pennsylvanian delegation was led by Joseph Galloway, a man in the prime of life, full of force and learning, who had been Speaker of the provincial House these eight years by the almost unanimous choice of his colleagues, and who now stood forth to utter the real voice of his colony in proposing measures of accommodation. He proposed that the home government be asked to sanction the establishment of a confederate parliament for America, composed of delegates to be chosen every third year by the legislatures of the several colonies, and acting under a governor-general to be appointed by the crown. Edward Rutledge, of South Carolina, hot orator for liberty though he was, declared it an "almost perfect plan," and was eager to see it adopted; influential members from almost every quarter gave it their hearty support, Mr. John Jay, of New York, among the rest; and it was defeated only by the narrow majority of a single colony's vote. Chatham might very justly commend the congress of 1774 as conspicuous among deliberative bodies for its "decency, firmness, and wisdom," its "solidity of reasoning, force of sagacity, and wisdom of conclusion, under such a complication of circumstances," for the complication of circumstances was such as even he did not fully comprehend. For seven weeks of almost continuous session did it hammer its stiff business into shape, never wearying of deliberation or debate, till

it could put forth papers to the world—an address to
the King, memorials to the people of Great Britain and
to the people of British America, their fellow-subjects,
and a solemn declaration of rights—which should mark
it no revolutionary body, but a congress of just and
thoughtful Englishmen, in love, not with license or rebellion, but with right and wholesome liberty. Their
only act of aggression was the formation of an "American Association" pledged against trade with Great
Britain till the legislation of which they complained
should be repealed. Their only intimation of intention
for the future was a resolution to meet again the next
spring, should their prayers not meanwhile be heeded.

Washington turned homeward from the congress
with thoughts and purposes every way deepened and
matured. It had been a mere seven weeks' conference;
no one had deemed the congress a government, or had
spoken of any object save peace and accommodation;
but no one could foresee the issue of what had been
done. A spirit had run through those deliberations
which gave thoughtful men, as they pondered it, a new
idea of the colonies. It needed no prophet to discern
beyond all this sober and anxious business a vision
of America united, armed, belligerent for her rights.
There was no telling what form of scornful rejection
awaited that declaration of rights or the grave plead-
ing of that urgent memorial to the crown. It behooved
every man to hold himself in readiness for the worst;
and Washington saw as clearly as any man at how nice
a hazard things stood. He had too frank a judgment
upon affairs to cheat himself with false hopes. "An
innate spirit of freedom first told me that the measures
which administration hath for some time been and now

are most violently pursuing are repugnant to every principle of natural justice," had been his earnest language
to Bryan Fairfax ere he set out for the congress;
" whilst much abler heads than my own hath fully convinced me that it is not only repugnant to natural right,
but subversive of the laws and constitution of Great
Britain itself, in the establishment of which some of
the best blood of the kingdom hath been spilt. . . . I
could wish, I own," he had added, "that this dispute
had been left to posterity to determine"; but he knew
more clearly than ever before, as he rode homeward
from the congress through the autumn woods, that it
had not been; that Lee and Henry and Mason were
rightly of the same mind and purpose with the men
from Massachusetts; that conference had only united
and heartened those who stood for liberty in every colony; that there could be no compromise—perhaps no
yielding either—and that every man must now take his
soberest resolution for the times to come.

He turned steadily to his private business for the
winter, nevertheless, as was his wont—pushed forward
the preparation and settlement of his western lands,
and stood guard, as before, over the soldiers' grants
upon the Ohio, against official bad faith and negligence.
" For a year or two past there has been scarce a moment that I could properly call my own," he declared
to a friend who solicited his promise to act as guardian
to his son.   " What with my own business, my present
ward's, my mother's, which is wholly in my hands,
Colonel Fairfax's, Colonel Mercer's, and the little assistance I have undertaken to give in the management of
my brother Augustine's concerns, together with the
share I take in public affairs, I have been constantly

engaged in writing letters, settling accounts, and nego-
tiating one piece of business or another ; by which means
I have really been deprived of every kind of enjoyment,
and had almost fully resolved to engage in no fresh matter till I had entirely wound up the old." He promised
to undertake the new charge, nevertheless. It was
stuff of his nature to spend himself thus, and keep his
powers stretched always to a great compass.

With the new year (1775) public affairs loomed big
again, and ominous. The petitions of the congress at
Philadelphia had been received in England almost with
contempt. Chatham, indeed, with that broad and noble sagacity which made him so great a statesman, had
proposed that America's demands should be met, to the
utmost length of repeal and withdrawal of menace, and
that she should be accorded to the full the self-government she demanded in respect of taxation and every
domestic concern. " It is not cancelling a piece of parchment," he cried, " that can win back America," the old
fire burning hot within him ; " you must respect her
fears and her resentments." The merchants, too, in fear
for their trade, urged very anxiously that there should
be instant and ample concession. But the King's stubborn anger, the Parliament's indifference, the ministry's
incapacity, made it impossible anything wise or generous should be done. Instead of real concession there
was fresh menace. The ministry did, indeed, offer to
exempt from taxation every colony that would promise
that by its own vote it would make proper contribution
to the expenses of public defence and imperial administration — in the hope thereby to disengage the luke-
warm middle colonies from the plot now thickening
against the government. But Massachusetts was at

once proclaimed in rebellion, every port in New England was declared closed against trade, New England fishermen were denied access to the Newfoundland fisheries, and ten thousand fresh troops were ordered to Boston. Neither the pleas of their friends nor the threats of their enemies reached the ears of the colonists promptly from over sea that portentous spring; but they were not slow to perceive that they must look for no concessions; and they did not wait upon Parliament in their preparation for a doubtful future. Upon the very day the "congress of committees" at Philadelphia adjourned, a "provincial congress" in Massachusetts, formed of its own authority in the stead of the House of Delegates the Governor had but just now dissolved, had voted to organize and equip the militia of the colony and to collect stores and arms. Virginia had been equally bold, and almost equally prompt, far away as she seemed from the King's troops at Boston. By the end of January Charles Lee could write from Williamsburg: "The whole country is full of soldiers, all furnished, all in arms. . . . Never was such vigor and concord heard of, not a single traitor, scarcely a silent dissentient."

"Every county is now arming a company of men for the avowed purpose of protecting their committees," Dunmore had reported to the ministry before the year 1774 was out, "and to be employed against government if occasion require. As to the power of government which your lordship directs should be exerted to counteract the dangerous measures pursuing here, I can assure your lordship that it is entirely disregarded, if not wholly overturned. There is not a justice of peace in Virginia that acts except as a committeeman; the abolishing of courts of justice was the first step taken, in which the men of fortune and pre-eminence joined equally with the lowest and meanest." Company after company, as it formed, asked Colonel Washington to assume command over it, not only in his own county of Fairfax, but in counties also at a distance—and he accepted the responsibility as often as it was offered to him. "It is my full intention," he said, simply, "to devote my life and fortune to the cause we are engaged in, if needful"; and he had little doubt any longer what was to come. He found time, even that stirring year, to quicken his blood once and again, nevertheless, while winter held, by a run with the hounds: for he was not turned politician so sternly even yet as to throw away his leisure upon anything less wholesome than the hale sport he loved.

On the 20th of May, 1775, the second Virginian convention met, not in Williamsburg, but at Richmond, and its chief business was the arming of the colony. Maryland had furnished the ironical formula with which to justify what was to be done : " Resolved, unanimously, that a well-regulated militia, composed of the gentlemen freeholders and other freemen, is the natural strength and only stable security of a free government ; and that such militia will relieve our mother-country from any expense in our protection and defence, will obviate the pretence of a necessity for taxing us on that account, and render it unnecessary to keep any standing army — ever dangerous to liberty — in this province." Mr. Henry accepted the formula with great relish, in the convention at Richmond, in his resolution " that the colony be immediately put into a posture of defence," but he broke with it in the speech with which he sup-

ported his measures of preparation. In that there was
no plan or pretence of peace, but, instead, a plain declaration of war. Once more did Edmund Pendleton,
Richard Bland, Mr. Nicholas, and Colonel Harrison
spring to their feet to check him, as in the old days of
the Stamp Act. Once more, nevertheless, did he have
his way, completely, triumphantly. What he had proposed was done, and his very opponents served upon
the committee charged with its accomplishment. It
was not doing more than other colonies had done; it
was only saying more; it was only dealing more fearlessly and frankly with fortune. Even slow, conservative men like John Dickinson, of Pennsylvania, shielded
themselves behind only an "if." "The first act of violence on the part of administration in America," they
knew, "or the attempt to reinforce General Gage this
winter or next year, will put the whole continent in
arms, from Nova Scotia to Georgia."

What they feared very speedily came to pass. 'Twas
hardly four weeks from the day Mr. Henry proclaimed
a state of war in the convention at Richmond before
the King's regulars were set upon at Lexington and
Concord and driven back in rout to their quarters by
the swarming militia-men of Massachusetts. On the
19th of April they had set out across a peaceful country
to seize the military stores placed at Concord. Before
the day was out they had been fairly thrown back into
Boston, close upon three hundred of their comrades
gone to a last reckoning; and the next morning disclosed a rapidly growing provincial army drawn in
threatened siege about them. In the darkness of that
very night (April 20th), at the command of Dunmore,
a force of marines was landed from an armed sloop that

lay in James River, in Virginia, to seize the gunpowder
stored at Williamsburg. The Virginians in their turn
sprang to arms, and Dunmore was forced, ere he could
rid himself of the business, to pay for the powder taken
—pay Captain Patrick Henry, at the head of a body of
militia under arms.

On the 10th of May the second Continental Congress
met at Philadelphia, with business to transact vastly
different from that to which the first "congress of committees" had addressed itself — not protests and re-
solves, but quick and efficient action. The very day it
met, a body of daring provincials under Ethan Allen
had walked into the open gates at Ticonderoga and
taken possession of the stout fortress "in the name of
the Great Jehovah and the Continental Congress"; and
two days later a similar exploit secured Crown Point to
the insurgents. Active war had begun; an army was
set down before Boston—a rude army that had grown
to be sixteen thousand strong within the first week of
its rally; the country was united in a general resistance,
and looked to the congress to give it organization and
guidance. Colonel Washington had come to the congress in his provincial uniform, and found himself a
great deal sought after in its committees. Not only
the drawing of state papers which would once more
justify their cause and their resort to arms in the eyes
of the world, but the actual mustering and equipment
of an army, quick fortification, the gathering of muni-
tions and supplies, the raising of money and the organization of a commissariat, the restraint of the Indians
upon the frontier, was the business in hand, and Washington's advice was invaluable when such matters were
afoot. He showed no hesitation as to what should be

done. His own mind had long ago been made up; and the sessions of the congress were not ended before Virginia was committed beyond all possibility of drawing back. The 1st of June saw her last House of Burgesses convene; for by the 8th of the month Dunmore was a fugitive — had seen the anger of a Williamsburg mob blaze hot against him, and had taken refuge upon a man - of - war lying in the river. The province was in revolution, and Washington was ready to go with it.

It meant more than he thought that he had come to Philadelphia habited like a soldier. It had not been his purpose to draw all eyes upon him: it was merely his instinctive expression of his own personal feeling with regard to the crisis that had come. But it was in its way a fulfilment of prophecy. When the first Virginian convention chose delegates to attend the congress of 1774, "some of the tickets on the ballot assigned reasons for the choice expressed in them. Randolph should preside in congress; Lee and Henry should display the different kinds of eloquence for which they were renowned; Washington should command the army, if an army should be raised; Bland should open the treasures of ancient colonial learning; Harrison should utter plain truths; and Pendleton should be the penman for business." No wonder the gentlemen from Virginia, coming with such confidence to the congress, made the instant impression they did for mastery and self - poise! "There are some fine fellows come from Virginia," Joseph Reed had reported, "but they are very high. We understand they are the capital men of the colony." Washington alone awaited his cue. Now he was to get it, without expecting it. The irregular army swarming before Boston was without standing or government. It had run hastily together out of four colonies; was subject to no common authority; hardly knew what allegiance it bore; might fall to pieces unless it were adequately commanded. The congress in Philadelphia was called upon to recognize and adopt it, give it leave and authority to act for all the colonies, give it a commander, and summon the whole country to recruit it. There was an obvious political necessity that the thing should be done, and done promptly. Massachusetts did not wish to stand alone; New England wanted the active assistance of the other colonies; something must be attempted to secure common action. The first thing to do was to choose an acceptable and efficient leader, and to choose him outside New England. To John Adams the choice seemed simple enough. There was no soldier in America, outside New England —nor inside either—to be compared, whether in experience or distinction, with Washington, the gallant, straightforward, earnest Virginian he had learned so to esteem and trust there in Philadelphia. He accordingly moved that congress " adopt the army at Cambridge," and declared that he had " but one gentleman in mind " for its command—"a gentleman from Virginia, who was among us," he said, " and very well known to all of us; a gentleman whose skill and experience as an officer, whose independent fortune, great talents, and excellent universal character, would command the approbation of all America, and unite the cordial exertions of all the colonies better than any other person in the union." Washington, taken unawares, rose and slipped in confusion from the room. Some of his own friends doubted the expediency of putting a Virginian at the head of a New England army, but the more clear-sighted among the New-Englanders did not, and the selection was made, after a little hesitation, unanimously.

Washington accepted his commission with that mixture of modesty and pride that made men love and honor him. "You may believe me, my dear Patsy," were his simple words to his wife, "when I assure you in the most solemn manner, that, so far from seeking this appointment, I have used every endeavor in my power to avoid it, not only from my unwillingness to part with you and the family, but from a consciousness of its being a trust too great for my capacity. . . . But as it has been a kind of destiny that has thrown me upon this service, I shall hope that my undertaking it is designed to answer some good purpose. . . . It was utterly out of my power to refuse this appointment, without exposing my character to such censures as would have reflected dishonor upon myself and given pain to my friends." He spoke in the same tone to the congress. "I beg it may be remembered," he said, "by every gentleman in this room, that I this day declare with the utmost sincerity I do not think myself equal to the command I am honored with." His commission was signed on the 19th of June; on the 21st he was on the road to the north—the road he had travelled twenty years ago to consult with Governor Shirley in Boston upon questions of rank, and to fall into Mary Philipse's snare by the way; the road he had ridden after the races, but three years ago, to put Jacky Custis at college in New York. "There is something charming to me in the conduct of Washington," exclaimed John Adams; and it was wholesome for the whole country that such a man should be put at the head of affairs. Many ignoble things were being done in the name of liberty, and an ugly tyranny had been brought to every man's door—"the tyranny of his next-door neighbor." There were men by the score in the colonies who had no taste or sympathy for the rebellion they now saw afoot— common men who knew little or nothing of the mother-country, as well as gentlemen of culture who loved her traditions and revered her crown; farmers and village lawyers, as well as merchants at the ports who saw their living gone and ruin staring them in the face. But the local committees and the "Sons of Liberty" everywhere saw to it that such men should know and dread and fearfully submit to the views of the majority. Government was suspended: there was nowhere so much as a justice of the peace acting under the authority of the crown. There might have been universal license had the rabble not seen their leaders so noble, so bent upon high and honorable purposes. It was an object-lesson in the character of the revolution to see Washington ride through the colonies to take charge of an insurgent army. And no man or woman, or child even, was likely to miss the lesson. That noble figure drew all eyes to it; that mien as if the man were a prince; that sincere and open countenance, which every man could see was lighted by a good conscience; that cordial ease in salute, as of a man who felt himself brother to his friends. There was something about Washington that quickened the pulses of a crowd at the same time that it awed them, that drew cheers which were a sort of voice of worship. Children desired sight of him, and men felt lifted after he had passed. It was good to have such a man ride all the open way from Philadelphia to Cambridge in sight of the people to assume command of the people's army. It gave character to the thoughts of all who saw him.

GENERAL WASHINGTON

MATTERS had not stood still before Boston to await a commander sent by congress. While Washington waited for his commission and made ready for his journey there had been fighting done which was to simplify his task. General William Howe had reached Boston with reinforcements on the 25th of May, and quite ten thousand troops held the city, while a strong fleet of men-of-war lay watchfully in the harbor. There was no hurry, it seemed, about attacking the sixteen thousand raw provincials, whose long lines were drawn loosely about the town from Charlestown Neck to Jamaica Plain. But commanding hills looked across the water on either hand—in Charlestown on the north and in Dorchester on the southeast—and it would be well, Howe saw, to secure them, lest they should be occupied by the insurgents. On the morning of the 17th of June, however, while leisurely preparations were a-making in Boston to occupy the hills of Charlestown, it was discovered that the provincials had been beforehand in the project. There they were in the clear sun, working diligently at redoubts of their own upon the height. Three thousand men were put across the water to drive them off. Though they mustered only seventeen hundred behind their unfinished works, three several assaults and the loss of a thousand men was the cost of dislodging them.

They withheld their fire till the redcoats were within fifty—nay, thirty—yards of them, and then poured out a deadly, blazing fire which no man could face and live. They were ousted only when they failed of powder and despaired of reinforcements. Veteran officers who had led the assault declared the regulars of France were not more formidable than these militia-men, whom they had despised as raw peasants. There was no desire to buy another American position at that price; and Washington had time enough for the complimentary receptions and addresses and the elaborate parade of escort and review that delayed his journey to headquarters.

He reached Cambridge on the 2d of July, and bore himself with so straightforward and engaging a courtesy in taking command that the officers he superseded could not but like him: jealousy was disarmed. But he found neither the preparations nor the spirit of the army to his liking. His soldierly sense of order was shocked by the loose discipline, and his instinct of command by the free and easy insolence of that irregular levy; and his authority grew stern as he labored to bring the motley host to order and effective organization. " The people of this government have obtained a character," his confidential letters declared, " which they by no means deserved—their officers, generally speaking, are the most indifferent kind of people I ever saw. I dare say the men would fight very well (if properly officered), although they are an exceedingly dirty and nasty people. . . . It is among the most difficult tasks I ever undertook in my life to induce these people to believe that there is, or can be, danger till the bayonet is pushed at their breasts. Not that it proceeds from any uncommon prowess, but rather from an unaccounta-

ble kind of stupidity in the lower class of these people,
which, believe me, prevails but too generally among the
officers of the Massachusetts part of the army, who are
nearly of the same kidney with the privates." He had
seen like demoralization and slackness in the old days at
Winchester, on the wild frontier, but he had expected
to find a better spirit and discipline in the New England
levies.

His first disgust, however, soon wore off. He was
not slow to see how shrewd and sturdy these uncouth,
intractable ploughboys and farmers could prove themselves upon occasion. "I have a sincere pleasure in
observing," he wrote to congress, "that there are
materials for a good army, a great number of able-
bodied men, active, zealous in the cause, and of unques-
tionable courage." There was time enough and to
spare in which to learn his army's quality. "Our lines
of defence are now completed," he could tell Lund
Washington on the 20th of August, "as near so at least
as can be—we now wish them to come out as soon as
they please; but they discover no inclination to quit
their own works of defence; and as it is almost impossible for us to get at them, we do nothing but watch
each other's motions all day at the distance of about a
mile." He could even turn away from military affairs
to advise that "spinning should go forward with all
possible despatch" on the estate at home, and to say,
"I much approve of your sowing wheat in clean ground,
although you should be late in doing it." Once more
he settled to the old familiar work, this time upon a
great scale, of carrying a difficult enterprise forward by
correspondence. Letters to the Continental Congress
at Philadelphia, letters to the provincial congresses of

the New England colonies, letters to subordinate (sometimes insubordinate) officers at distant posts, letters to
intimate friends and influential men everywhere, setting
forth the needs and situation of the army, advising
measures of organization, supply, and defence, pointing
out means that might be used and mistakes that must
be avoided, commanding, dissuading, guiding, forecast-
ing, poured steadily forth from those busy headquarters,
where the commander-in-chief was always to be found,
intent, deeply employed, calmly imperative, never tir-
ing, never hesitating, never storming, a leader and master of men and affairs. He was in his prime, and all
the forty-three years of his strenuous life he had been
at school to learn how such a task as this was to be
performed. He had found the army not only without
proper discipline and equipment, but actually without
powder; and the winter had come and was passing
away before even that primary and perilous need could
be supplied. The men of that extemporized army had
been enlisted but for a few months' service. When
their brief terms of enlistment ran out they inconti-
nently took themselves off; and Washington's most
earnest appeals to the continental and provincial congresses to provide for longer enlistments and an adequate
system of recruitment did not always suffice to prevent
his force from perilously dwindling away under his very
eyes. It was a merciful providence that disposed the
British to lie quiet in Boston.

Such authority as he had, Washington used to the utmost, and with a diligence and foresight which showed
all his old policy of Thorough. Under his orders a few
fast vessels were fitted out and armed as privateers at
the nearest safe ports. Marblehead volunteers in the

army were put aboard them for crews, and the enemy's supplies were captured upon the seas and brought over-land—the much-needed powder and all—into the American camp, while men-of-war which might have swept the coast lay just at hand in the harbor. No opportunity was missed either to disturb the British or to get what the army needed; and the ministers at home, as well as the commanders in Boston, grew uneasy and apprehensive in the presence of so active and watchful an opponent. He was playing the game boldly, even a bit desperately at times. More than once, as the slow months of siege dragged by, he would have hazarded a surprise and sought to take the city by storm, had not the counsel of his officers persistently restrained him.

Only in the north was there such fighting as he wished to see. Montgomery had pushed through the forests and taken Montreal (November 12th, 1775). At the same time Washington had sent a force of some twelve hundred men, under Benedict Arnold, to see what could be done against the little garrison at Quebec. The journey had cost Arnold four hundred men; but with what he had left he had climbed straight to the Heights of Abraham and summoned the British at their gates. When they would neither surrender nor fight, he had sat down to wait for Montgomery; and when he came, with barely five hundred men, had stormed the stout defences, in a driving snow-storm, in the black darkness that came just before the morning on the last day of the year. Had Montgomery not been killed in the assault, the surprise would have succeeded; and Arnold had no cause to be ashamed of the gallant affair. Failure though it was, it heartened the troops before Boston to think what might be done under such officers.

The monotony of the long, anxious season was broken at Cambridge by a touch now and again of such pleasures as spoke of home and gracious peace. In midwinter Mrs. Washington had driven into camp, come all the way from Virginia, with proper escort, in her coach and four, her horses bestridden by black postilions in their livery of scarlet and white; and she had seemed to bring with her to the homely place not only the ceremonious habit, but the genial and hospitable air of Virginia as well. Many a quiet entertainment at headquarters coaxed a little ease of mind out of the midst of even that grim and trying winter's work while she was there.

With the first month of spring Washington determined to cut inaction short and make a decisive stroke. He had been long enough with the army now to presume upon its confidence and obedience, though he followed his own counsels. Siege cannon had been dragged through the unwilling forests all the way from Ticonderoga; the supplies and the time had come; and on the morning of the 5th of March, 1776, the British stared to see ramparts and cannon on Dorchester Heights. "It was like the work of the genii of Aladdin's wonderful lamp," declared one of their astonished officers. Why they had themselves neglected to occupy the hills of Dorchester, and had waited so patiently till Washington should have time and such guns as he needed, was a question much pressed at home in England; and their stupidity was rewarded now. They had suffered themselves to be amused all night by a furious cannonading out of Roxbury, Somerville, and East Cambridge, while two thousand men, a battery of heavy ordnance, and hundreds of wagons and ox-carts with timber, bales of hay, spades, crowbars, hatchets, hammers, and nails, had been gotten safely to the Dorchester hills. When they saw what had happened they thought of the assault upon Bunker's Hill, and hesitated what to do. A violent storm blew up while they waited, rendering an attack across the water impracticable, and when the calmer morning of the 6th dawned it was too late; the American position was too strong. Neither the town nor the harbor could safely be held under fire from Dorchester Heights. There was nothing for it but to evacuate the place, and no one gainsaid their departure. By the 17th they were all embarked, eight thousand troops and nine hundred loyalist citizens of Boston, and had set sail towards the north for Halifax. They were obliged to leave behind them more than two hundred cannon and a great quantity of military stores of every kind—powder, muskets, gun-carriages, small-arms — whatever an army might need. When Washington established himself in General Howe's headquarters, in Mrs. Edwards's comfortable lodging-house at the head of State Street, he could congratulate himself not only on a surprising victory brilliantly won, but on the possession, besides, of more powder and better stores and equipments than he could have dreamed of in his camp at Cambridge. He caught up his landlady's little granddaughter one day, set her on his knee, as he liked to do, and asked her, smiling, which she liked the better, the redcoats or the provincials.

"The redcoats," said the child.

"Ah, my dear," said the young general, a blithe light in his blue eyes, "they look better, but they don't fight. The ragged fellows are the boys for fighting."

But he did not linger at Boston. He knew that its capture did not end, but only deepened, the struggle.

Reinforcements would be poured out of England with the spring, and the next point of attack would unquestionably be New York, the key to the Hudson. Here again was a city flanked about on either hand by water, and commanded by heights—the heights of Brooklyn. A garrison must be left in Boston, and New York must be held for the most part by a new levy, as raw, as ill organized and equipped, as factious, as uncertain in capacity and purpose, as that which had awaited his discipline and guidance before Boston. It was an army always a-making and to be made. The sea was open, moreover. The British could enter the great harbor when they pleased. The insurgents had no naval force whatever with which to withstand them on the water. There were a score of points to be defended which were yet without defence on the long island where the town lay, and round about the spreading arms of the sea that enclosed it; and there were but eighteen thousand militia-men mustered for the formidable task, in the midst of an active loyalist population. The thing must be attempted, nevertheless. The command of the Hudson would very likely turn out to be the command of the continent, and the struggle was now to be to the death.

It was too late to draw back. The royal authority had, in fact, been everywhere openly thrown off, even in the middle colonies, where allegiance and opinion hung still at so doubtful a balance. For Washington the whole situation must have seemed to be summed up in what had taken place in his own colony at home. Dunmore, when he fled to the men-of-war in the bay, had called upon all who were loyal to follow him; had even offered freedom to all slaves and servants who would enlist in the force he should collect for the purpose of "reducing the colony to a proper sense of its duty." Unable to do more, he had ravaged the coasts on either hand upon the Bay, and had put men ashore within the rivers to raid and burn, making Norfolk, with its loyalist merchants, his headquarters and rendezvous. Driven thence by the provincial militia, he had utterly destroyed the town by fire, and was now refuged upon Gwynn's Island, striking when he could, as before, at the unprotected hamlets and plantations that looked everywhere out upon the water. Virginia's only executive, these nine months and more, had been her Committee of Safety, of which Edmund Pendleton was president.

Washington had hardly begun his work of organization and defence at New York before North Carolina (April 12th, 1776) authorized her delegates in the congress at Philadelphia to join in a declaration of independence; and the next month (May 15th) the congress advised the colonies to give over all show and pretence of waiting for or desiring peace or accommodation: to form complete and independent governments of their own, and so put an end to "the exercise of every kind of authority under the crown." The next step was a joint Declaration of Independence, upon a motion made in congress by Richard Henry Lee, in eager obedience to the express bidding of a convention met in the hall of the Burgesses at Williamsburg to frame a constitution for Virginia. His motion was adopted by the votes of every colony except New York. It was a bitter thing to many a loyal man in the colonies to see such things done, and peace rendered impossible. Not even those who counted themselves among the warmest friends of the colonial cause were agreed that it was wise thus to throw off one government before another was put in its place—while there was as yet no better guidance in that distracted time than might be had from a body of gentlemen in Philadelphia who possessed no power but to advise. But the radicals were in the saddle. Washington himself came down from New York to urge that the step be taken. He deemed such radicalism wise ; for he wished to see compromise abandoned, and all minds set as sternly as his own in the resolve to fight the fight out to the bitter end. " I have never entertained an idea of an accommodation," he said, "since I heard of the measures which were adopted in consequence of the Bunker's Hill fight "; and his will hardened to the contest after the fashion that had always been characteristic of him when once the heat of action was upon him. He grew stern, and spoke sometimes with a touch of harshness, in the presence of his difficulties at New York ; because he knew that they were made for him in no small part by Americans who were in the British interest, and whom he scorned even while scrupulous to be just in what he did to thwart and master them. " It requires more serenity of temper, a deeper understanding, and more courage than fell to the lot of Marlborough to ride in this whirlwind," said John Adams ; and the young commander-in-chief had them all. But his quiet was often that of a metal at white heat, and he kindled a great fire with what he touched.

No strength of will, however, could suffice to hold New York and its open harbor against a powerful enemy with such troops as Washington could drill and make between April and July. On the 28th of June British transports began to gather in the lower bay. Within a few days they had brought thirty thousand

men, armed and equipped as no other army had ever
been in America. It was impossible to prevent their
landing, and they were allowed to take possession of
Staten Island unopposed. Men-of-war passed untouched
through the Narrows, and made their way at will up the
broad Hudson, unhurt by the batteries upon either shore.
General Howe remembered Dorchester and Charlestown
Heights, and directed his first movement against Washington's intrenched position on the hills of Brooklyn,
where quite half the American army lay. For a little
space he waited, till his brother, Admiral Lord Howe,
should come to act with him in negotiation and command. Lord Howe was authorized to offer pardon for
submission, and very honorably used a month and more
of good fighting time in learning that the colonists had
no desire to be pardoned. "No doubt we all need pardon from Heaven for our manifold sins and transgres-
sions," was Governor Trumbull's Connecticut version of
the general feeling, "but the American who needs the
pardon of his Britannic Majesty is yet to be found."
On the 22d of August, accordingly, General Howe put
twenty thousand men ashore at Gravesend Bay. On
the 27th, his arrangements for an overwhelming attack
succeeding at every point, he drove the five thousand
Americans thrown out to oppose him back into their
works upon the heights, with a loss of four hundred
killed and wounded and a thousand taken. Still mind-
ful of Bunker's Hill, he would not storm the intrenchments, to which Washington himself had brought reinforcements which swelled his strength upon the heights
to ten thousand. He determined, instead, to draw lines
of siege about them, and at his leisure take army, position, stores, and all. Washington, seeing at once what

Howe intended, and how possible it was, decided to withdraw immediately, before a fleet should be in the river and his retreat cut off. It was a masterly piece of work. The British commander was as much astounded to see Brooklyn Heights empty on the morning of August 30th as he had been to see Dorchester Heights occupied that memorable morning six months before. Washington had taken ten thousand men across that broad river, with all their stores and arms, in a single night, while a small guard kept up a sharp fire from the breastworks, and no sound of the retreat reached the dull ears of the British sentries.

But the sharp fighting and bitter defeat of the 27th had sadly, even shamefully, demoralized Washington's raw troops, and he knew he must withdraw from New York. All through September and a part of October he held what he could of the island, fighting for it almost mile by mile as he withdrew—now cut to the quick and aflame with almost uncontrollable anger to see what cowards his men could be; again heartened to see them stand and hold their ground like men, even in the open. The most that he could do was to check and thwart the powerful army pressing steadily upon his front and the free fleet threatening his flanks. He repulsed the enemy at Harlem Heights (September 16th); he kept his ground before them at White Plains, despite the loss of an outpost at Chatterton Hill (October 28th); he might possibly have foiled and harassed them the winter through had not General Greene suffered a garrison of three thousand of the best-trained men in the army to be penned up and taken, with a great store of artillery and small-arms besides, in Fort Washington, on the island (November 16th). After such a blow there was

nothing for it but to abandon the Hudson and retreat
through New Jersey. His generals growing insubordinate, Washington could not even collect his divisions and
unite his forces in retreat. His men deserted by the
score; whole companies took their way homeward as
their terms of enlistment expired with the closing of the
year; barely three thousand men remained with him by
the time he had reached Princeton. Congress, in its
fright, removed to Baltimore; hundreds of persons hurried to take the oath of allegiance upon Howe's offer of
pardon; and the British commanders deemed the rebellion at an end.

They did not understand the man they were fighting.
When he had put the broad Delaware between his
dwindling regiments and the British at his heels, he
stopped, undaunted, to collect force and give his opponents a taste of his quality. Such an exigency only stif-
fened his temper, and added a touch of daring to his
spirit. Charles Lee, his second in command, hoping to
make some stroke for himself upon the Hudson, had
withheld full half the army in a safe post upon the river,
in direct disobedience to orders, while the British drove
Washington southward through New Jersey; but Lee
was now happily in the hands of the enemy, taken at an
unguarded tavern where he lodged, and most of the
troops he had withheld found their way at last to Washington beyond the Delaware. Desperate efforts at recruiting were made. Washington strained his authority
to the utmost to keep and equip his force, and excused
himself to congress very nobly. " A character to lose,"
he said, " an estate to forfeit, the inestimable blessing of
liberty at stake, and a life devoted must be my excuse."
What he planned and did won him a character with his

foes. Before the year was out he had collected six thousand men, and was ready to strike a blow at the weak, extended line—Hessian mercenaries for the most part—which Howe had left to hold the Delaware.

On Christmas Day he made his advance, and ordered a crossing to be made in three divisions, under cover of the night. Only his own division, twenty-five hundred strong, effected the passage. 'Twas ten hours' perilous work to cross the storm-swept river in the pitchy darkness, amidst the hazards of floating ice, but not a man or a gun was lost. There was a nine miles' march through driving snow and sleet after the landing before Trenton could be reached, the point of attack, and two men were frozen to death as they went. General Sullivan sent word that the guns were wet: "Tell him to use the bayonet," said Washington, "for the town must be taken." And it was taken—in the early morning, at the point of the bayonet, with a loss of but two or three men. The surprise was complete. Colonel Rahl, the commander of the place, was mortally wounded at the first onset, and nine hundred Hessians surrendered at discretion.

When he had gotten his prisoners safe on the south side of the river, Washington once more advanced to occupy the town. It was a perilous place to be, no doubt, with the great unbridged stream behind him; but the enemy's line was everywhere broken, now that its centre had been taken; had been withdrawn from the river in haste, abandoning its cannon even and its baggage at Burlington; and Washington calmly dared to play the game he had planned. It was not Howe who came to meet him, but the gallant Cornwallis, no mean adversary, bringing eight thousand men. Washington let him come all the way to the Delaware without himself stirring, except to put a small tributary stream between his men and the advancing columns; and the confident Englishman went to bed that night exclaiming, "At last we have run down the old fox, and we'll bag him in the morning." Then, while a small force kept the camp-fires burning and worked audibly at the ramparts the cold night through, the fox was up and away. He put the whole of his force upon the road to Princeton and New Brunswick, where he knew Cornwallis's stores must be. As the morning's light broadened into day (January 3d, 1777) he met the British detachment at Princeton in the way, and drove it back in decisive rout, a keen ardor coming into his blood as he saw the sharp work done. "An old-fashioned Virginia fox-hunt, gentlemen," he exclaimed, shouting the view-halloo. Had his troops been fresh and properly shod to outstrip Cornwallis at their heels, he would have pressed on to New Brunswick and taken the stores there; but he had done all that could be done with despatch, and withdrew straight to the heights of Morristown. Cornwallis could only hasten back to New York. By the end of the month the Americans were everywhere afoot; the British held no posts in New Jersey but Paulus Hook, Amboy, and New Brunswick; and Washington had issued a proclamation commanding all who had accepted General Howe's offer of pardon either to withdraw within the British lines or to take oath of allegiance to the United States. Men loved to tell afterwards how Frederick the Great had said that it was the most brilliant campaign of the century.

Congress took steps before the winter was over to

secure long enlistments, and substitute a veritable army
for the three months' levies with which Washington
had hitherto been struggling to make shift.   After the
affair at Trenton, Washington had been obliged to
pledge his own private fortune for their pay to induce
the men whose terms of enlistment were to expire on
New Year's Day—more than half his force — to stay
with him but a few weeks more, till his plan should be
executed.   Now he was authorized to raise regiments
enlisted till the war should end, and to exercise almost
dictatorial powers in everything that might affect the
discipline, provisioning, and success of his army.   There
was need, for the year witnessed fighting of tremendous
consequence.   The British struck for nothing less than
complete possession of the whole State of New York,
throughout the valleys of the Hudson and the Mohawk.
General Howe, who had above twenty thousand men
in New York city, was to move up the Hudson; General Burgoyne, with eight thousand men, from Canada
down Lake Champlain; Colonel St. Leger, with a small
but sufficient force, down into the valley of the Mohawk, striking from Oswego, on Ontario; and the colonies were to be cut in twain, New England hopelessly separated from her confederates, by the converging
sweep of three armies, aggregating more than thirty-
three thousand men.   But only the coast country, it
turned out, was tenable ground for British troops.   Sir
Guy Carleton had attempted Champlain out of Canada
the year before, and had gone back to Quebec without
touching Ticonderoga, so disconcerted had he been by
the price he had had to pay for his passage up the lake
to a small force and an extemporized fleet under Benedict Arnold.   This time Burgoyne, with his splendid

army, made short work of Ticonderoga (July, 1777),
and drove General Schuyler and his army back to their
posts beyond the Hudson; but the farther he got from
his base upon the lake into the vast forests of that wide
frontier, the more certainly did he approach disaster.
No succor came. St. Leger was baffled, and sent in
panic back the way he had come. Howe did not ascend
the river. The country swarmed with gathering militia. They would not volunteer for distant campaigns;
but this invading host, marching by their very homes
into the deep forest, roused and tempted them as they
had been roused at Concord, and they gathered at its
rear and upon its flanks as they had run together to in-
vest Boston. A thousand men Burgoyne felt obliged
to leave in garrison at Ticonderoga; a thousand more,
sent to Bennington to seize the stores there, were overwhelmed and taken (August 16th). Quite twenty thousand provincials presently beset him, and he had but six
thousand left wherewith to save himself. He crossed
the river, for he still expected Howe; and there was
stubborn fighting about Saratoga (September 19th, October 7th), in which Arnold once more made his name
in battle. But the odds were too great; Burgoyne's supplies were cut off, his troops beaten; there was nothing
for it but capitulation (October 17th). He had been
trapped and taken by a rising of the country.

Howe had not succored him, partly because he lacked
judgment and capacity, partly because Washington had
thwarted him at every turn. From his position at Morristown, Washington could send reinforcements to the
north or recall them at will, without serious delay; and
Howe, in his hesitation, gave him abundant time to do
what he would. It was Sir William's purpose to occupy

the early summer, ere Burgoyne should need him, in an
attack on Philadelphia. On the 12th of June, accordingly, he threw a force of eighteen thousand men into
New Jersey. But Washington foiled him at each attempt to advance by hanging always upon his flank in
such a position that he could neither be safely ignored
nor forced to fight; and the prudent Howe, abandoning
the march, withdrew once more to New York. But he
did not abandon his project against Philadelphia. He
deemed it the "capital" of the insurgent confederacy,
and wished to discredit congress and win men of doubtful allegiance to his standard by its capture; and he
reckoned upon some advantage in drawing Washington
after him to the southward, away from Burgoyne's field
of operations in the north. Though July had come,
therefore, and Burgoyne must need him presently, he
put his eighteen thousand men aboard the fleet and
carried them by sea to the Chesapeake. Washington
was sorely puzzled. He had taken it for granted
that Howe would go north, and he had gone south!
"Howe's in a manner abandoning Burgoyne is so un-
accountable," he said, "that I cannot help casting my
eyes continually behind me;" and he followed very
cautiously, ready upon the moment to turn back, lest
the movement should prove a feint. But there was no
mistake. Howe entered the Delaware, and, being fright-
ened thence by reports of obstructions in the river, went
all the long four hundred miles about the capes of
Chesapeake, and put his army ashore at Elkton for its
advance upon Philadelphia. It was then the 25th of
August. Washington met him (September 11th) behind
the fords of the Brandywine, and, unable to check
Cornwallis on his flank, was defeated. But for him

defeat was never rout: his army was still intact and
steady; and he held his foe yet another fortnight on
the road ere the "capital" could be entered (September
27th). Burgoyne was by that time deep within the net
spread for him at Saratoga. On the morning of the 4th
of October, in a thick mist, Washington threw himself
upon Howe's main force encamped across the village
street of Germantown, and would have overwhelmed it
in the surprising onset had not two of his own columns
gone astray in the fog, attacked each other, and so lost
the moment's opportunity. General Howe knew very
soon how barren a success he had had. The end of
November came before he had made himself master of
the forts upon the Delaware below the " capital " and
removed the obstructions from the river to give access
to his fleet; the British power was broken and made an
end of in the north ; and Washington was still at hand
as menacing and dangerous as ever. Dr. Franklin was
told in Paris that General Howe had taken Philadelphia. " Philadelphia has taken Howe," he laughed.

Philadelphia kept Howe safely through the winter,
and his officers made themselves easy amidst a round of
gayeties in the complacent town, while Washington
went to Valley Forge to face the hardships and the in-
trigues of a bitter season. A deep demoralization fell
that winter, like a blight, upon all the business of the
struggling confederacy. The congress, in its exile at
York, had lost its tone and its command in affairs. It
would have lost it as completely in Philadelphia, no
doubt, for it was no longer the body it had been. Its
best members were withdrawn to serve their respective
states in the critical business, now everywhere in hand,
of reorganizing their governments ; and it itself was no

government at all, but simply a committee of advice, which the states heeded or ignored as they pleased. Oftentimes but ten or twelve members could be got together to transact its business. It suffered itself to fall into the hands of intriguers and sectional politicians. It gave commissions in the army not according to merit, but upon a plan carefully devised to advance no more officers from one section than from another—even men like John Adams approving. Adams denounced claims of seniority and service as involving "one of the most putrid corruptions of absolute monarchy," and suggested that the officers who did not relish the idea of seeing the several states given "a share of the general officers," proportioned to the number of troops they had sent to the army, had better take themselves off, and see how little they would be missed. Worst of all, an ugly plot was hatched to displace Washington ; and the various distempers of different men for a brief season gave it a chance to succeed. Some were impatient of Washington's "Fabian policy," as they called it, and would have had him annihilate, instead of merely checking, these invading hosts. "My toast," cried John Adams, "is a short and violent war." Others envied Washington his power and his growing fame, resented their own subordination and his supremacy, and intrigued to put General Gates in his place. Had not Gates won at Saratoga, and Washington lost at the Brandywine and at Germantown? Schuyler had prepared the victory in the north ; Arnold and Morgan had done the fighting that secured it ; but Gates had obtained the command when all was ready, and was willing to receive the reward. With a political committee-congress in charge of affairs, nothing was impossible.

Washington and his army were starving the while
at Valley Forge, in desperate straits to get anything
to eat or anything to cover them in that bitter season—
not because there were no supplies, but because congress
had disorganized the commissary department, and the
supplies seldom reached the camp. The country had
not been too heavily stricken by the war. Abundant
crops were everywhere sown and peacefully reaped, and
there were men enough to do the work of seed-time and
harvest. It was only the army that was suffering for
lack of food and lack of men. The naked fact was that
the confederacy was falling apart for lack of a government. Local selfishness had overmastered national feeling, and only a few men like Washington held the
breaking structure together. Washington's steadfastness was never shaken ; and Mrs. Washington, stanch
lady that she was, joined him even at Valley Forge.
The intrigue against him he watched in stern silence
till it was ripe and evident, then he crushed it with
sudden exposure, and turned away in contempt, hardly
so much as mentioning it in his letters to his friends.
" Their own artless zeal to advance their views has
destroyed them," he said. His soldiers he succored and
supplied as he could, himself sharing their privations,
and earning their love as he served them. " Naked and
starving as they are," he wrote, " we cannot sufficiently
admire the incomparable patience and fidelity of the
soldiers." And even out of that grievous winter some
profit was wrung. Handsome sums of French money
had begun of late to come slowly into the confederate
treasury—for France, for the nonce, was quick with
sympathy for America, and glad to lend secret aid
against an old foe. Presently, she promised, she would

recognize the independence of the United States, and
herself grapple once more with England. Meanwhile
French, German, and Polish officers hurried over sea
to serve as volunteers with the raw armies of the confederacy — adventurers, some of them; others sober
veterans, gentlemen of fortune, men of generous and
noble quality—among the rest the boyish Lafayette
and the distinguished Steuben. Baron von Steuben
had won himself a place on the great Frederick's staff
in the Seven Years' War, and was of that studious race
of soldiers the world was presently to learn to fear. He
joined Washington at Valley Forge, and turned the
desolate camp into a training-school of arms, teaching,
what these troops had never known before, promptness
and precision in the manual of arms, in massed and
ordered movement, in the use of the bayonet, the drill
and mastery of the charge and of the open field. Neither Washington nor any of his officers had known how
to give this training. The commander-in-chief had not
even had a properly organized staff till this schooled
and thorough German supplied it, and he was valued
in the camp as he deserved. " You say to your soldier,
' Do this,' and he doeth it," he wrote to an old comrade
in Prussia; " I am obliged to say to mine, ' This is the
reason why you ought to do that,' and then he does
it." But he learned to like and to admire his new comrades soon enough when he found what spirit and
capacity there was in them for the field of action.

The army came out of its dismal winter quarters
stronger than it had ever been before, alike in spirit
and in discipline; more devoted to its commander than
ever, and more fit to serve him. At last the change to
a system of long enlistments had transformed it from

a levy of militia into an army steadied by service, un-
afraid of the field. The year opened, besides, with a
new hope and a new confidence. They were no longer
a body of insurgents even to the eye of Europe. News
came to the camp late in the night of the 4th of May
(1778) that France had entered into open alliance with
the United States, and would send fleets and an army
to aid in securing their independence. Such an alliance
changed the whole face of affairs. England would no
longer have the undisputed freedom of the seas, and
the conquest of her colonies in America might turn out
the least part of her task in the presence of European
enemies. She now knew the full significance of Saratoga and Germantown. Washington's splendid audacity and extraordinary command of his resources in
throwing himself upon his victorious antagonist at Germantown as the closing move of a long retreat had
touched the imagination and won the confidence of foreign soldiers and statesmen hardly less than the taking
of Burgoyne at Saratoga. Parliament at last (February, 1778) came to its senses: resolved to renounce the
right to tax the colonies, except for the regulation of
trade, and sent commissioners to America to offer such
terms for submission. But it was too late; neither congress nor the states would now hear of anything but
independence.

With a French fleet about to take the sea, it was
necessary that the British commanders in America
should concentrate their forces. Philadelphia, they had
at last found out, was a burden, not a prize. It had
no strategic advantage of position; was hard to defend,
and harder to provision; was too far from the sea, and
not far enough from Washington's open lines of opera-

tion. Before the summer's campaign began, Sir William Howe resigned his command and bade the town good-bye, amidst elaborate festivities (May 18th, 1778). General Clinton, who succeeded him, received orders from England to undo Howe's work at once, abandon Philadelphia, and concentrate his forces at New York. 'Twas easier said than done. There were not transports enough to move his fifteen thousand men by sea; only the three thousand loyalists who had put themselves under his protection could be sent in the ships, with a portion of his stores; he must cross the hostile country; and his march was scarcely begun (June 18th) before Washington was at his heels, with a force but little inferior to his own either in numbers or in discipline. He might never have reached New York at all had not Charles Lee been once more second in command in the American army. He had come out of captivity, exchanged, and now proved himself the insubordinate poltroon he was. He had never had any real heart in the cause. He owned estates in Virginia, but he was not of the great Virginian family of the Northern Neck. He was only a soldier of fortune, strayed out of the British service on half-pay to seek some profit in the colonies, and cared for no interest but his own. While a prisoner he had secretly directed Howe's movement against Philadelphia, and now he was to consummate his cowardly treachery. Washington outstripped his opponent in the movement upon New York, and determined to fall upon him at Monmouth Court House, where, on the night of the 27th of June, Clinton's divisions lay separate, offering a chance to cut them asunder. On the morning of the 28th, Lee was ordered forward with six thousand men to enfold Clinton's left wing—eight thousand men, the flower of the British force—by gaining its flank, while Washington held his main body ready to strike in his aid at the right moment. The movement was perfectly successful, and the fighting had begun, when, to the amazement and chagrin alike of officers and men, Lee began to withdraw. Lafayette sent a messenger hot-foot for Washington, who rode up to find his men, not attacking, but pursued. " What is the meaning of all this ?" he thundered, his wrath terrible to see. When Lee would have made some excuse, he hotly cursed him, in his fury, for a coward, himself rallied the willing troops, and led them forward again to a victory : won back the field Lee had abandoned, and drove the enemy to the cover of a morass. In the night that followed, Clinton hastily withdrew, leaving even his wounded behind him, and Washington's chance to crush him was gone.

" Clinton gained no advantage except to reach New York with the wreck of his army," commented the observant Frederick over sea ; " America is probably lost for England." But a great opportunity had been treacherously thrown away, and the war dragged henceforth with every painful trial of hope deferred. A scant three weeks after Clinton had reached New York, the Count d'Estaing was off Sandy Hook, with a French fleet of twelve ships of the line and six frigates, bringing four thousand troops. The British fleet within the harbor was barely half as strong ; but the pilots told the cautious Frenchman that his larger ships could not cross the bar, and he turned away from New York to strike at Newport, the only other point now held by the British in all the country. That place had hardly been invested, however, when Lord Howe appeared with a

stronger fleet than the French. D'Estaing was obliged
to draw off to meet him ; a great storm sent both fleets
into port to refit instead of to fight ; and the disgusted
militia-men and continentals, who had come to take the
town with the French, withdrew in high choler to see
the fleet, without which they could do nothing, taken
off to Boston.   When the autumn came Clinton felt
free to send thirty-five hundred men to the Southern
coast, and Savannah was taken (December 29th, 1778).
Only in the far West, at the depths of the great wilderness beyond the mountains, was anything done that
promised decisive advantage.   George Rogers Clark,
that daring Saxon frontiersman, who moved so like a
king through the far forests, swept the whole country
of the Illinois free from British soldiers and British authority that winter of 1778–9, annexing it to the states
that meant to be independent ; and a steady stream of
immigration began to pour into the opened country, as
if to prepare a still deeper task of conquest for the British at far New York.

But few noted in the East what gallant men were doing in the valley of the Mississippi.   They saw only
that the British, foiled in New England and the middle
colonies, had changed their plans, and were now minded
to try what could be done in the South.   There at last
their campaigns seemed about to yield them something.
Savannah taken, they had little trouble in overrunning
Georgia, and every effort to dislodge them failed ; for
Washington could not withdraw his army from before
Clinton at New York.   Spain joined France in offensive
alliance in April, 1779 ; in August a combined French
and Spanish fleet attempted an invasion of England ; all
Europe seemed about to turn upon the stout little king-

dom in its unanimous fear and hatred of her arrogant supremacy upon the seas. Everywhere there was war upon the ocean highways—even America sending forth men of desperate valor, like John Paul Jones, to ravage and challenge Britain upon her very coasts. But England's spirit only rose with the danger, and Washington waited all the weary year through for his French allies. In 1780 it looked for a little as if the British were indeed turned victors. In the spring Clinton withdrew the force that had held Newport to New York, and, leaving General Knyphausen there with a powerful force to keep Washington and the city, carried eight thousand men southward to take Charleston. There were forces already in the South sufficient to swell his army to ten thousand ere he invested the fated town ; and on the 12th of May (1780) it fell into his hands, with General Lincoln and three thousand prisoners. Washington had sent such succor as he could, but the British force was overwhelming, and South Carolina was lost. South Carolina teemed with loyalists. The whole country was swept and harried by partisan bands. The men who should have swelled General Lincoln's force knew not when their homes might be plundered and destroyed, if they were to leave them. The planters of the low country dared not stir for fear of an insurrection of their slaves. In June, Clinton could take half his force back to New York, deeming the work done. General Gates completed the disastrous record. On the 13th of June he was given chief command in the South, and was told that the country expected another " Burgoynade." His force was above three thousand, and he struck his blow, as he should, at Camden, where Cornwallis had but two thousand men, albeit trained and

veteran troops; but the end was total, shameful rout
(August 16th, 1780), and men knew at last the incapacity
of their "hero of Saratoga." "We look on America as
at our feet," said Horace Walpole.

Certainly things looked desperate enough that dark
year. The congress was sinking into a more and more
helpless inefficiency. Definitive articles of confederation
had been submitted to the states nearly three years ago
(November, 1777), but they had not been adopted yet,
and the states had almost ceased to heed the requisitions
of the congress at all. Unable to tax, it paid its bills
and the wages of its troops in paper, which so rapidly
fell in value that by the time the hopeless year 1780 was
out, men in the ranks found a month's pay too little
with which to buy even a single bushel of wheat.
Washington was obliged to levy supplies from the country round him to feed his army; and in spite of their
stanch loyalty to him, his men grew mutinous, in sheer
disgust with the weak and faithless government they
were expected to serve. Wholesale desertion began, as
many as one hundred men a month going over to the
enemy, to get at least pay and food and clothing. The
country seemed not so much dismayed as worn out and
indifferent; weary of waiting and hoping; looking stol-
idly to see the end come. Washington was helpless.
Without the co-operation of a naval force, it was impossible to do more than hold the British in New York.
France, it was true, was bestirring herself again. On
the 10th of July a French fleet put in at Newport and
landed a force of six thousand men, under Count Rochambeau, a most sensible and capable officer, who was
directed to join Washington and put himself entirely
under his command. But a powerful British fleet pres-

ently made its appearance in the Sound; the French admiral dared not stir; Rochambeau dared not leave him without succor; and the reinforcements that were to have followed out of France were blockaded in the harbor of Brest.

Then, while things stood so, treason was added. Benedict Arnold, the man whom Washington trusted with a deep affection, and whom the army loved for his gallantry, entered into correspondence with the enemy; arranged to give West Point and the posts dependent upon it into their hands; and, his treason suddenly detected, escaped without punishment to the British sloop of war that waited in the river for the British agent in the plot. Washington was at hand when the discovery was made. His aides were breakfasting with Arnold when the traitor was handed the note which told him he was found out; and Arnold had scarcely excused himself and made good his flight when the commander-in-chief reached the house. When Washington learned what had happened, it smote him so that mighty sobs burst from him, as if his great heart would break; and all the night through the guard could hear him pacing his room endlessly, in a lonely vigil with his bitter thoughts. He did not in his own grief forget the stricken wife upstairs. "Go to Mrs. Arnold," he said to one of his officers, "and tell her that, though my duty required that no means should be neglected to arrest General Arnold, I have great pleasure in acquainting *her* that he is now safe on board a British vessel." Arnold had deemed himself wronged and insulted by congress—but what officer that Washington trusted might not? Who could be confided in if such men turned traitors?

But a sudden turning of affairs marked the close of the year. Cornwallis had penetrated too far into the Carolinas; had advanced into North Carolina, and was beset, as Burgoyne had been, by a rising of the country. He lost twelve hundred men at King's Mountain (October 7th, 1780), as Burgoyne had lost a thousand at Bennington; and everywhere, as he moved, he found himself checked by the best officers the long war had bred —Nathanael Greene, who had been Washington's right hand the war through; Henry Lee, the daring master of cavalry, whom Washington loved; the veteran Steuben; Morgan, who had won Saratoga with Arnold; and partisan leaders a score, whom he had learned to dread in that wide forested country. He was outgeneralled; his forces were taken in detail and beaten, and he himself was forced at last into Virginia. By midsummer, 1781, all his interior posts were lost, and he was cut off from Charleston and Savannah by a country he dared not cross again. In Virginia, though at first he raided as he pleased, he was checked more and more as the season advanced by a growing force under Lafayette; and by the first week in August he had taken counsel of prudence, and established himself, seven thousand strong, at Yorktown, near the sea, his base of supplies. Then it was that Washington struck the blow which ended the war. At last Rochambeau was free to move; at last a French fleet was at hand to block the free passage of the sea. The Count de Grasse, with twenty-eight ships of the line, six frigates, and twenty thousand men, was in the West Indies, and in August sent word to Washington that he was about to bring his whole fleet to the Chesapeake, as Washington had urged. Either the Chesapeake or New York, had been

Washington's prayer to him. Making as if he were but moving about New York from north to south for some advantage of position, Washington suddenly took two thousand Continentals and four thousand Frenchmen, under Rochambeau, all the long four hundred miles to York River in Virginia, to find Cornwallis already entrapped there, as he had planned, between Grasse's fleet in the bay and Lafayette intrenched across the peninsula with eight thousand men, now the French had loaned him three thousand. A few weeks' siege and the decisive work was done, to the admiration of Cornwallis himself. The British army was taken. The generous Englishman could not withhold an expression of his admiration for the extraordinary skill with which Washington had struck all the way from New York with six thousand men as easily as if with six hundred. "But, after all," he added, "your Excellency's achievements in New Jersey were such that nothing could surpass them."

THE STRESS OF VICTORY

THE victory at Yorktown brought neither peace nor ease in affairs. The revolution was indeed accomplished —that every man could see who had the candor to look facts in the face; but its accomplishment brought tasks harder even than the tasks of war. Hostilities slackened—were almost wholly done with before another spring had come. No more troops came over sea. The ministry in England were discredited and ousted. Every one knew that the proud mother country must yield, for all her stout defiance of the world. But a long year dragged by, nevertheless, before even preliminary articles of accommodation were signed; and still another before definitive peace came, with independence and the full fruits of victory. Meanwhile there was an army to be maintained, despite desperate incompetence on the part of the congress and a hopeless indifference among the people; and a government to be kept presentably afoot, despite lack of money and lack of men. The Articles of Confederation proposed at the heart of the war time (November 15th, 1777) had at last been adopted (March 1st, 1781), in season to create at least a government which could sign treaties and conclude wars, but neither soon enough nor wisely enough to bring order out of chaos. The states, glad to think the war over, would do nothing for the army, nothing for the public credit, nothing even for the maintenance of order ; and the Articles of Confederation only gave the congress written warranty for offering advice : they did not make its shadowy powers real.

It was beyond measure fortunate that at such a critical time as this Washington still kept his command, still held affairs under the steady pressure of his will. His successes had at last given him a place of authority in the thoughts and affections of his countrymen in some sort commensurate with his capacity and his vision in affairs. He had risen to a very safe footing of power among all the people as the war drew towards its close, filling their imaginations, and reigning among them as securely as among his troops, who for so long had felt his will wrought upon them day by day. His very reserve, and the large dignity and pride of his stately bearing, made him seem the more like a hero in the people's eyes. They could understand a man made in this ample and simple kind, give them but time enough to see him in his full proportions. It answered to their thought of him to find him too proud to dissemble, too masterful to brook unreasonable faults, and yet slow to grow impatient, though he must wait a whole twelve-month to see a plan mature, or coax a half-score states to get a purpose made good. And they could not deem him cold, though they found him self-possessed, keeping his own counsel ; for was not the country full of talk how passionately he was like to act at a moment of crisis and in the field? They only feared to lose a leader so reckless of himself when danger was sharpest. "Our army love their general very much," one of his officers had said, " but they have one thing against him, which is the little care he takes of himself in any

action "; for he had seen how Washington pressed at
Trenton and at Princeton to the points that were most
exposed, thinking of his troops, not of himself. The
spirit of fight had run high in him the whole war
through. Even during those dismal weeks of 1776,
when affairs looked darkest, and he had but a handful
of men about him as he all but fled before Howe
through New Jersey, he had spoken, as if in the very
pleasantry of daring, of what he would do should things
come to the worst with him. His thought turned to
those western fastnesses he knew so well, where the
highlands of his own state lay, and he spoke calmly of
a desperate venture thither. "Reed," he exclaimed, to
one of his aides, "my neck does not feel as though it
was made for a halter. We must retire to Augusta
County, in Virginia, and if overpowered, must pass the
Alleghany Mountains." And when the last movement
of the war came, it was still with the same feeling that
he drew his lines about Cornwallis. "We may be
beaten by the English," he said ; "it is the chance of
war ; but there is the army they will never conquer."

"The privates are all generals, but not soldiers," the
gallant Montgomery had cried, in his hot impatience
with the heady militia-men he was bidden command ;
but it was not so in the presence of Washington, when
once these men had taken his measure. They were
then "rivals in praising him," the Abbé Robin declared, "fearing him even when he was silent, and retaining their full confidence in him after defeats and
disgrace." The singular majesty and poise of this revolutionary hero struck the French officers as infinitely
more remarkable than his mastery in the field and his
ascendency in council. They had looked to find him

great in action, but they had not thought to see in him
a great gentleman, a man after their own kind in grace
and courtesy and tact, and yet so lifted above the manner of courts and drawing-rooms by an incommunicable
quality of grave sincerity which they were at a loss how
to describe. No one could tell whether it were a gift of
the mind or of the heart. It was certain only that it
constituted the atmosphere and apotheosis of the man.
The Marquis de Chastellux noted, with a sort of reverent awe for this hero not yet turned of fifty, how
perfect a union reigned between his physical and moral
qualities. " One alone," he declared, " will enable you
to judge of all the rest." " It is not my intention to
exaggerate," he said; " I wish only to express my impression of a perfect whole, which cannot be the product of enthusiasm, since the effect of proportion is
rather to diminish the idea of greatness."

Strangers who had noted his appearance in the earlier
years of the war had remarked the spirit and life that
sat in Washington's eyes: but when the war was over,
and its strain relaxed, they found those eyes grown
pensive, " more attentive than sparkling"; steady still,
and noble in their frankness and good feeling, but
touched a little with care, dimmed with watching. The
Prince de Broglie found him "still as fresh and active
as a young man " in 1782, but thought " he must have
been much handsomer three years ago," for " the gentlemen who had remained with him during all that
time said that he seemed to have grown much older."
'Twould have been no marvel had he broken under the
burden he had carried, athletic soldier and hardened
campaigner though he was. " This is the seventh year
that he has commanded the army and that he has

obeyed the congress : more need not be said," the Marquis de Chastellux declared, unconsciously uttering a very bitter gibe against the government, when he meant only to praise its general.

Such service told the more heavily upon Washington because he had rendered it in silence. No man among all the Revolutionary leaders, it is true, had been more at the desk than he. Letters of command and persuasion, reports that carried every detail of the army's life and hopes in their careful phrases, orders of urgency and of provident arrangement, writings of any and every sort that might keep the hard war afoot, he had poured forth incessantly, and as if incapable of fatigue or discouragement. No one who was under orders, no man who could lend the service a hand or take a turn at counsel, was likely to escape seeing the commander-in-chief's handwriting often enough to keep him in mind of his tireless power to foresee and to direct. Washington seemed present in every transaction of the war. And yet always and to every one he seemed a silent man. What he said and what he wrote never touched himself. He spoke seldom of motives, always of what was to be done and considered; and even his secretaries, though they handled the multitude of his papers, were left oftentimes to wonder and speculate about the man himself—so frank and yet so reserved, so straightforward and simple and yet so proud and self-contained, revealing powers, but somehow not revealing himself. It must have seemed at times to those who followed him and pondered what they saw that he had caught from Nature her own manner while he took his breeding as a boy and his preparation as a man amidst the forests of a wild frontier; that his character spoke in

what he did and without self-consciousness; that he
had no moods but those of action.

Nor did men know him for what he really was until
the war was over. His own officers then found they
had something more to learn of the man they had
fought under for six years—and those six, all of them,
years such as lay bare the characters of men. What
remained to be done during the two trying, anxious
years 1782 and 1783 seemed as if intended for a supreme
and final test of the qualities of the man whose genius
and character had made the Revolution possible. "At
the end of a long civil war," said the Marquis de Chastellux, with a noble pride for his friend, "he had nothing with which he could reproach himself"; but it was
these last years which were to crown this perfect praise
with its full meaning. In the absence of any real government, Washington proved almost the only prop of
authority and law. What the crisis was no one knew
quite so thoroughly or so particularly as he. It consisted in the ominous fact that the army was the only
organized and central power in the country, and that
it had deep reason for discontent and insubordination.
When once it had served its purpose greatly at Yorktown, and the war seemed ended at a stroke, the country turned from it in indifference—left it without money;
talked of disbanding it without further ceremony, and
with no provision made for arrears of pay; seemed
almost to challenge it to indignation and mutiny. It
was necessary, for every reason of prudence and good
statesmanship, to keep the army still upon a war footing.
There were sure signs of peace, no doubt, but no man
could foretell what might be the course of politics ere
England should have compounded her quarrel with

France and Spain, and ended the wars with which the
Revolution had become inextricably involved. 'Twere
folly to leave the English army at New York unchecked.
Premature confidence that peace had come might bring
some sudden disaster of arms, should the enemy take
the field again. The army must be ready to fight, if
only to make fighting unnecessary. Washington would
have assumed the offensive again, would have crushed
Clinton where he lay in New York; and the congress
was not slack—as slackness was counted there—in sus-
taining his counsels. But the congress had no power
to raise money; had no power to command. The
states alone could make it possible to tax the country
to pay the army : their thirteen governments were the
only civil authority, and they took the needs and the
discontents of the army very lightly, deemed peace secure and war expenses unnecessary, and let matters drift
as they would.

They came very near drifting to another revolution
—a revolution such as politicians had left out of their
reckoning, and only Washington could avert. After
Yorktown, Washington spent four months in Philadelphia, helping the congress forward with the business of
the winter; but as March of the new year (1782) drew
towards its close, he rejoined the army at Newburgh,
to resume his watch upon New York. He had been
scarcely two months at his post when a letter was
placed in his hands which revealed, more fully than any
observations of his own could have revealed it, the pass
to which affairs had come. The letter was from Colonel
Lewis Nicola, an old and respected officer, who stood
nearer than did most of his fellow-officers to the commander-in-chief in intimacy and affection, and who felt

it his privilege to speak plainly. The letter was calm
in temper, grave and moderate in tone, with something
of the gravity and method of a disquisition written
upon abstract questions of government; did not broach
its meaning like a revolutionary document. But what
it proposed was nothing less, when read between the
lines, than that Washington should suffer himself to be
made king, and that so an end should be put to the
incompetency and ingratitude of a band of weak and
futile republics. Washington met the suggestion with
a rebuke so direct and overwhelming that Colonel Nicola
must himself have wondered how he had ever dared
make such a venture. " Be assured, sir," said the indignant commander, " no occurrence in the course of the
war has given me more painful sensations than your information of there being such ideas existing in the army.
. . . I am much at a loss to conceive what part of my
conduct could have given encouragement to an address
which to me seems big with the greatest mischiefs that
can befall my country. If I am not deceived in the
knowledge of myself, you could not have found a person
to whom your schemes are more disagreeable. . . . Let
me conjure you, if you have any regard for your country,
concern for yourself or posterity, or respect for me, to
banish these thoughts from your mind, and never communicate, as from yourself or any one else, a sentiment
of the like nature." He was cut to the quick that his
own officers should deem him an adventurer, willing to
advance his own power at the expense of the very
principles he had fought for. His thought must have
gone back at a bound to his old comradeship with his
brother Lawrence, with the Fairfaxes, George Mason,
and the Lees, and all that free company of gentlemen

in the Northern Neck who revered law, loved liberty, and hated a usurper.

But he could not blink the just complaints and real grievances of the army; nor did he wish to. Though others were angry after a manner he scorned, no man's grief or indignation was deeper than his that the army should be left penniless after all it had suffered and done, and be threatened, besides, with being turned adrift without reward or hope of provision for the future. "No man possesses a more sincere wish to see ample justice done to the army than I do," he had declared to Colonel Nicola; "and as far as my power and influence, in a constitutional way, extend, they shall be employed to the utmost of my abilities to effect it." The pledge was fulfilled in almost every letter he wrote, private or public. He urged the states, as he urged the congress, in season and out of season, to see justice done the men who had won the Revolution, and whom he loved as if they had been of his own blood. But even his great voice went too long unheeded. "The spirit of party, private interest, slowness, and national indolence slacken, suspend, and overthrow the best concerted measures," the Abbé Robin had observed, upon his first coming with Rochambeau; and now measures were not so much as concerted until a final menace from the army brought the country to its senses. A troubled summer came and went, and another winter of anxious doubt and ineffectual counsel. The very approach of peace, as it grew more certain, quickened the angry fears of the army, lest peace should be made a pretext, when it came, to disperse them before their demands could be driven home upon the demoralized and reluctant government they were learning to despise.

Another spring and the mischief so long maturing was
ripe; it looked as if even Washington could not prevent
it. It had been rumored in Philadelphia, while the
winter held, "that the army had secretly determined
not to lay down their arms until due provision and a
satisfactory prospect should be afforded on the subject
of their pay," and that Washington had grown unpop-
ular among almost all ranks because of his harshness
against every unlawful means of securing justice. "His
extreme reserve, mixed sometimes with a degree of as-
perity of temper, both of which were said to have increased of late, had contributed to the decline of his
popularity"—so ran the report—and it grew every
week the more unlikely he could check the treasonable
purposes of his men.

In March, 1783, the mine was sprung; and then men
learned, by a new sign, what power there was in the
silent man: how he could handle disaffection and dis-
arm reproach. An open address was spread broadcast
through the camp, calling upon the army to use its
power to obtain its rights, and inviting a meeting of the
officers to devise a way. "Can you consent to be the
only sufferers by this Revolution? . . . If you can, . . go,
. . carry with you the ridicule, and, what is worse, the
pity of the world. Go, starve, and be forgotten. . . .
But if you have sense enough to discover, and spirit
enough to oppose, tyranny, . . awake; attend to your
situation, and redress yourselves." Such were its kind-
ling phrases; and no man need deceive himself with
thinking they would go unheeded. Washington showed
his tact and mastery by assuming immediate control of
the movement, with a sharp rebuke for such a breach
of manly propriety and soldierly discipline, but with no

thought to stay a righteous protest. He himself summoned the officers ; and when they had come together
stepped to the desk before them, with no show of anger
or offended dignity, but very gravely, with a sort of
majesty it moved one strangely to see, and taking a
written paper from his pocket, adjusted his spectacles
to read it. " Gentlemen," he said, very simply, " you
will permit me to put on my spectacles, for I have not
only grown gray, but almost blind, in the service of my
country." There were wet eyes upon the instant in the
room ; no man stirred while he read — read words of
admonition, of counsel, and of hope which burned at
the ear; and when he was done, and had withdrawn,
leaving them to do what they would, they did nothing
of which he could be ashamed. They spoke manfully,
as was right, of what they deemed it just and imperative the congress should do for them; but they "Resolved, unanimously, that at the commencement of the
present war the officers of the American army engaged
in the service of their country from the purest love and
attachment to the rights and liberties of human nature,
which motives still exist in the highest degree ; and that
no circumstances of distress or danger shall induce a
conduct that may tend to sully the reputation and glory
which they have acquired at the price of their blood
and eight years' faithful services."

Washington knew, nevertheless, how black a danger
lurked among these distressed men ; did not fail to
speak plainly of it to the congress ; and breathed freely
again only when the soldiers' just demands had at last
in some measure been met, by any rate the proper
legislation. He grew weary with longing for peace,
when the work seemed done and his thoughts had lei-

sure to turn towards his home again. But once in all the lengthened days of fighting had he seen Mount Vernon. He had turned aside to spend a night or two there on his way to Yorktown, and he had seen the loved place again for a little after the victory was won. Now, amidst profitless days at Newburgh, or in counsel with the committees of the congress upon business that was never finished, while affairs stood as it were in a sort of paralysis, waiting upon the interminable conferences of the three powers who haggled over definitive terms of peace at Paris, home seemed to him, in his weariness, more to be desired than ever before. Private griefs had stricken him at the very moment of his triumph. Scarcely had the victory at Yorktown been celebrated when he was called (November, 1781) to the death-bed of Jack Custis, his wayward but dearly loved step-son, and had there to endure the sight of his wife's grief and the young widow's hopeless sorrow added to his own. The two youngest children he claimed for himself, with that wistful fatherly longing that had always marked him ; and Mount Vernon seemed to him more like a haven than ever, where to seek rest and solace. The two years he had yet to wait may well have seemed to him the longest of his life, and may have added a touch of their own to what strangers deemed his sternness.

He had seldom seemed so stern, indeed, as in one incident of those trying months. An officer of the American army had been taken in a skirmish, and the English had permitted a brutal company of loyalists, under one Captain Lippincott, to take him from his prison in New York and wantonly hang him in broad daylight on the heights near Middletown. Washington at once notified the British commander that unless the murderers were delivered up to be punished, a British officer would be chosen by lot from among his prisoners to suffer in their stead; and, when reparation was withheld, proceeded without hesitation to carry his threat into execution. The lot fell upon Captain Charles Asgill, an engaging youth of only nineteen, the heir of a great English family. Lady Asgill, the lad's mother, did not stop short of moving the very French court itself to intervene to save her son, and at last the congress counselled his release, the English commander having disavowed the act of the murderers in whose place he was to suffer, and Washington himself having asked to be directed what he should do. "Captain Asgill has been released," Washington wrote to Vergennes, in answer to the great minister's intercession. "I have no right to assume any particular merit from the lenient manner in which this disagreeable affair has terminated. But I beg you to believe, sir, that I most sincerely rejoice, not only because your humane intentions are gratified, but because the event accords with the wishes of his Most Christian Majesty." It lifted a great weight from his heart to have the innocent boy go unhurt from his hands, and he wrote almost tenderly to him in acquainting him with his release; but it was of his simple nature to have sent the lad to the gallows, nevertheless, had things continued to stand as they were at the first. He was inexorable to check perfidy and vindicate the just rules of war. Men were reminded, while the affair pended, of the hanging of André, Arnold's British confederate in treason, and how pitiless the commander-in-chief had seemed in sending the frank, accomplished, lovable gentleman to his disgraceful death, like any

common spy, granting him not even the favor to be
shot, like a soldier.   It seemed hard to learn the inflex-
ible lines upon which that consistent mind worked, as if
it had gone to school to Fate.

But no one deemed him hard or stern, or so much as
a thought more or less than human, when at last the
British had withdrawn from New York, and he stood
amidst his officers in Fraunce's Tavern to say good-bye.
He could hardly speak for emotion : he could only lift
his glass and say : " With a heart full of love and gratitude, I now take my leave of you, most devoutly wishing that your latter days may be as prosperous and
happy as your former ones have been glorious and honorable. . . . I cannot come to each of you and take my
leave," he said, " but shall be obliged if you will come
and take me by the hand."   When General Knox, who
stood nearest, approached him, he drew him to him with
a sudden impulse and kissed him, and not a soldier
among them all went away without an embrace from
this man who was deemed cold and distant.   After the
parting they followed him in silence to Whitehall Ferry,
and saw him take boat for his journey.

And then, standing before the congress at Annapolis
to resign his commission, he added the crowning touch
of simplicity to his just repute as a man beyond others
noble and sincere.   " I have now the honor of offering
my sincere congratulations to congress," he said, as he
stood amidst the august scene they had prepared for
him, " and of presenting myself before them to surrender into their hands the trust committed to me, and
to claim the indulgence of retiring from the service of
my country.   Happy in the confirmation of our independence and sovereignty, and pleased with the op-

portunity afforded the United States of becoming a
respectable nation, I resign with satisfaction the appointment I accepted with diffidence — a diffidence in
my abilities to accomplish so arduous a task, which,
however, was superseded by a confidence in the recti-
tude of our cause, the support of the supreme power of
the Union, and the patronage of Heaven. The successful termination of the war has verified the most sanguine
expectations; and my gratitude for the interposition of
Providence and the assistance I have received from my
countrymen increases with every review of the momentous contest. . . . I consider it my indispensable duty
to close this last solemn act of my official life by com-
mending the interests of our dearest country to the protection of Almighty God, and those who have the superintendence of them to His holy keeping." It was as if
spoken on the morrow of the day upon which he accepted his commission : the same diffidence, the same trust
in a power greater and higher than his own. The
plaudits that had but just now filled his ears at every
stage of his long journey from New York seemed utterly
forgotten ; he seemed not to know how his fellow countrymen had made of him an idol and a hero ; his simplicity was once again his authentic badge of genuineness.
He knew, it would seem, no other way in which to act.
A little child remembered afterwards how he had prayed
at her father's house upon the eve of battle ; how he had
taken scripture out of Joshua, and had cried, " The Lord
God of gods, the Lord God of gods, He knoweth, and
Israel he shall know ; if it be in rebellion, or if in trans-
gression against the Lord (save us not this day)." There
was here the same note of solemnity and of self-forgetful devotion, as if duty and honor were alike inevitable.

On Christmas Eve, 1783, he was once more at Mount
Vernon, to resume the life he loved more than victory
and power. He had a zest for the means and the labor
of succeeding, but not for the mere content of success.
He put the Revolution behind him as he would have laid
aside a book that was read ; turned from it as quietly as
he had turned from receiving the surrender of Cornwallis at Yorktown—interested in victory not as a pageant
and field of glory, but only as a means to an end. He
looked to find very sweet satisfaction in the peace which
war had earned, as sufficient a scope for his powers at
home as in the field. Once more he would be a Virginian, and join his strength to his neighbors' in all the
tasks of good citizenship. He had seen nothing of the
old familiar places since that far-away spring of the
year 1775, when he had left his farming and his fox-
hunting, amidst rumors of war, to attend the congress
which was to send him to Cambridge. He had halted
at Fredericksburg, indeed, with the Count de Rochambeau, two years ago, ere he followed his army from
York to its posts upon the Hudson. Mrs. Lewis, his
sister, had returned one day from visiting a neighbor in
the quiet town to look in astonishment upon an officer's
horses and attendants at her door, and had entered to
find her beloved brother stretched upon her own bed
within, sound asleep in his clothes, like a boy returned
from hunting. There had been a formal ball given, too,
in celebration of the victory, before the French officers
and the commander-in-chief left Fredericksburg to go
northward again, and Washington had had the joy of
entering the room in the face of the gay company with
his aged mother on his arm, not a whit bent for all her
seventy-four years, and as quiet as a queen at receiving

the homage of her son's comrades in arms. He had got his imperious spirit of command from her. A servant had told her that "Mars George" had put up at the tavern. "Go and tell George to come here instantly," she had commanded; and he had come, masterful man though he was. He had felt every old affection and every old allegiance renew itself as he saw former neighbors crowd around him; and that little glimpse of Virginia had refreshed him like a tonic—deeply, and as if it renewed his very nature, as only a silent man can be refreshed. But a few days in Fredericksburg and at Mount Vernon then had been only an incident of campaigning, only a grateful pause on a march. Now at last he had come back to keep his home and be a neighbor again, as he had not been these nine years.

FIRST IN PEACE

It was not the same Virginia, nor even the same home and neighborhood he had gone from, that Washington came back to when the war was done. He had left Mount Vernon in the care of Lund Washington, his nephew, while the war lasted, and had not forgotten amidst all his letter writing to send seasonable directions and maintain a constant oversight upon the management of his estate. It was part of his genius to find time for everything; and Mount Vernon had suffered something less than the ordinary hazards and neglects of war. It had suffered less upon one occasion, indeed, than its proud owner could have found it in his heart to wish. In the spring of 1781 several British vessels had come pillaging within the Potomac, and the anxious Lund had regaled their officers with refreshments from Mount Vernon to buy them off from mischief. "It would have been a less painful circumstance to me," his uncompromising uncle had written him, "to have heard that, in consequence of your non-compliance with their request, they had burnt my house and laid the plantation in ruin. You ought to have considered yourself as my representative." Kept though it was from harm, however, the place had suffered many things for lack of his personal care. There was some part of the task to be done over again that had con-

fronted him when he came to take possession of the
old plantation with his bride after the neglects of the
French war.

But Virginia was more changed than Mount Vernon.
He had left it a colony, at odds with a royal Governor;
he returned to find it a State, with Benjamin Harrison,
that stout gentleman and good planter, for Governor,
by the free suffrages of his fellow Virginians. There
had been no radical break with the aristocratic traditions of the past. Mr. Harrison's handsome seat at
Lower Brandon lay where the long reaches of the James
marked the oldest regions of Virginia's life upon broad,
half-feudal estates; where there were good wine and
plate upon the table, and gentlemen kept old customs
bright and honored in the observance. But the face
of affairs had greatly changed, nevertheless. The old
generation of statesmen had passed away, almost with
the colony, and a younger generation was in the saddle,
notwithstanding a gray-haired figure here and there.
Richard Bland had died in the year of the Declaration;
Peyton Randolph had not lived to see it. Edmund
Pendleton, after presiding over Virginia's making as a
State, as chairman of her revolutionary Committee of
Safety, was now withdrawn from active affairs to the
bench, his fine figure marred by a fall from his horse,
his old power as an advocate transmuted into the cooler
talents of the judge. Patrick Henry, the ardent leader
of the Revolution, had been chosen the State's first
Governor, in the year of the Declaration of Independence; three years later Thomas Jefferson had succeeded him in the office, the philosophical radical of
times of change; the choice of Mr. Harrison had but
completed the round of the new variety in affairs. Men

who, like Richard Henry Lee, had counselled revolution
and the breaking of old bonds, were now in all things
at the front of the State's business; and younger men,
of a force and power of origination equal to their own,
were pressing forward, as if to hurry a new generation
to the stage which had known nothing but independence and a free field for statesmanship. Among the
rest, James Madison, only a little more than ten years
out of college, but already done with serving his no-
vitiate in the Congress of the Confederation, a pub-
licist and leader in the Old Dominion at thirty-two.
Edmund Randolph, of the new generation of the commonwealth's great family of lawyers, like his forebears
in gifts and spirit, was already received, at thirty, into
a place of influence among public men. John Marshall,
just turned of twenty-eight, but a veteran of the long
war none the less, having been at the thick of the fighting, a lieutenant and a captain among the Virginian
forces, from the time Dunmore was driven from Norfolk till the eve of Yorktown, was, now that that duty
was done, a lawyer in quiet Fauquier, drawing to himself the eyes of every man who had the perception to
note qualities of force and leadership. James Monroe
had come out of the war at twenty-five to go at once
into the public councils of his State, an equal among his
elders. Young men came forward upon every side to
take their part in the novel rush of affairs that followed
upon the heels of revolution.

Washington found himself no stranger in the new
State, for all it had grown of a sudden so unlike that
old community in which his own life had been formed.
He found a very royal welcome awaiting him at his
home-coming. The old commonwealth loved a hero

still as much as ever; was as loyal to him now as it
had been in the far-away days of the French war, when
Dinwiddie alone fretted against him; received him
with every tribute of affection; offered him gifts, and
loved him all the better for refusing them. But he
must have felt that a deep change had come upon his
life, none the less, and even upon his relations with his
old familiars and neighbors. He had gone away honored indeed, and marked for responsible services among
his people—a Burgess as a matter of course, a notable
citizen, whose force no man who knew him could fail
to remark; but by no means accounted greatest, even
among the men who gathered for the colony's business
at Williamsburg; chosen only upon occasion for special services of action; no debater or statesman, so far
as ordinary men could see; too reserved to be popular
with the crowd, though it should like his frankness
and taking address, and go out of its way to see him
on horseback; a man for his neighbors, who could know
him, not for the world, which he refused to court. But
the war had suddenly lifted him to the view of all
mankind; had set him among the great captains of the
world; had marked him a statesman in the midst of
affairs—more a statesman than a soldier even, men
must have thought who had read his letters or heard
them read in Congress, on the floor or in the committee rooms; had drawn to himself the admiration of the
very men he had been fighting, the very nation whose
dominion he had helped to cast off. He had come home
perhaps the most famous man of his day, and could
not take up the old life where he had left it off, much
as he wished to; was obliged, in spite of himself, to
play a new part in affairs.

For a few weeks, indeed, after he had reached Mount
Vernon, Nature herself assisted him to a little privacy
and real retirement. The winter (1783-4) was an un-
commonly severe one. Snow lay piled, all but impas-
sable, upon the roads; frosts hardened all the country
against travel; he could not get even to Fredericksburg
to see his aged mother; and not many visitors, though
they were his near neighbors, could reach him at Mount
Vernon. "At length, my dear Marquis," he could write
to Lafayette in his security, "I am become a private
citizen on the banks of the Potomac; and under the
shadow of my own vine and my own fig-tree, free from
the bustle of a camp and the busy scenes of public life,
I am solacing myself with those tranquil enjoyments
of which the soldier, who is ever in pursuit of fame, the
statesman, whose watchful days and sleepless nights are
spent in devising schemes to promote the welfare of his
own, perhaps the ruin of other countries, as if this globe
was insufficient for us all, and the courtier, who is always watching the countenance of his prince, can have
very little conception. I have not only retired from
all public employments, but I am retiring within myself.
. . . Envious of none, I am determined to be pleased
with all; and this, my dear friend, being the order of
my march, I will move gently down the stream of time
until I sleep with my fathers." The simple gentleman
did not yet realize what the breaking up of the frosts
would bring.

With the spring the whole life of the world seemed to
come pouring in upon him. Men of note everywhere
pressed their correspondence upon him; no stranger
visited America but thought first of Mount Vernon in
planning where he should go and what he should see;

new friends and old sat every day at his table; a year
and a half had gone by since his home-coming before he
could note in his diary (June 30th, 1785): " Dined with
only Mrs. Washington, which, I believe, is the first instance of it since my retirement from public life"—for
some visitors had broken their way even through the
winter roads.   Authors sent him what they wrote; in-
ventors submitted their ideas and models to him; everything that was being said, everything that was being
done, seemed to find its way, if nowhere else, to Mount
Vernon — till those who knew his occupations could
speak of Washington, very justly, as " the focus of political intelligence for the New World."   He would not
alter his way of living even in the face of such overwhelming interruptions.   His guests saw him for a little after dinner, and once and again, it might be, in the
evening also; but he kept to his business throughout
all the working hours of the day; was at his desk even
before breakfast, and after breakfast was always early
in the saddle and off to his farms.

Only at table did he play the host, lingering over the
wine to give and call for toasts and relax in genial conversation, losing, as the months passed by, some of the
deep gravity that had settled upon him in the camp,
and showing once more an enjoying relish for " a pleasant story, an unaffected sally of wit, or a burlesque de-
scription," as in the old days after hunting.   Strangers
were often in awe of him.   It did not encourage talk in
those who had little to say to sit in the presence of a
man who so looked his greatness in the very proportions
of his strong figure even, and whose grave and steady
eyes so challenged the significance of what was said.
Young people would leave off dancing and romping

when he came into the room, and force him to withdraw, and peep at the fun from without the door, unob-
served. It was only among his intimates that he was
suffered and taken to be the simple, straightforward,
sympathizing man he was, exciting, not awe, but only a
warm and affectionate allegiance. "The General, with
a few glasses of champagne, got quite merry," a young
Englishman could report who had had the good luck
to be introduced by Richard Henry Lee, "and, being
with his intimate friends, laughed and talked a good
deal."

As much as he could, he resumed the old life, and the
thoughts and pastimes that had gone with it. Once
more he became the familiar of his hounds at the kennels, and followed them as often as might be in the
hunt at sunrise. He asked but one thing of a horse, as
of old, "and that was to go along. He ridiculed the
idea that he could be unhorsed, provided the animal
kept on his legs." The two little children, a tiny boy
and a romping, mischievous lassie, not much bigger,
whom he had adopted at Jack Custis's death-bed, took
strong hold upon his heart, and grew slowly to an intimacy with him such as few ventured to claim any longer
amidst those busy days in the guest-crowded house. It
seemed to Lafayette a very engaging picture when he
saw Washington and the little toddling boy together—
"a very little gentleman with a feather in his hat, holding fast to one finger of the good General's remarkable
hand, which (so large that hand!)" was all the tiny fellow could manage. These children took Washington
back more completely than anything else to the old
days when he had brought his bride home with her own
little ones. He felt those days come back, too, when he

was on his horse in the open, going the round of good
twelve miles and more that carried him to all the quarters of his plantation.

Once more he was the thorough farmer, ransacking
books, when men and his own observation failed him,
to come at the best methods of cultivation. Once more
he took daily account of the character of his slaves and
servants, and of the progress of their work, talking with
them when he could, and gaining a personal mastery
over them. Contracts for work he drew up with his
own hand, with a minuteness and particularity which
were sometimes whimsical and shot through with a
gleam of grim humor. He agreed with Philip Barter
that if he would serve him faithfully as gardener and
keep sober at all other times, he would allow him "four
dollars at Christmas, with which to be drunk four days
and four nights; two dollars at Easter, to effect the
same purpose; two dollars at Whitsuntide, to be drunk
for two days; a dram in the morning, and a drink of
grog at dinner, at noon"; and the contract was drawn,
signed, and witnessed with all formality. Philip no
doubt found short shrift of consideration from his
thorough-going master if there was any drunkenness
in the garden beyond the limit of the eight days nomi-
nated in the bond, and found the contract no jest in the
end, for Washington had small patience and no soft
words for a breach of agreement, whatever its kind.
He would help men in distress with a generosity and
wise choice of means which few took the pains to exercise, but he had only sharp rebuke for carelessness or
neglect or any slackness in the performance of a duty.
Men who had cheated or sought to impose upon him
deemed him harsh and called him a hard master, so

sharply did they smart after he had reckoned with them. He exacted the uttermost farthing. But he spent it, with the other hand, to relieve genuine suffering and real want, though it were deserved and the fruit of a crying fault. In his home dealings, as in everything else, his mind kept that trait by which men had been awed in the camp — that trick, as if of Fate, of letting every act come at its consequences and its full punishment or reward, as if he but presided at a process which was just Nature's own. When he succored distress, he did it in pity, not in justice—not excusing fault, but giving leave to mercy. If he urged the government to pension and reward the soldiers of the war, who had only done their duty, he himself set an example. There were black pensioners not a few about his own homestead. Bishop, his old body-servant, lived like a retired gentleman in his cottage there; even Nelson, the good sorrel who had borne him so bravely in the field till Yorktown, now went forever unsaddled, free in his own pasture.

But, much as he loved his home and courted retirement amidst the duties of a planter, the old life would not come back, was gone forever. He was too famous, and there was an end on 't. He could not go abroad without drawing crowds about him. If he attended service on a Sunday away from home, though it were in never so quiet a parish, the very walls of the church groaned threateningly under the unaccustomed weight of people gathered in the galleries and packed upon the floor to see the hero of the Revolution. Not even a ride into the far west, to view his lands and pull together his neglected business on the Ohio, was long enough to take him beyond the reach of public affairs. On the

1st of September, 1784, with Dr. Craik for company, he set out on horseback to go by Braddock's road again into the west. For nearly five weeks he was deep in the wilderness, riding close upon seven hundred miles through the forested mountains, and along the remote courses of the long rivers that ran into the Mississippi; camping out as in the old days when he was a surveyor and a soldier in his 'prenticeship in these very wilds; renewing his zest for the rough life and the sudden adventures of the frontiersman. But, though he had come upon his own business, it was the seat of a future empire he saw rather than his own acres scattered here and there.

When last he had ridden the long stages from settlement to settlement and cabin to cabin in this far country of the Ohio, he had been a Virginian and nothing more, a colonial colonel merely, come to pick out lands for his comrades and himself, their reward for serving the crown against the French. A transformation had been worked upon him since then. He had led the armies of the whole country; had been the chief instrument of a new nation in winning independence; had carried its affairs by his own counsels as no other man had done; had seen through all the watches of those long campaigns the destinies and the hopes that were at stake. Now he saw the crowding immigrants come into the west with a new solicitude he had not felt before. A new vision was in his thought. This western country was now a "rising world," to be kept or lost, husbanded or squandered, by the raw nation he had helped put upon its feet. His thought was stretched at last to a continental measure; problems of statesmanship that were national, questions of policy that had a scope great as schemes of empire, stood foremost in his view. He returned home more engrossed than ever by interests not his own, but central to public affairs, and of the very stuff of politics.

And so not the letters merely which poured in with every mail, not only his host of visitors, great and small —the Governor of the State, the President of Congress, foreign noblemen, soldiers, diplomatists, travellers, neighbors, friends, acquaintances, intruders — but his own unbidden thoughts as well, and the very suggestions of his own interest as a citizen and land-owner, drew him from his dreams of retirement and forced him upon the open stage again. Even hunting ceased before many seasons were out. The savage boar-hounds which Lafayette had sent, in his kindness, from the Old World, proved too fierce and great a breed for even the sharp sport with the gray fox; the old hunting companions were gone—the Fairfaxes over sea ; Belvoir deserted and burned ; George Mason too much engaged— none but boys and strangers left to ride with. 'Twas poor sport, after all, without the right sportsmen. It must needs give way before a statesman's cares.

Upon his first home-coming, Washington had found it hard to break himself of his habit of waking very early in the morning with a sense of care concerning the affairs of the day, as if he were still in camp and in the midst of public duties. Now a new sense of responsibility possessed him, and more and more gained ascendency over him. He began to feel a deep anxiety lest a weak government should make independence little better than a reproach, and the country should fall into a hopeless impotency. At first he had been very sanguine. " Notwithstanding the jealous and contracted

temper which seems to prevail in some of the States,"
he wrote to Jonathan Trumbull in January, 1784, "yet
I cannot but hope and believe that the good sense of
the people will ultimately get the better of their prejudices, and that order and sound policy, though they do
not come so soon as one could wish, will be produced
from the present unsettled and deranged state of public
affairs. . . . Everything, my dear Trumbull, will come
right at last, as we have often prophesied. My only
fear is that we shall lose a little reputation first." But
the more he observed the temper of the time, the more
uneasy he grew. "Like a young heir," he cried, "come
a little prematurely to a large inheritance, we shall
wanton and run riot until we have brought our reputation to the brink of ruin, and then, like him, shall have
to labor with the current of opinion, when compelled,
perhaps, to do what prudence and common policy point-
ed out, as plain as any problem in Euclid, in the first
instance. . . . I think we have opposed Great Britain,
and have arrived at the present state of peace and independency, to very little purpose, if we cannot conquer our own prejudices."

For the present he saw little that could be done beyond holding up the hands of the Congress, and increasing, as it might prove possible to do so, the meagre
powers of the Confederation. "My political creed," he
said, "is to be wise in the choice of delegates, support
them like gentlemen while they are our representatives,
give them competent powers for all federal purposes,
support them in the due exercise thereof, and, lastly, to
compel them to close attendance in Congress during
their delegation." But his thoughts took wider scope as
the months passed; and nothing quickened them more

than his western trip. He saw how much of the future
travelled with those slow wagon trains of immigrants into
the west ; realized how they were leaving behind them
the rivers that ran to the old ports at the sea, and going
down into the valleys whose outlet was the great highway of the Mississippi and the ports of the Gulf; how
the great ridge of the Alleghanies lay piled between
them and the older seats of settlement, with only here
and there a gap to let a road through, only here and
there two rivers lying close enough at their sources to
link the east with the west ; and the likelihood of a
separation between the two populations seemed to him
as obvious as the tilt of the mountains upon either
slope. " There is nothing which binds one country or
one State to another but interest," he said. " Without
this cement the western inhabitants, who more than
probably will be composed in a great degree of foreigners, can have no predilection for us, and a commercial
connection is the only tie we can have upon them."
" The western settlers," he declared, while still fresh
from the Ohio, " stand as it were upon a pivot. The
touch of a feather would turn them any way "—down
the Mississippi to join their interests with those of the
Spaniard, or back to the mountain roads and the head-
waters of the eastern streams, to make for themselves
a new allegiance in the east. He was glad to see the
Spaniard so impolitic as to close the Mississippi against
the commerce offered him, and hoped that things might
stand so until there should have been " a little time allowed to open and make easy the ways between the Atlantic States and the western territory."

The opening of the upper reaches of the Potomac to
navigation had long been a favorite object with Wash-

ington; now it seemed nothing less than a necessity. It had been part of the original scheme of the old Ohio Company to use this means of winning a way for commerce through the mountains. Steps had been taken more than twenty years ago to act in the matter through private subscription; and active measures for securing the necessary legislation from the Assemblies of Virginia and Maryland were still in course when Washington was called to Cambridge and revolution drew men's minds imperatively off from the business. In 1770 Washington had written to Jefferson of the project as a means of opening a channel for "the extensive trade of a rising empire"; now the empire of which he had had a vision was no longer Britain's, but America's own, and it was become a matter of exigent political necessity to keep that western country against estrangement, winning it by commerce and close sympathy to join itself with the old colonies in building up a free company of united States upon the great continent.

Already the west was astir for the formation of new States. Virginia had taken the broad and national view of her duty that Washington himself held, and had ceded to the Confederation all her ancient claims to the lands that lay northwest of the Ohio River, reserving for herself only the fair region that stretched south of that great stream, from her own mountains to the Mississippi. North Carolina would have ceded her western lands beyond the mountains also, had they been empty and unclaimed, like the vast territory that lay beyond the Ohio. But for many a year settlers had been crossing the mountains into those fertile valleys, and both this region and that which Virginia still kept showed many a clearing now and many a rude hamlet where hardy frontiersmen were making a new home for civilization. Rather than be handed over to Congress, to be disposed of by an authority which no one else was bound to obey, North Carolina's western settlers declared they would form a State of their own, and North Carolina had to recall her gift of their lands to the Confederation before their plans of defiance could be checked and defeated. Virginia found her own frontiersmen no less ready to take the initiative in whatever affair touched their interest. Spain offered the United States trade at her ports, but refused to grant them the use of the lower courses of the Mississippi, lest territorial aggression should be pushed too shrewdly in that quarter; and news reached the settlers beyond the mountains, in the far counties of North Carolina and Virginia, that Mr. Jay, the Confederation's Secretary for Foreign Affairs, had proposed to the Congress to yield the navigation of the Mississippi for a generation in exchange for trade on the seas. They flatly declared they would give themselves, and their lands too, into the hands of England again rather than submit to be so robbed, cramped, and deserted. The New England States, on their part, threatened to withdraw from the Confederation if treaties were to be made to wait upon the assent of frontiersmen on the far Mississippi.

The situation was full of menace of no ordinary sort. It could profit the Confederation little that great States like Virginia and New York had grown magnanimous, and were endowing the Confederation with vast gifts of territory in the west, if such gifts were but to loosen still further the already slackened bonds of the common government, leaving settlers in the unclaimed lands no allegiance they could respect. Without a national government spirited and strong enough to frame policies and command obedience, "we shall never establish a national character or be considered as on a respectable footing by the powers of Europe," Washington had said from the first. He had made a most solemn appeal to the States in his last circular to them, ere he resigned his commission, urging them to strengthen the powers of Congress, put faction and jealousy away, and make sure of "an indissoluble union under one federal head." "An option is still left to the United States of America," he had told them, with all his plain and stately eloquence; "it is in their choice, and depends upon their conduct, whether they will be respectable and prosperous, or contemptible and miserable, as a nation. This is the time of their political probation." The hazards of that probation had been a burden upon his heart through all the toil of the Revolution, and now it seemed as if the States must needs make every evil choice in meeting them. Congress could not so much as carry out the provisions of the treaty of peace, for its commissioners had made promises in the name of the States which the States would not redeem. England consequently refused to keep her part of the agreement and relinquish the western posts. She levied commercial war against the country, besides, without fear of reprisal; for Congress had no power to regulate trade, and the States were too jealous of each other to co-operate in this or any other matter. English statesmen had consented to give up the colonies, and recognize their independence as a nation, rather than face any longer the world in arms; but they now looked to see them presently drop back into their hands again, out of sheer helplessness and hopeless division in counsel; and there were observant men in America who deemed the thing possible, though it brought an intolerable fire into their blood to think of it.

Other nations, too, were fast conceiving a like contempt for the Confederation. It was making no provision for the payment of the vast sums of money it had borrowed abroad, in France and Holland and Spain; and it could not make any. It could only ask the States for money, and must count itself fortunate to get enough to pay even the interest on its debts. It was this that foreign courts were finding out, that the Confederation was a mere " government of supplication," as Randolph had dubbed it; and its credit broke utterly down. Frenchman and Spaniard alike would only have laughed in contemptuous derision to see the whole fabric go to pieces, and were beginning to interest themselves with surmises as to what plunder it would afford. The States which lay neighbors to each other were embroiled in boundary disputes, and were fallen to levying duties on each other's commerce. They were individually in debt, besides, and were many of them resorting to issues of irredeemable paper money to relieve themselves of the inevitable taxation that must sooner or later pay their reckonings. " We are either a united people, or we are not so," cried Washington. " If the former, let us in all matters of general concern act as a nation which has a national character to support; if we are not, let us no longer act a farce by pretending to it." As the months passed it began to look as if the farce might be turned into a tragedy.

The troubles of the country, though he filled his letters with them and wrung his heart for phrases of protest and persuasion that would tell effectually in the deep labor of working out the sufficient remedy of a roused and united opinion, though he deemed them personal to himself, and knew his own fame in danger to be undone by them, did not break the steady self-possession of Washington's life at Mount Vernon. "It's astonishing the packets of letters that daily come for him, from all parts of the world," exclaimed an English visitor; but it was not till he had struggled to keep pace with his correspondence unassisted for a year and a half that he employed a secretary to help him. "Letters of friendship require no study," he wrote to General Knox; "the communications are easy, and allowances are expected and made. This is not the case with those that require researches, consideration, recollection, and the de—l knows what to prevent error, and to answer the ends for which they are written." He grew almost docile, nevertheless, under the gratuitous tasks of courtesy thrust upon him. His gallantry, bred in him since a boy, the sense of duty to which he was born, his feeling that what he had done had in some sort committed him to serve his countrymen and his friends everywhere, though it were only in answering questions, disposed him to sacrifice his comfort and his privacy to every one who had the slightest claim upon his attention. He even found sitting for his portrait grow easy at last. "*In for a penny, in for a pound*, is an old adage," he laughed, writing to Francis Hopkinson. "I am so hackneyed to the touches of the painter's pencil that I am *now* altogether at their beck; and sit 'like Patience on a monument' whilst they are delineating the lines of my face. . . . At first I was as impatient at the request, and as restive under the operation, as a colt is of the saddle. The next time I submitted very re-

luctantly, but with less flouncing. Now no dray-horse
moves more readily to his thill than I do to the painter's
chair." Besides the failure of the public credit, it concerned him to note the fact that, though he kept a hundred cows, he was obliged to buy butter for his innu-
merable guests. He saw to it that there should be at
least a very definite and efficient government upon his
own estate, and, when there was need, put his own hand
to the work. He "often works with his men himself—
strips off his coat and labors like a common man," measures with his own hands every bit of building or con-
struction that is going forward, and "shows a great turn
for mechanics," one of his guests noted, amidst com-
ments on his greatness and his gracious dignity. It was
such constancy and candor and spirit in living that took
the admiration of all men alike upon the instant; and
his neighbors every day saw here the same strenuous
and simple gentleman they had known before ever the
war began.

It was through the opening of the Potomac, after all
—the thing nearest his hand—that a way was found to
cure the country of its malady of weakness and disorder.
Washington had been chosen president of the Potomac
Company, that it might have the advantage both of his
name and of his capacity in affairs; and he had gone
upon a tour of inspection, with the directors of the company, to the falls of the river in the summer of 1785,
keeping steadily to the business he had come upon, and
insisting upon being in fact a private gentleman busy
with his own affairs, despite the efforts made everywhere
he went to see and to entertain him; and it presently
became evident even to the least sanguine that the
long-talked-of work was really to be carried through. A

visitor at Mount Vernon in the autumn of 1785 found
Washington "quite pleased at the idea of the Baltimore
merchants laughing at him, and saying it was a ridicu-
lous plan, and would never succeed. They begin now,
says the General, to look a little serious about the matter, as they know it must hurt their commerce amaz-
ingly."

The scheme had shown its real consequence in the
spring of that very year, when it brought commissioners
from the two States that lay upon the river together in
conference to devise plans of co-operation. Both Virginia and Maryland had appointed commissioners, and
a meeting had been set for March, 1785, at Alexandria.
For some reason the Virginian commissioners were not
properly notified of the place and time of conference.
The meeting was held, nevertheless, a minority of the
Virginian commissioners being present ; and, as if to
give it more the air of a cordial conference of neighbors, Washington invited the representatives of both
States to adjourn from Alexandria to Mount Vernon.
There they sat, his guests, from Friday to Monday. He
was not formally of the commission ; but conference
was not confined to their formal sessions, and his counsel entered into their determinations. It was evident
that two States were not enough to decide the questions
submitted to them. Pennsylvania, at least, must be
consulted before the full line of trade they sought could
be drawn from the head - waters of the Ohio to the
head - waters of the Potomac ; and if three States
were to consult upon questions of trade which concerned the whole continent, why should not more be
invited, and the conference be made general? Such
was the train of suggestion, certainly, that ran in

Washington's mind, and which the commissioners carried home with them. Every sign of the time served to deepen its significance for Washington. Just before quitting the army he had ridden upon a tour of inspection into the valley of the Mohawk, where a natural way, like this of the Potomac, ran from the northern settlements into the west. He knew that the question of joining the Potomac with the Ohio was but one item of a policy which all the States must consider and settle—nothing less than the policy which must make them an empire or doom them to remain a weak and petty confederacy.

The commissioners did not put all that they had heard at Mount Vernon into their reports to their respective Assemblies. They recommended only that, besides co-operating with each other and with Pennsylvania in opening a way to the western waters, Virginia and Maryland should adopt a uniform system of duties and of commercial regulations, and should establish uniform rules regarding their currency. But the Maryland Assembly itself went further. It presently informed the Virginian Legislature that it had not only adopted the measures recommended by the commissioners, but thought it wise to do something more. Delaware ought to be consulted, with a view to carrying a straight watercourse, by canal, from Chesapeake Bay to the Delaware River; and, since conference could do no harm and bind nobody, it would be as well to invite all the States to confer with them, for the questions involved seemed far-reaching enough to justify it, if not to make it necessary. Governor Bowdoin, of Massachusetts, had that very year urged his Legislature to invite a general convention of the States in the interest of trade. The whole country was in a tangle of disagreement about granting to Congress the power to lay imposts; Gardoqui, it was rumored, was insisting, for Spain, upon closing the Mississippi: 'twas evident enough conference was needed. Every thoughtful man might well pray that it would bring peace and accommodation. When Maryland's suggestion was read in the Virginian Assembly, there was prompt acquiescence. Virginia asked all the States of the Union (January, 1786) to send delegates to a general conference to be held at Annapolis on the first Monday in September, to consider and recommend such additions to the powers of Congress as might conduce to a better regulation of trade. "There is more wickedness than ignorance in the conduct of the States, or, in other words, in the conduct of those who have too much influence in the government of them," Washington wrote hotly to Henry Lee, upon hearing to what lengths contempt of the authority of Congress had been carried; "and until the curtain is withdrawn, and the private views and selfish principles upon which these men act are exposed to public notice, I have little hope of amendment without another convulsion." Perhaps the conference at Annapolis would withdraw the curtain and give the light leave to work a purification; and he waited anxiously for the issue.

But when the commissioners assembled they found only five States represented—Virginia, Pennsylvania, Delaware, New Jersey, and New York. Maryland had suddenly fallen indifferent, and had not appointed delegates. New Hampshire, Massachusetts, Rhode Island, and North Carolina had appointed delegates, but they had not taken the trouble to come. Connecticut, South

Carolina, and Georgia had ignored the call altogether. The delegates who were in attendance, besides, had come with only the most jealously restricted powers; only New Jersey, in her great uneasiness at being neighbor to the powerful States of New York and Pennsylvania, had authorized her representatives to "consider how far a uniform system in their commercial regulations *and other important matters* might be necessary to the common interest and permanent harmony of the several States." The other delegates had no such scope; all deemed it futile to attempt their business in so small a convention; and it was resolved to make another opportunity. Alexander Hamilton, of New York, drew up their address to the States, and in it made bold to adopt New Jersey's hint, and ask for a conference which should not merely consider questions of trade, but also "devise such further provisions as should appear to them necessary to render the constitution of the federal government adequate to the exigencies of the Union." Hamilton held with Washington for a national government. He had been born, and bred as a lad, in the West Indies, and had never received the local pride of any colony-state into his blood. He had served with the army, too, in close intimacy with Washington, and, though twenty-five years his captain's junior, had seen as clearly as he saw the deep hazards of a nation's birth.

The Congress was indifferent, if not hostile, to the measures which the address proposed; and the States would have acted on the call as slackly as before, had not the winter brought with it something like a threat of social revolution, and fairly startled them out of their negligent humor. The central counties of Massachu-

setts broke into violent rebellion, under one Shays, a
veteran of the Revolution—not to reform the government, but to rid themselves of it altogether; to shut
the courts and escape the payment of debts and taxes.
The insurgents worked their will for weeks together;
drove out the officers of the law, burned and plundered at pleasure through whole districts, living upon
the land like a hostile army, and were brought to a
reckoning at last only when a force thousands strong
had been levied against them. The contagion spread
to Vermont and New Hampshire; and, even when
the outbreak had been crushed, the States concerned
were irresolute in the punishment of the leaders.
Rhode Island declared her sympathy with the insurgents; Vermont offered them asylum; Massachusetts
brought the leaders to trial and conviction only to pardon and set them free again. Congress dared do no
more than make covert preparation to check a general
rising. " You talk, my good sir," wrote Washington to
Henry Lee, in Congress, "of employing influence to
appease the present tumults in Massachusetts. I know
not where that influence is to be found, or, if attainable,
that it would be a proper remedy for the disorders.
Influence is no *government*. Let us have one by which
our lives, liberties, and properties will be secured, or let
us know the worst at once." It was an object-lesson
for the whole country ; the dullest and the most lethar-
gic knew now what slack government and financial disorder would produce. The States one and all—save
Rhode Island—bethought them of the convention called
to meet in Philadelphia on the second Monday in May,
1787, and delegates were appointed. Even Congress took
the lesson to heart, and gave its sanction to the conference.

The Legislature of Virginia put Washington's name at the head of its own list of delegates, and after his name the names of Patrick Henry, Edmund Randolph, John Blair, James Madison, George Mason, and George Wythe—the leading names of the State, no man could doubt. But Washington hesitated. He had already declined to meet the Society of the Cincinnati in Philadelphia about the same time, he said, and thought it would be disrespectful to that body, to whom he owed much, "to be there on any other occasion." He even hinted a doubt whether the convention was constitutional, its avowed purposes being what they were, until Congress tardily sanctioned it. His real reason his intimate friends must have divined from the first. They knew him better in such matters than he knew himself. He not only loved his retirement; he deemed himself a soldier and man of action, and no statesman. The floor of assemblies had never seemed to him his principal sphere of duty. He had thought of staying away from the House of Burgesses on private business twenty years ago, when he knew that the Stamp Act was to be debated. But it was not for the floor of the approaching convention that his friends wanted him; they told him from the first he must preside. He was known to be in favor of giving the Confederation powers that would make it a real government, and he thought that enough; but they wanted the whole country to see him pledged to the actual work, and, when they had persuaded him to attend, knew that they had at any rate won the confidence of the people in their patriotic purpose. His mere presence would give them power.

Washington and the other Virginians were prompt to be in Philadelphia on the day appointed, but only the Pennsylvanian delegates were there to meet them. They had to wait an anxious week before so many as seven States were represented. Meanwhile, those who gathered from day to day were nervous and apprehensive, and there was talk of compromise and halfway measures, should the convention prove weak or threaten to miscarry. They remembered for many a long year afterwards how nobly Washington, "standing self-collected in the midst of them," had uttered brave counsels of wisdom in their rebuke. "It is too probable," he said, "that no plan we propose will be adopted. Perhaps another dreadful conflict is to be sustained. If, to please the people, we offer what we ourselves disapprove, how can we afterwards defend our work? Let us raise a standard to which the wise and honest can repair. The event is in the hand of God." It was an utterance, they knew, not of statesmanship merely, but of character; and it was that character, if anything could, that would win the people to their support. When at last seven States were represented—a quorum of the thirteen—an organization was effected, and Washington unanimously chosen president of the convention. He spoke, when led to the chair, "of the novelty of the scene of business in which he was to act, lamented his want of better qualifications, and claimed the indulgence of the house towards the involuntary errors which his inexperience might occasion"; but no mere parliamentarian could have given that anxious body such steadiness in business or such grave earnestness in counsel as it got from his presence and influence in the chair. Five more States were in attendance before deliberation was very far advanced; but he had the satisfaction to see his own friends lead upon the floor.

It was the plan which Edmund Randolph proposed, for his fellow Virginians, which the convention accepted as a model to work from; it was James Madison, that young master of counsel, who guided the deliberations from day to day, little as he showed his hand in the work or seemed to put himself forward in debate. No speeches came from the president; only once or twice did he break the decorum of his office to temper some difference of opinion or facilitate some measure of accommodation. It was the 17th of September when the convention at last broke up; the 19th when the Constitution it had wrought out was published to the country. All the slow summer through, Washington had kept counsel with the rest as to the anxious work that was going forward behind the closed doors of the long conference; it was a grateful relief to be rid of the painful strain, and he returned to Mount Vernon like one whose part in the work was done.

" I never saw him so keen for anything in my life as he is for the adoption of the new scheme of government," wrote a visitor at Mount Vernon to Jefferson; but he took no other part than his correspondence afforded him in the agitation for its acceptance. Throughout all those long four months in Philadelphia he had given his whole mind and energy to every process of difficult counsel by which it had been wrought to completion; but he was no politician. Earnestly as he commended the plan to his friends, he took no public part either in defence or in advocacy of it. He read not only the *Federalist* papers, in which Hamilton and Madison and Jay made their masterly plea for the adoption of the Constitution, but also " every performance which has been printed on the one side and the other on the

great question," he said, so far as he was able to obtain
them; and he felt as poignantly as any man the deep
excitement of the momentous contest. It disturbed him
keenly to find George Mason opposing the Constitution
—the dear friend from whom he had always accepted
counsel hitherto in public affairs—and Richard Henry
Lee and Patrick Henry, too, in their passionate attachment to what they deemed the just sovereignty of Virginia. He could turn away with all his old self - possession, nevertheless, to discuss questions of culture and
tillage, in the midst of the struggle, with Arthur Young
over sea, and to write very gallant compliments to the
Marquis de Chastellux on his marriage. "So your day
has at length come," he laughed. "I am glad of it with
all my heart and soul. It is quite good enough for you.
Now you are well served for coming to fight in favor of
the American rebels all the way across the Atlantic
Ocean, by catching that terrible contagion — domestic
felicity—which, like the small-pox or the plague, a man
can have only once in his life, because it commonly lasts
him (at least with us in America — I don't know how
you manage such matters in France) for his whole lifetime."

Ten months of deep but quiet agitation — the forces
of opinion in close grapple—and the future seemed to
clear. The Constitution was adopted, only two States
dissenting. It had been a tense and stubborn fight: in
such States as Massachusetts and New York, the concerted action of men at the centres of trade against the
instinctive dread of centralization or change in the regions that lay back from the rivers and the sea; in States
like Virginia, where the mass of men waited to be led,
the leaders who had vision against those who had

only the slow wisdom of caution and presentiment. But, though she acted late in the business, and some home-keeping spirits among even her greater men held back, Virginia did not lose the place of initiative she had had in all this weighty business of reform. Something in her air or her life had given her in these latter years an extraordinary breed of public men—men liberated from local prejudice, possessed of a vision and an efficacy in affairs worthy of the best traditions of statesmanship among the English race from which they were sprung, capable of taking the long view, of seeing the permanent lines of leadership upon great questions, and shaping ordinary views to meet extraordinary ends. Even Henry and Mason could take their discomfiture gracefully, loyally, like men bred to free institutions; and Washington had the deep satisfaction to see his State come without hesitation to his view and hope.

The new Constitution made sure of, and a time set by Congress for the elections and the organization of a new government under it, the country turned as one man to Washington to be the first President of the United States. " We cannot, sir, do without you," cried Governor Johnson, of Maryland, "and I and thousands more can explain to anybody but yourself why we cannot do without you." To make any one else President, it seemed to men everywhere, would be like crowning a subject while the king was by. But Washington held back, as he had held back from attending the Constitutional Convention. He doubted his civil capacity, called himself an old man, said "it would be to forego repose and domestic enjoyment for trouble, perhaps for public obloquy." " The acceptance," he declared, " would be attended with more diffidence and reluctance than I ever experienced before in my life." But he was not permitted to decline. Hamilton told him that his attendance upon the Constitutional Convention must be taken to have *pledged* him in the view of the country to take part also in the formation of the government. "In a matter so essential to the well-being of society as the prosperity of a newly instituted government," said the great advocate, "a citizen of so much consequence as yourself to its success has no option but to lend his services, if called for. Permit me to say it would be inglorious, in such a situation, not to hazard the glory, however great, which he might have previously acquired."

Washington of course yielded, like the simple-minded gentleman and soldier he was, when it was made thus a matter of duty. When the votes of the electors were opened in the new Congress, and it was found that they were one and all for him, he no longer doubted. He did not know how to decline such a call, and turned with all his old courage to the new task.

THE FIRST PRESIDENT OF THE
UNITED STATES

THE members of the new Congress were so laggard in coming together that it was the 6th of April, 1789, before both Houses could count a quorum, though the 4th of March had been appointed the day for their convening. Their first business was the opening and counting of the electoral votes; and on the 7th Charles Thomson, the faithful and sedulous gentleman who had been clerk of every congress since that first one in the old colonial days fifteen years ago, got away on his long ride to Mount Vernon to notify Washington of his election. Affairs waited upon the issue of his errand. Washington had for long known what was coming, and was ready and resolute, as of old. There had been no formal nominations for the presidency, and the votes of the electors had lain under seal till the new Congress met and found a quorum; but it was an open secret who had been chosen President, and Washington had made up his mind what to do. Mr. Thomson reached Mount Vernon on the 14th, and found Washington ready to obey his summons at once. He waited only for a hasty ride to Fredericksburg to bid his aged mother farewell. She was not tender in the parting. Her last days had come, and she had set herself to bear with grim resolution the fatal disease that had long been upon her. She had never been tender, and these

latter days had added their touch of hardness. But it
was a tonic to her son to take her farewell, none the
less; to hear her once more bid him God-speed, and
once more command him, as she did, to his duty. On
the morning of the 16th he took the northern road
again, as so often before, and pressed forward on the
way for New York.

The setting out was made with a very heavy heart;
for duty had never seemed to him so unattractive as it
seemed now, and his diffidence had never been so distressing. "For myself the delay may be compared to
a reprieve," he had written to Knox, when he learned
how slow Congress was in coming together, "for in
confidence I tell you that my movements to the chair
of government will be accompanied by feelings not
unlike those of a culprit who is going to the place of
execution." When the day for his departure came, his
diary spoke the same heaviness of heart. "About ten
o'clock," he wrote, "I bade adieu to Mount Vernon, to
private life, and to domestic felicity; and, with a mind
oppressed with more anxious and painful sensations
than I have words to express, set out for New York."
He did not doubt that he was doing right; he doubted
his capacity in civil affairs, and loved the sweet retirement and the free life he was leaving behind him.
Grief and foreboding did not in the least relax his
proud energy and promptness in action. He was not
a whit the less resolute to attempt this new rôle, and
stretch his powers to the uttermost to play it in masterful fashion. He was only wistful and full of a sort
of manly sadness; lacking not resolution, but only
alacrity.

He had hoped to the last that he would be suffered

to spend the rest of his days at Mount Vernon; he knew the place must lack efficient keeping, and fall once more out of repair under hired overseers; he feared his strength would be spent and his last years come ere he could return to look to it and enjoy it himself again. He had but just now been obliged to borrow a round sum of money to meet pressing obligations; and the expenses of this very journey had made it necessary to add a full hundred pounds to the new debt. If the estate brought money so slowly in while he farmed it, he must count upon its doing even less while he was away; and yet he had determined to accept no salary as President, but only his necessary expenses while in the discharge of his official duties, as in the old days of the war. It had brought distressing perplexities upon him to be thus drawn from his private business to serve the nation. Private cares passed off, no doubt, and were forgotten as the journey lengthened. But the other anxiety, how he should succeed in this large business of statesmanship to which he had been called, did not pass off; the incidents of that memorable ride only served to heighten it. When he had ridden to Cambridge that anxious summer of 1775, he had been hailed by cheering crowds upon the way, who admired the fine figure he made, and shouted for the cause he was destined to lead; but he knew himself a soldier then, was but forty-three, and did not fear to find his duty uncongenial. The people had loved him and had thronged about him with looks and words it had quickened his heart to see and hear as he made his way from New York to Annapolis to resign his commission but six years ago; but that was upon the morrow of a task accomplished, and the plaudits he heard upon the way

were but greetings to speed him the more happily
homeward. Things stood very differently now. Though
he felt himself grown old, he had come out to meet a
hope he could not share, and it struck a subtle pain to
his heart that the people should so trust him—should
give him so royal a progress as he fared on his way to
attempt an untried task.

No king in days of kings' divinity could have looked
for so heartfelt a welcome to his throne as this modest
gentleman got to the office he feared to take. Not only
were there civil fête and military parade at every stage
of the journey; there was everywhere, besides, a running together from all the country roundabout of people who bore themselves not as mere sight-seers, but as
if they had come out of love for the man they were to
see pass by. It was not their numbers but their manner
that struck their hero with a new sense of responsibility : their earnest gaze, their unpremeditated cries of
welcome, their simple joy to see the new government
put into the hands of a man they perfectly trusted. He
was to be their guarantee of its good faith, of its respect
for law and its devotion to liberty ; and they made him
know their hope and their confidence in the very tone of
their greeting. There was the manifest touch of love in
the reception everywhere prepared for him. Refined
women broke their reserve to greet him in the open
road ; put their young daughters forward, in their enthusiasm, to strew roses before him in the way ; brought
tears to his eyes by the very artlessness of their affection. When at last the triumphal journey was ended,
the display of every previous stage capped and outdone
by the fine pageant of his escort of boats from Newark
and of his reception at the ferry stairs in New York,

the demonstration seemed almost more than he could bear. "The display of boats which attended and joined us," he confessed to his diary, "the decorations of the ships, the roar of the cannon, and the loud acclamations of the people which rent the skies as I walked along the streets, filled my mind with sensations as painful as they are pleasant"; for his fears foreboded scenes the opposite of these, when he should have shown himself unable to fulfil the hopes which were the burden of all the present joy.

It was the 27th of April when he reached New York. Notwithstanding his executive fashion of making haste, the rising of the country to bid him God-speed had kept him four days longer on the way than Mr. Thomson had taken to carry the summons to Mount Vernon. Three days more elapsed before Congress had completed its preparations for his inauguration. On the 30th of April, in the presence of a great concourse of people, who first broke into wild cheers at sight of him, and then fell silent again upon the instant to see him so moved, Washington stood face to face with the Chancellor of the State upon the open balcony of the Federal Hall in Wall Street, and took the oath of office. "Do you solemnly swear," asked Livingston, "that you will faithfully execute the office of President of the United States, and will, to the best of your ability, preserve, protect, and defend the Constitution of the United States?" "I do solemnly swear," replied Washington, "that I will faithfully execute the office of President of the United States, and will, to the best of my ability, preserve, protect, and defend the Constitution of the United States," and then, bending to kiss the Bible held before him, bowed his head and said "So help me God!" in tones no man could mistake, so deep was their thrill of feeling. "Long live George Washington, President of the United States!" cried Livingston to the people; and a great shout went up with the booming of the cannon in the narrow streets.

Washington was profoundly moved, and, with all his extraordinary mastery of himself, could not hide his agitation. It was a company of friends, the Senators and Representatives who stood about him within the Senate chamber as he read his address, after the taking of the oath. Some very old friends were there—men who had been with him in the first continental congress, men who had been his intimate correspondents the long years through, men who were now his close confidants and sworn supporters. Not many strangers could crowd into the narrow hall; and it was not mere love of ceremony, but genuine and heartfelt respect, that made the whole company stand while he read. He visibly trembled, nevertheless, as he stood in their presence, strong and steadfast man though he was, "and several times could scarce make out to read"; shifted his manuscript uneasily from hand to hand; gestured with awkward effort; let his voice fall almost inaudible; was every way unlike himself, except for the simple majesty and sincerity that shone in him through it all. His manner but gave emphasis, after all, to the words he was reading. "The magnitude and difficulty of the trust," he declared, "could not but overwhelm with despondence one who, inheriting inferior endowments from nature, and unpractised in the duties of civil administration, ought to be peculiarly conscious of his own deficiencies"; and no one there could look at him and deem him insincere when he added, "All I dare

aver is that it has been my faithful study to collect my
duty from a just appreciation of every circumstance by
which it might be affected. All I dare hope is that, if
in executing this task I have been too much swayed by
a grateful remembrance of former instances, or by an
affectionate sensibility to this transcendent proof of the
confidence of my fellow-citizens, and have thence too
little consulted my incapacity as well as disinclination
for the weighty and untried cares before me, my error
will be palliated by the motives which misled me, and
its consequences be judged by my country with some
share of the partiality with which they originated."
His hearers knew how near the truth he struck when he
said, " The smiles of Heaven can never be expected on a
nation that disregards the eternal rules of order and
right which Heaven itself has ordained ; and the pres-
ervation of the sacred fire of liberty, and the destiny of
the republican model of government, are justly considered as *deeply*, perhaps as *finally*, staked on the experiment intrusted to the hands of the American people."
It was, no doubt, " a novelty in the history of society to
see a great people turn a calm and scrutinizing eye upon
itself," as the people of America had done; " to see it
carefully examine the extent of the evil " into which dis-
union and disorder had brought it ; " patiently wait for
two years until a remedy was discovered "; and at last
voluntarily adopt a new order and government " without having wrung a tear or a drop of blood from mankind." But Washington knew that the praise deserved
for such mastery and self-possession would be short-
lived enough if the new government should fail or be
discredited. It was the overpowering thought that he
himself would be chiefly responsible for its success or

failure that shook his nerves as he stood there at the
beginning of his task; and no man of right sensibility
in that audience failed to like him the better and trust
him the more implicitly for his emotion. " It was a
very touching scene," wrote Fisher Ames, of Massachusetts. " It seemed to me an allegory in which
virtue was personified as addressing those whom she
would make her votaries. Her power over the heart
was never greater, and the illustration of her doctrine
by her own example was never more perfect." " I
feel how much I shall stand in need of the countenance
and aid of every friend to myself, of every friend to
the Revolution, and of every lover of good government," were Washington's words of appeal to Edward
Rutledge, of South Carolina; and he never seemed
to his friends more attractive or more noble than
now.

The inauguration over, the streets fallen quiet again,
the legislative business of the Houses resumed, Washington regained his old self - possession, and turned to
master his new duties with a calm thoroughness of purpose which seemed at once to pass into the action of the
government itself. Perhaps it was true, as he thought,
that he had been no statesman hitherto; though those
who had known him would have declared themselves of
another mind. He had carried the affairs of the Confederation upon his own shoulders, while the war lasted,
after a fashion the men of that time were not likely to
forget, so full of energy had he been, so provident and
capable upon every point of policy. His letters, too,
since the war ended, had shown his correspondents the
country over such an appreciation of the present, so
sure a forecast of the future, so masculine an under-

standing of what waited to be done and of the means at hand to do it, that they, at least, accounted him their leader in peace no less than in war.   But statesmanship hitherto had been only incidental to his duties as a soldier and a citizen.   It had been only an accident of the Revolution that he had had himself, oftentimes, to supply the foresight and the capacity in action which the halting congress lacked.   He had had no experience at all in actual civil administration.   He did not know his own abilities, or realize how rich his experience in affairs had, in fact, been.   He went about his new tasks with diffidence, therefore, but with the full-pulsed heartiness, too, of the man who thoroughly trusts himself, for the capacity at any rate of taking pains. Statesmanship was now his duty—his whole duty—and it was his purpose to understand and execute the office of President as he had understood and administered the office of General.

He knew what need there was for caution.   This was to be, "in the first instance, in a considerable degree, a government of accommodation as well as a government of laws.   Much was to be done by prudence, much by conciliation, much by firmness."   "I walk," he said, "on untrodden ground.   There is scarcely an action the motive of which may not be subjected to a double interpretation.   There is scarcely any part of my conduct which may not hereafter be drawn into precedent." But, though he sought a prudent course, he had no mind to be timid; though he asked advice, he meant to be his own master.

Washington had, no doubt, a more precise understanding of what the new government must be made to mean than any other man living, except, perhaps, Hamilton and Madison, the men whom he most consulted. The Confederation had died in contempt, despised for its want of dignity and power. The new government must deserve and get pre-eminent standing from the first. Its policy must make the States a nation, must stir the people out of their pettiness as colonists and provincials, and give them a national character and spirit. It was not a government only that was to be created, but the definite body of opinion also which should sustain and perfect it. It must be made worth believing in, and the best spirits of the country must be rallied to its support. It was not the question simply of how strong the government should be. Its action must, as Washington said, be mixed of firmness, prudence, and conciliation, if it would win liking and loyalty as well as respect. It must cultivate tact as well as eschew weakness; must win as well as compel obedience. It was of the first consequence to the country, therefore, that the man it had chosen to preside in this delicate business of establishing a government which should be vigorous without being overbearing was a thoroughbred gentleman, whose instincts would carry him a great way towards the solution of many a nice question of conduct. While he waited to be made President he called upon every Senator and Representative then in attendance upon Congress, with the purpose to show them upon how cordial and natural a basis of personal acquaintance he wished, for his part, to see the government conducted; but, the oath of office once taken, he was no longer a simple citizen, as he had been during those two days of waiting; the dignity of the government had come into his keeping with the office. Henceforth he would pay no more calls, accept no invitations. On a day fixed he would receive calls; and he would show himself once a week at Mrs. Washington's general receptions. He would invite persons of official rank or marked distinction to his table at suitable intervals. There should be no pretence of seclusion, no parade of inaccessibility. The President should be a republican officer, the servant of the people. But he would not be common. It should be known that his office and authority were the first in the land. Every proper outward form of dignity, ceremony, and self-respect should be observed that might tell wholesomely upon the imagination of the people; that might be made to serve as a visible sign, which no man could miss, that there was here no vestige of the old federal authority, at which it had been the fashion to laugh, but a real government, and that the greatest in the land.

It was not that the President was not to be seen by anybody who had the curiosity to wish to see him. Many a fine afternoon he was to be seen walking, an unmistakable figure, upon the Battery, whither all persons of fashion in the town resorted for their daily promenade, his secretaries walking behind him, but otherwise unattended. Better still, he could be seen almost any day on horseback, riding in his noble way through the streets. People drew always aside to give him passage wherever he went, whether he walked or rode; no doubt there was something in his air and bearing which seemed to expect them to do so; but their respect had the alacrity of affection, and he would have borne himself with a like proud figure in his own Virginia. Some thought him stiff, but only the churlish could deem him unrepublican, so evident was it to every candid man that it was not himself but his office he was exalting. His old passion for success was upon him, and he meant that this government of which he had been made the head should have prestige from the first. Count de Moustier, the French Minister to the United States, deeming America, no doubt, a protégé of France, claimed the right to deal directly with the President in person, as if upon terms of familiar privilege, when conducting his diplomatic business; but was checked very promptly. It was not likely a man bred in the proud school of Virginian country gentlemen would miss so obvious a point of etiquette as this. To demand intimacy was to intimate superiority, and Washington's reply drew from the Count an instant apology. That the United States had every reason to hold France in loyal affection Washington gladly admitted with all stately courtesy ; but affection became servility when it lost self-respect, and France must approach the President of the United States as every other country did, through the properly constituted department. "If there are rules of proceeding," he said, quietly, "which have originated from the wisdom of statesmen, and are sanctioned by the common assent of nations, it would not be prudent for a young state to dispense with them altogether," — particularly a young state (his thought added) which foreign states had despised and might now try to patronize. These small matters would carry an infinite weight of suggestion with them, as he knew, and every suggestion that proceeded from the President should speak of dignity and independence.

For the first few months of the new government's life these small matters that marked its temper and its self-respect were of as much consequence as its laws or its efficient organization for the tasks of actual adminis-

tration. The country evidently looked to Washington
to set the tone and show what manner of government
it was to have. Congress, though diligent and purpose-
ful enough, could linger, meanwhile, the whole summer
through upon its task of framing the laws necessary for
the erection and organization of Departments of State,
for Foreign Affairs, of the Treasury, and of War, and
the creation of the office of Attorney-General—a simple
administrative structure to suffice for the present. In
the interval the treasury board of the Confederation and
its secretaries of war and foreign affairs were continued
in service, and the President found time to digest the
business of the several departments preparatory to their
reorganization. He sent for all the papers concerning
their transactions since the treaty of peace of 1783, and
mastered their contents after his own thorough fashion,
making copious notes and abstracts as he read.

He had been scarcely six weeks in office when he was
stricken with a sharp illness. A malignant tumor in
his thigh seemed to his physicians for a time to threaten
mortification. It was three weeks before he could take
the air again, stretched painfully at length in his coach ;
even his stalwart strength was slow to rally from the
draught made upon it by the disease, and its cure with
the knife. There was deep anxiety for a little among
those who knew, so likely did it seem that the life of
the government was staked upon his life. He himself
had looked very calmly into the doctor's troubled face,
and had bidden him tell him the worst with that placid
firmness that always came to him in moments of danger. " I am not afraid to die," he said. " Whether to-
night or twenty years hence makes no difference. I
know that I am in the hands of a good Providence." A

chain had been stretched across the street in front of
the house where he lay, to check the noisy traffic that
might have disturbed him more deeply in his fever.
But the government had not stood still the while. He
had steadily attended to important matters as he could.
'Twas scarcely necessary he should be out of bed and
abroad again to make all who handled affairs feel his
mastery ; and by the time the summer was ended that
mastery was founded upon knowledge. He understood
the affairs of the new government, as of the old, better
than any other man ; knew the tasks that waited to be
attempted, the questions that waited to be answered,
the difficulties that awaited solution, and the means at
hand for solving them, with a grasp and thoroughness
such as made it impossible henceforth that any man
who might be called to serve with him in executive
business, of whatever capacity in affairs, should be more
than his counsellor. He had made himself once for all
head and master of the government.

By the end of September (1789) Congress had completed its work of organization and Washington had
drawn his permanent advisers about him. The federal
courts, too, had been erected and given definitive jurisdiction. The new government had taken distinct shape,
and was ready to digest its business in detail. Washington chose Alexander Hamilton to be Secretary of the
Treasury, Henry Knox to be Secretary of War, Thomas
Jefferson Secretary of State, and Edmund Randolph
Attorney - General — young men all, except Jefferson,
and he was but forty-six.

The fate of the government was certain to turn, first
of all, upon questions of finance. It was hopeless pov-
erty that had brought the Confederation into deep dis-

grace; the new government had inherited from it nothing but a great debt; and the first test of character to which the new plan in affairs would be put, whether at home or abroad, was the test of its ability to sustain its financial credit with businesslike thoroughness and statesmanlike wisdom. Alexander Hamilton was only thirty-two years old. He had been a spirited and capable soldier and an astute and eloquent advocate; but he had not had a day's experience in the administration of a great governmental department, and had never handled—so far as men knew, had never studied—questions of public finance. Washington chose him, nevertheless, without hesitation, for what must certainly turn out to be the most critical post in his administration. No man saw more clearly than Washington did how large a capacity for statesmanship Hamilton had shown in his masterly papers in advocacy of the Constitution. He had known Hamilton, moreover, through all the quick years that had brought him from precocious youth to wise maturity; had read his letters and felt the singular power that moved in them; and was ready to trust him with whatever task he would consent to assume.

Henry Knox, that gallant officer of the Revolution, had been already four years Secretary of War for the Confederation. In appointing him to the same office under the new Constitution, Washington was but retaining a man whom he loved and to whom he had for long been accustomed to look for friendship and counsel. He chose Thomas Jefferson to handle the delicate questions of foreign affairs which must press upon the young state because, John Adams being Vice-President, there was no other man of equal gifts available who had

had so large an experience in the field of diplomacy. Again and again Jefferson had been chosen for foreign missions under the Confederation; he was American Minister to France when Washington's summons called him to the Secretaryship of State; and he came of that race of Virginian statesmen from whom Washington might reasonably count upon receiving a support touched with personal loyalty. Richard Henry Lee, Patrick Henry, and George Mason were home-keeping spirits, and doubted of the success of the new government; but Jefferson, though he had looked upon its making from across the sea, approved, and was ready to lend his aid to its successful establishment. In appointing Edmund Randolph to be Attorney - General, Washington was but choosing a brilliant young man whom he loved out of a great family of lawyers who had held a sort of primacy at the bar in Virginia ever since he could remember — almost ever since she had been called the Old Dominion. Knox was thirty-nine, Edmund Randolph thirty-six; but if Washington chose young men to be his comrades and guides in counsel, it was but another capital proof of his own mastery in affairs. Himself a natural leader, he recognized the like gift and capacity in others, even when fortune had not yet disclosed or brought them to the test.

It was hard, in filling even the greater offices, to find men of eminence who were willing to leave the service of their States or the security and ease of private life to try the untrodden paths of federal government. The States were old and secure—so men thought—the federal government was new and an experiment. The stronger sort of men, particularly amongst those bred to the law, showed, many of them, a great reluctance to identify themselves with new institutions set up but five or six months ago; and Washington, though he meant to make every liberal allowance for differences of opinion, would invite no man to stand with him in the new service who did not thoroughly believe in it. He was careful to seek out six of the best lawyers to be had in the country when he made up the Supreme Court, and to choose them from as many States—John Jay, of New York, to be chief justice; John Rutledge, of South Carolina; William Cushing, of Massachusetts; John Blair, of Virginia; James Wilson, of Pennsylvania, and R. H. Harrison, of Maryland — for he knew that the government must draw its strength from the men who administered it, and that the common run of people must learn to respect it in the persons of its officers. But he was equally careful to find out in advance of every appointment what the man whom he wished to ask thought of the new government and wished its future to be. Many to whom he offered appointment declined; minor offices seemed almost to go a-begging amongst men of assured position such as it was his object to secure. It needed all the tact and patience he could command to draw about him a body of men such as the country must look up to and revere. His letters again went abroad by the hundred, as so often before, to persuade men to their duty, build a bulwark of right opinion round about the government, make his purposes clear and his plans effective. He would spare no pains to make the government both great and permanent.

In October, 1789, his principal appointments all made, the government in full operation, and affairs standing still till Congress should meet again, he went upon a four weeks' tour through the eastern States, to put the people in mind there, by his own presence, of the existence and dignity of the federal government, and to make trial of their feeling towards it. They received him with cordial enthusiasm, for he was secure of their love and admiration; and he had once more a royal progress from place to place all the way to far New Hampshire and back again. He studiously contrived to make it everywhere felt, nevertheless, by every turn of ceremonial and behavior, that he had come, not as the hero of the Revolution, but as the President of the United States. At Boston Governor Hancock sought by cordial notes and pleas of illness to force Washington to waive the courtesy of a first call from him, and so give the executive of Massachusetts precedence, if only for old friendship's sake. But Washington would not be so defeated of his errand; forced the perturbed old patriot to come to him, swathed as he was in flannels and borne upon men's shoulders up the stairs, received him with grim courtesy, and satisfied the gossips of the town once and for all that precedence belonged to the federal government—at any rate, so long as George Washington was President. Having seen him and fêted him, the eastern towns had seen and done homage to the new authority set over them. Washington was satisfied, and returned with a noticeable accession of spirits to the serious work of federal administration.

No man stood closer to him in his purpose to strengthen and give prestige to the government than Hamilton; and no man was able to discover the means with a surer genius. Hamilton knew who the well-wishers of the new government were, whence its strength was to be drawn, what it must do to approve itself great and permanent, with an insight and thoroughness Washington himself could not match : for Hamilton knew Washington and the seats of his strength in the country as that self-forgetful man himself could not. He knew that it was the commercial classes of the country — such men as he had himself dwelt amongst at the great port at New York — who were bound by self-interest to the new government, which promised them a single policy in trade, in the stead of policies a half-score; and that the men who were standing to its support out of a reasoned prudence, out of a high-minded desire to secure good government and a place of consideration for their country amongst the nations of the world, were individuals merely, to be found only in small groups here and there, where a special light shone in some minds. He knew that Washington was loved most for his national character and purpose amongst the observant middle classes of substantial people in the richer counties of Pennsylvania, New Jersey, New York, and New England, while his neighbors in the South loved him with an individual affection only, and rather as their hero than as their leader in affairs. He saw that the surest way to get both popular support and international respect was to give to the government at once and in the outset a place of command in the business and material interests of the country. Such a policy every man could comprehend, and a great body of energetic and influential men would certainly support; that alone could make the government seem real from the first—a veritable power, not an influence and a shadow merely.

Here was a man, unquestionably, who had a quick genius in affairs; and Washington gave him leave and initiative with such sympathy and comprehension and support as only a nature equally bold and equally originative could have given. Hamilton's measures jumped with Washington's purpose, ran with Washington's perception of national interests; and they were with Washington's aid put into execution with a promptness and decision which must have surprised the friends of the new government no less than it chagrined and alarmed its enemies.

Having done its work of organization during its first summer session, the Congress came together again, January 4th, 1790, to attempt the formulation of a policy of government, and Hamilton at once laid before it a " plan for the settlement of the public debt" which he had drawn and Washington had sanctioned. He proposed that provision should be made for the payment of the foreign debt in full—that of course; that the domestic debt, the despised promises and paper of the Confederation, should be funded and paid; and that the debts contracted by the several States in the prosecution of the war for independence should be assumed by the general government as the debt of the nation. No one could doubt that the foreign debt must be paid in full: to that Congress agreed heartily and without hesitation. But there was much in the rest of the plan to give prudent men pause. To pay off the paper of the Confederation would be to give to the speculators, who had bought it up in the hope of just such a measure, a gratuity of many times what they had paid for it. To assume the State debts would be taken to mean that the States were bankrupt or delinquent, that the federal government was to be their guardian and financial providence, and that the capital of the country must

look only to the government of the nation, not to the
government of the States, for security and profitable
employment. This was nationalizing the government
with a vengeance, and was a plain bid, besides, to win
the moneyed class to its support. Members whose con-
stituencies lay away from the centres of trade looked
askance at such measures, and deemed them no better
than handing the government over to the money lenders
of the towns. But boldness and energy prevailed, as
they had prevailed in the adoption of the Constitution
itself, and both measures were carried through the
Houses—the first at once, the second after a close and
doubtful struggle—by stratagem and barter.

Jefferson had been in France when Washington called
him to assume the headship of foreign affairs at home;
had not reached New York on his return voyage until
December 23d, 1789 ; and did not take his place in Washington's council till March 21st, 1790. All of Hamilton's
great plan had by that time passed Congress, except the
assumption of the State debts. Upon that question a
crisis had been reached. It had wrought Congress to
a dangerous heat of feeling. Members from the South,
where trade was not much astir and financial interests
told for less than local pride and sharp jealousy of a too
great central power, were set hotly against the measure;
most of the Northern members were as hotly resolved
upon its adoption. Mr. Jefferson must have caught
echoes and rumors of the great debate as he lingered
at Monticello in order to adjust his private affairs before entering upon his duties in the cabinet. The measure had been lost at last in the House by the narrow
margin of two votes. But the minority were in no
humor to submit. They declined to transact any busi-

ness at all till they should be yielded to in this matter.
There were even ugly threats to be heard that some
would withdraw from Congress and force a dissolution
of the Union rather than make concessions upon the
one side or the other.

It was to this pass that things had come when Mr.
Jefferson reached the seat of government; and his
arrival gave Hamilton an opportunity to show how
consummate a politician he could be in support of his
statesmanship. The Southern members wanted the seat
of the federal government established within their
reach, upon the Potomac, where Congress might at least
be rid of importunate merchants and money lenders
clamoring at its doors, and of impracticable Quakers
with their petitions for the abolition of slavery; and
were almost as hot at their failure to get their will in
that matter as the Northern men were to find themselves defeated upon the question of the State debts.
Mr. Jefferson was fresh upon the field, was strong
among the Southern members, was not embroiled or
committed in the quarrel. Hamilton besought him to
intervene. The success of the government was at stake,
he said, and Mr. Jefferson could pluck it out of peril.
Might it not be that the Southern men would consent
to vote for the assumption of the State debts if the
Northern members would vote for a capital on the
Potomac? The suggestion came as if upon the thought
of the moment, at a chance meeting on the street, as
the two men walked and talked of matters of the day;
but it was very eloquently urged. Mr. Jefferson declared he was " really a stranger to the whole subject,"
but would be glad to lend what aid he could. Would
not Mr. Hamilton dine with him the next day, to meet

and confer with a few of the Southern members? In
the genial air of the dinner-table the whole difficulty
was talked away. Two of the diners agreed to vote
for the assumption of the State debts if Mr. Hamilton
could secure a majority for a capital on the Potomac;
and Congress presently ratified the bargain. There was
not a little astonishment at the sudden clearing of the
skies. The waters did not go down at once; hints of
a scandal and of the shipwreck of a fair name or two
went about the town and spread to the country. But
Congress had come out of its angry tangle of factions,
calm had returned to the government, and Hamilton's
plan stood finished and complete. He had nationalized
the government as he wished.

It was this fact that most struck the eye of Jefferson
when he had settled to his work and had come to see
affairs steadily and as a whole at the seat of government. He saw Hamilton supreme in the cabinet and in
legislation — not because either the President or Congress was weak, but because Hamilton was a master in
his new field, and both Congress and the President had
accepted his leadership. It chagrined Jefferson deeply
to see that he had himself assisted at Hamilton's triumph, had himself made it complete, indeed. He could
not easily brook successful rivalry in leadership; must
have expected to find himself, not Hamilton, preferred
in the counsels of a Virginian President; was beyond
measure dismayed to see the administration already in
the hands, as it seemed, of a man just two months turned
of thirty-three. He began ere long to declare that he
had been "most ignorantly and innocently made to hold
the candle" to the sharp work of the Secretary of the
Treasury, having been "a stranger to the circum-

stances." But it was not the circumstances of which
he had been ignorant; it was the effect of what he had
done upon his own wish to play the chief rôle in the
new government. When he came to a calm scrutiny of
the matter, he did not like the assumption of the State
debts, and, what was more serious for a man of political ambition, it was bitterly distasteful to the very men
from whom he must look to draw a following when parties should form. He felt that he had been tricked; he
knew that he had been outrun in the race for leadership.

What he did not understand or know how to reckon
with was the place and purpose of Washington in the
government. Hamilton had been Washington's aide
and confidant when a lad of twenty, and knew in what
way those must rule who served under such a chief. He
knew that Washington must first be convinced and
won; did not for a moment doubt that the President
held the reins and was master; was aware that his own
plans had prospered both in the making and in the
adoption because the purpose they spoke was the purpose
Washington most cherished. Washington had adopted
the fiscal measures as his own; Hamilton's strength
consisted in having his confidence and support. Jefferson
had slowly to discover that leadership in the cabinet was
to be had, not by winning a majority of the counsellors
who sat in it, but by winning Washington. That masterful man asked counsel upon every question of consequence, but took none his own judgment did not approve. He had chosen Hamilton because he knew his
views, Jefferson only because he knew his influence,
ability, and experience in affairs. When he did test
Jefferson's views he found them less to his liking than
he had expected.

He had taken Jefferson direct from France, where for five years he had been watching a revolution come on apace, hurried from stage to stage, not by statesmen who were masters in the art and practice of freedom, like those who had presided in the counsels of America, but by demagogues and philosophers rather; and the subtle air of that age of change had crept into the man's thought. He had come back a philosophical radical rather than a statesman. He had yet to learn, in the practical air of America, what plain and steady policy must serve him to win hard-headed men to his following; and Washington found him a guide who needed watching. Foreign affairs, over which it was Jefferson's duty to preside, began of a sudden to turn upon the politics of France, where Jefferson's thought was so much engaged. The year 1789, in which America gained self-possession and set up a government soberly planned to last, was the year in which France lost self-possession and set out upon a wild quest for liberty which was to cost her both her traditional polity and all the hopes she had of a new one. In that year broke the storm of the French revolution.

It was a dangerous infection that went abroad from France in those first days of her ardor, and nowhere was it more likely to spread than in America.

> "Bliss was it in that dawn to be alive,
>   But to be young was very heaven ! O times
>   In which the meagre, stale, forbidding ways
>   Of custom, law, and statute took at once
>   The attraction of a country in romance !
>   When Reason seemed the most to assert her rights
>   When most intent on making of herself
>   A prime Enchantress, to assist the work

> Which then was going forward in her name!
> Not favored spots alone, but the whole earth,
> The beauty wore of promise, that which sets
> (As at some moments might not be unfelt
> Among the bowers of paradise itself)
> The budding rose above the rose full blown."

Was not this spirit that had sprung to such sudden might in France the very spirit that had made America free, her people sovereign, her government liberal as men could dream of? Was not France now more than ever America's friend and close ally against the world? 'Twould be niggardly to grudge her aid and love to the full in this day of her emulation of America's great example. The Bastile was down, tyranny at an end, Lafayette the people's leader. The gallant Frenchman himself could think of nothing more appropriate than to send the great key of the fallen fortress to Washington.

But Washington's vision in affairs was not obscured. He had not led revolutionary armies without learning what revolution meant. "The revolution which has been effected in France," he said, "is of so wonderful a nature that the mind can hardly realize the fact"—his calm tones ringing strangely amidst the enthusiastic cries of the time. "I fear, though it has gone triumphantly through the first paroxysm, it is not the last it has to encounter before matters are finally settled. The revolution is of too great a magnitude to be effected in so short a space and with the loss of so little blood." He hoped, but did not believe, that it would run its course without fatal disorders; and he meant, in any case, to keep America from the infection. She was herself but "in a convalescent state," as he said, after her own great struggle. She was too observant still, more-

over, of European politics and opinion, like a province
rather than like a nation—inclined to take sides as if she
were still a child of the European family, who had flung
away from her mother England to cling in pique to an
ancient foe. Washington's first and almost single object, at every point of policy, was to make of the provincial States of the Union a veritable nation, independent, at any rate, and ready to be great when its
growth should come, and its self-knowledge. "Every
true friend to this country," he said, at last, "must *see*
and *feel* that the policy of it is not to embroil ourselves
with any nation whatever, but to avoid their disputes
and their politics, and, if they will harass one another,
to avail ourselves of the neutral conduct we have adopted. Twenty years' peace, with such an increase of population and resources as we have a right to expect,
added to our remote situation from the jarring powers,
will in all probability enable us, in a just cause, to bid
defiance to any power on earth"; and such were his
thought and purpose from the first. "I want an *American* character," he cried, "that the powers of Europe
may be convinced we act for *ourselves*, and not for
others." He had been given charge of a nation in the
making, and he meant it should form, under his care, an
independent character.

It was thus he proved himself no sentimentalist, but
a statesman. It was stuff of his character, this purpose
of independence. He would have played a like part of
self-respect for himself among his neighbors on the Virginian plantations; and he could neither understand nor
tolerate the sentiment which made men like Jefferson
eager to fling themselves into European broils. Truly
this man was the first American, the men about him

provincials merely, dependent still for their life and thought upon the breath of the Old World, unless, like Hamilton, they had been born and had stood aloof, or, like Gouverneur Morris, had divined Europe in her own capitals with clear, unenamoured eyes. Fortunately affairs could be held steadily enough to a course of wise neutrality and moderation at first, while France's revolution wrought only its work of internal overthrow and destruction; and while things went thus opinion began slowly to cool. 'Twas plain to be seen, as the months went by, that the work being done in France bore no real likeness at all to the revolution in America; and wise men began to see it for what it was, a social distemper, not a reformation of government — effective enough as a purge, no doubt; inevitable, perhaps; a cure of nature's own devising; but by no means to be taken part in by a people not likewise stricken, still free to choose. At first Washington and a few men of like insight stood almost alone in their cool self-possession. Every man of generous spirit deemed it his mere duty to extol the French, to join clubs after their manner, in the name of the rights of man, to speak everywhere in praise of the revolution. But by the time it became necessary to act—to declare the position and policy of the nation's government towards France—a sober second thought had come, and Washington's task was a little simplified.

The crisis came with the year 1793. In 1792 France took arms against her European neighbors, let her mobs sack the King's palace, declared herself a republic, and put her monarch on trial for his life. The opening days of 1793 saw Louis dead upon the scaffold; England, Holland, Spain, and the Empire joined with the alliance against the fevered nation; and war as it were spread suddenly to all the world. Would not America succor her old ally? Was there no compulsion in the name of liberty? Would she stand selfishly off to save herself from danger? There was much in such a posture of affairs to give pause even to imperative men like Washington. Those who favored France seemed the spokesmen of the country. The thoughtful men, to whom the real character of the great revolution over sea was beginning to be made plain, were silent. It would have required a veritable art of divination to distinguish the real sentiment of the country, upon which, after all, the general government must depend. "It is on great occasions only, and after time has been given for cool and deliberate reflection," Washington held, "that the real voice of the people can be known"; but a great risk must be run in waiting to know it.

The measures already adopted by the government, though well enough calculated to render it strong, had not been equally well planned to make it popular. The power to tax, so jealously withheld but the other day from the Confederation, the new Congress had begun promptly and confidently to exercise upon a great scale, not only laying duties upon imports, the natural resource of the general government, but also imposing taxes upon distilled spirits, and so entering the fiscal field of the States. Not only had the war debts of the States been assumed, but a national bank had been set up (1791), as if still further to make the general government sure of a complete mastery in the field of finance. Jefferson and Randolph had fought the measure in the cabinet, as many a moderate man had fought it in Congress, and Washington had withheld his signature from it till he should hear what they had to urge. But he had sent their arguments to Hamilton for criticism, and had accepted his answer in favor of the bank. Jefferson and Randolph had challenged the measure on the ground that it was without warrant in the Constitution, which nowhere gave Congress the right to create corporations, fiscal or other. Hamilton replied that, besides the powers explicitly enumerated, the Constitution gave to Congress the power to pass any measure "necessary and proper" for executing those set forth; that Congress was itself left to determine what might thus seem necessary; and that if it deemed the erection of a bank a proper means of executing the undoubted financial powers of the government, the constitutional question was answered. By accepting such a view Washington sanctioned the whole doctrine of "implied powers," which Jefferson deemed the very annulment of a written and explicit constitution. No bounds, Jefferson believed, could be set to the aggressive sweep of congressional pretension if the two Houses were to be given leave to do whatever they thought expedient in exercising their in any case great and commanding powers. No man could doubt, in the face of such measures, what the spirit and purpose of Hamilton were, or of the President whom Hamilton so strangely dominated.

Strong measures bred strong opposition. When the first Congress came together there seemed to be no parties in the country. All men seemed agreed upon a fair and spirited trial of the new Constitution. But an opposition had begun to gather form before its two years' term was out; and in the second Congress party lines began to grow definite—not for and against the Consti-

tution, but for and against an extravagant use of constitutional powers. There was still a majority for the
principal measures of the administration ; but the minority had clearly begun to gather force both in the votes
and in the debates. The reaction was unmistakable.
Even Madison, Washington's stanch friend and intimate counsellor, who had at first been his spokesman in
the House, began to draw back — first doubted and
then opposed the policy of the Treasury. He had led
the opposition to the bank, and grew more and more
uneasy to note the course affairs were taking. It looked
as if the administration were determined of set purpose
to increase the expenses of the government, in order
that they might add to the loans,which were so acceptable to influential men of wealth, and double the taxes
which made the power of the government so real in the
eyes of the people. Steps were urged to create a navy ;
to develop an army with permanent organization and
equipment; and the President insisted upon vigorous
action at the frontiers against the western Indians.
This was part of his cherished policy. It was his way
of fulfilling the vision that had long ago come to him,
of a nation spreading itself down the western slopes of
the mountains and over all the broad reaches of fertile
land that looked towards the Mississippi ; but to many a
member of Congress from the quiet settlements in the
east it looked like nothing better than a waste of men
and of treasure. The President seemed even a little too
imperious in the business: would sometimes come into
the Senate in no temper to brook delay in the consideration and adoption of what he proposed in such matters.
When things went wrong through the fault of the commanders he had sent to the frontier, he stormed in a

sudden fury, as sometimes in the old days of the war,
scorning soldiers who must needs blunder and fail. The
compulsion of his will grew often a little irksome to
the minority in Congress; and the opposition slowly
pulled itself together as the months went by to concert
a definite policy of action.

Washington saw as plainly as any man what was
taking place. He was sensitive to the movements of
opinion; wished above all things to have the government supported by the people's approval; was never
weary of writing to those who were in a position to know,
to ask them what they and their neighbors soberly
thought about the questions and policies under debate;
was never so impatient as to run recklessly ahead of
manifest public opinion. He knew how many men had
been repelled by the measures he had supported Hamilton in proposing; knew that a reaction had set in; that
even to seem to repulse France and to refuse her aid or
sympathy would surely strengthen it. The men who
were opposed to his financial policy were also the men
who most loved France, now she was mad with revolution. They were the men who dreaded a strong government as a direct menace to the rights alike of individuals and of the separate States; the men who held
a very imperative philosophy of separation and of revolt
against any too great authority. If he showed himself
cold towards France, he would certainly strengthen
them in their charge that the new government craved
power and was indifferent to the guarantees of freedom.

But Washington's spirit was of the majestic sort that
keeps a great and hopeful confidence that the right view
will prevail; that the " standard to which the wise and
honest will repair " is also the standard to which the

whole people will rally at last, if it be but held long and steadily enough on high to be seen of all. When the moment for action came he acted promptly, unhesitatingly, as if in indifference to opinion. The outbreak of war between France and England made it necessary he should let the country know what he meant to do. " War having actually commenced between France and Great Britain," he wrote to Jefferson in April, 1793, " it behooves the government of this country to use every means in its power to prevent the citizens thereof from embroiling us with either of those powers, by endeavoring to maintain a strict neutrality. I therefore require that you will give the subject mature consideration, that such measures as shall be deemed most likely to effect this desirable purpose may be adopted without delay. . . . Such other measures as may be necessary for us to pursue against events which it may not be in our power to avoid or control, you will also think of, and lay them before me at my arrival in Philadelphia; for which place I shall set out to-morrow." He was at Mount Vernon when he despatched these instructions; but it did not take him long to reach the seat of government, to consult his cabinet, and to issue a proclamation of neutrality whose terms no man could mistake. It contained explicit threat of exemplary action against any who should presume to disregard it.

That very month (April, 1793) Edmond Charles Genet, a youth still in his twenties whom the new republic over sea had commissioned Minister to the United States, landed at Charleston. It pleased him to take possession of the country, as if it were of course an appanage of France. He was hardly ashore before he had begun to arrange for the fitting out of privateers, to issue let-

ters of marque to American citizens, and to authorize
French consuls at American ports to act as judges of admiralty in the condemnation of prizes. As he journeyed
northward to Philadelphia he was joyfully confirmed in
his views and purposes by his reception at the hands of
the people. He was everywhere dined and toasted and
fêted, as if he had been a favorite prince returned to his
subjects. His speeches by the way rang in a tone of authority and patronage. He reached Philadelphia fairly
mad with the sense of power, and had no conception of
his real situation till he stood face to face with the President. Of that grim countenance and cold greeting
there could be but one interpretation; and the fellow
winced to feel that at last he had come to a grapple
with the country's government. It was, no doubt, in
the eyes of the sobering man, a strange and startling
thing that then took place. The country itself had not
fully known Washington till then—or its own dignity
either. It had deemed the proclamation of neutrality a
party measure, into which the President had been led
by the enemies of France, the partisans of England.
But the summer undeceived everybody, even Genet.
Not content with the lawless mischief he had set afoot
on the coasts by the commissioning of privateersmen,
that mad youth had hastened to send agents into
the south and west to enlist men for armed expedi-
tions against the Floridas and against New Orleans, on
the coveted Mississippi; but his work was everywhere
steadily undone. Washington acted slowly, deliberately
even, with that majesty of self-control, that awful courtesy and stillness in wrath, that had ever made him a
master to be feared in moments of sharp trial. One by
one the unlawful prizes were seized; justice was done

upon their captors; the false admiralty courts were shut up. The army of the United States was made ready to check the risings in the south and west, should there be need; the complaints of the British Minister were silenced by deeds as well as by words; the clamor of those who had welcomed the Frenchman so like provincials was ignored, though for a season it seemed the voice of the country itself; and the humiliating work, which ought never to have been necessary, was at last made effective and complete.

Towards the close of June, Washington ventured to go for a little while to Mount Vernon for rest. At once there was trouble. A privateer was found taking arms and stores aboard in the very river at Philadelphia; Jefferson allowed her to drop down to Chester, believing Genet instead of the agents of the government; and she was upon the point of getting to sea before Washington could reach the seat of government. Jefferson was not in town when the President arrived. "What is to be done in the case of the *Little Sarah*, now at Chester?" came Washington's hot questions after him. "Is the Minister of the French Republic to set the acts of this government at defiance *with impunity?* And then threaten the executive with an appeal to the people? What must the world think of such conduct, and of the United States in submitting to it? Circumstances press for decision; and as you have had time to consider them, I wish to know your opinion upon them, even before to-morrow, for the vessel may then be gone." It was indeed too late to stop her: a gross violation of neutrality had been permitted under the very eyes of the Secretary of State. Washington stayed henceforth in Philadelphia, in personal control of affairs.

It was an appeal to the people that finally delivered
Genet into his hands. Washington revoked the *exe-
quatur* of one Duplaine, French consul at Boston, for
continuing to ignore the laws of neutrality; Genet declared he would appeal from the President to the sovereign State of Massachusetts; rumors of the silly threat
got abroad, and Genet demanded of the President that
he deny them. Washington answered with a chilling
rebuke; the correspondence was given to the public
prints; and at last the country saw the French Minister
for what he was. A demand for his recall had been resolved upon in the cabinet in August; by February,
1794, the slow processes of diplomatic action were complete, and a successor had arrived. Genet did not venture to return to his distracted country; but he was as
promptly and as readily forgotten in America. Some
might find it possible to love France still; but no one
could any longer stomach Genet.

Washington had divined French affairs much too
clearly to be for a moment tempted to think with
anything but contempt of the French party who had
truckled to Genet. " The affairs of France," he said to
Lee, in the midst of Genet's heyday, " seem to me to be
in the highest paroxysm of disorder; not so much from
the presence of foreign enemies, but because those in
whose hands the government is intrusted are ready to
tear each other to pieces, and will more than probably
prove the worst foes the country has." It was his clear
perception what the danger would be should America
be drawn into the gathering European wars that had
led him to accept a second term as President. It had
been his wish to remain only four years in the arduous
office: but he had no thought to leave a task unfinished;

knew that he was in the very midst of the critical business of holding the country to the course which should
make it a self-respecting nation; and consented to
submit himself once more to the vote of the electors.
Parties were organizing, but there was no opposition to
Washington. He received again a unanimous vote; and
John Adams was again chosen Vice-President. The
second inauguration (March, 1793) seemed but a routine confirmation of the first. But the elections to
Congress showed a change setting in. In the Senate
the avowed supporters of the administration had still a
narrow majority; but in the House they fell ten votes
short of control; and Washington had to put his policy
of neutrality into execution against the mad Genet with
nothing but doubts how he should be supported. The
insane folly of Genet saved the President serious embarrassment, after all; made the evidence that Washington
was right too plain to be missed by anybody; and gave
the country at last vision enough to see what was in
fact the course of affairs abroad, within and without
unhappy France. Before that trying year 1793 was
out, an attack upon Hamilton in the House, though led
by Madison, had failed; Jefferson had left the cabinet;
and the hands of those who definitely and heartily supported the President were not a little strengthened.
There was sharp bitterness between parties—a bitterness sharper as yet, indeed, than their differences of
view; but the " federalists," who stood to the support
of Washington and Hamilton, were able, none the less,
to carry their more indispensable measures — even an
act of neutrality which made the President's policy the
explicit law of the land. The sober second thought of
the country was slowly coming about to their aid.

The air might have cleared altogether had the right method of dealing with France been the only question that pressed; but the ill fortune of the time forced the President to seem not only the recreant friend of France, but also the too complacent partisan of England. Great Britain seemed as mischievously bent upon forcing the United States to war as Genet himself had been. She would not withdraw her garrisons from the border posts; it was believed that she was inciting the Indians to their savage inroads upon the border, as the French had done in the old days; she set herself to destroy neutral trade by seizing all vessels that carried the products of the French islands or were laden with provisions for their ports; she would admit American vessels to her own West Indian harbors only upon sufferance, and within the limits of a most jealous restriction. It gave a touch of added bitterness to the country's feeling against her that she should thus levy as it were covert war upon the Union while affecting to be at peace with it, as if she counted on its weakness, especially on the seas; and Congress would have taken measures of retaliation, which must certainly have led to open hostilities, had not Washington intervened, despatching John Jay, the trusted Chief Justice, across sea as minister extraordinary, to negotiate terms of accommodation; and so giving pause to the trouble.

While the country waited upon the negotiation, it witnessed a wholesome object-lesson in the power of its new government. In March, 1791, Congress had passed an act laying taxes on distilled spirits: 'twas part of Hamilton's plan to show that the federal government could and would use its great authority. The act bore nowhere so hard upon the people as in the vast far counties of Pennsylvania and Virginia, beyond the mountains—and there the very allegiance of the people had been but the other day doubtful, as Washington very well knew. How were they to get their corn to market over the long roads if they were not to be permitted to reduce its bulk and increase its value by turning it into whiskey? The tax seemed to them intolerable, and the remedy plain. They would not pay it. They had not been punctilious to obey the laws of the States; they would not begin obedience now by submitting to the worst laws of the United States. At first they only amused themselves by tarring and feathering an exciseman here and there; but resistance could not stop with that in the face of a government bent upon having its own way. Opposition organized itself and spread, till the writs of federal courts had been defied by violent mobs and the western counties of Pennsylvania were fairly quick with incipient insurrection.

For two years Washington watched the slow gathering of the storm, warning those who resisted, keeping Congress abreast of him in preparation for action when the right time should come, letting all the country know what was afoot and prepare its mind for what was to come. It must have won him to a stern humor to learn that seven thousand armed men had gathered in massmeeting on Braddock's field to defy him. At last he summoned an army of militia out of the States, sent it straight to the lawless counties, going with it himself till he learned there would be no serious resistance— and taught the country what was back of federal law. Hamilton had had his way, the country its lesson. " The servile copyist of Mr. Pitt thought he must have his alarms, his insurrections and plots against the Constitution," sneered Jefferson. " It aroused the favorite purposes of strengthening government and increasing the public debt ; and therefore an insurrection was announced and proclaimed and armed against and marched against, but could never be found. And all this under the sanction of a name which has done too much good not to be sufficient to cover harm also." " The powers of the executive of this country are more definite and better understood, perhaps, than those of any other country," Washington had said, "and my aim has been, and will continue to be, neither to stretch nor to relax from them in any instance whatever, unless compelled to it by imperious circumstances," and that was what he meant the country to know, whether the law's purpose was good or bad.

The next year the people knew what Mr. Jay had done. He reached New York May 28th, 1796 ; and the treaty he brought with him was laid before the Senate on the 8th of June. On the 2d of July the country knew what he had agreed to and the Senate had ratified. There was an instant outburst of wrath. It swept from one end of the country to the other. The treaty yielded so much, gained so little, that to accept it seemed a veritable humiliation. The northwestern posts were, indeed, to be given up at last; the boundaries between English and American territory were to be determined by commissioners ; unrestricted commerce with England herself, and a free direct trade with her East Indian possessions, were conceded ; but not a word was said about the impressment of American seamen ; American claims for damages for unjust seizures in the West Indies were referred to a commission, along with American debts to Englishmen ; the coveted trade with the West Indian islands was secured only to vessels of seventy tons and under, and at the cost of renouncing the right to export sugar, molasses, coffee, cocoa, or cotton to Europe. Washington agreed with the Senate that ratifications of the treaty ought not to be exchanged without a modification of the clauses respecting the West Indian trade, and October had come before new and better terms could be agreed upon ; but he had no doubt that the treaty as a whole ought to be accepted. The opposition party in Congress had refused to vote money for an efficient navy, and so had made it impossible to check British aggressions : they must now accept this unpalatable treaty as better at any rate than war.

It was hard to stand steady in the storm. The country took fire as it had done at the passage of the Stamp Act. Harder things had never been said of king and parliament than were now said of Washington and his advisers. Many stout champions stood to his defence— none stouter or more formidable than Hamilton, no longer a member of the cabinet, for imperative private interests had withdrawn him these six months and more, but none the less redoubtable in the field of controversy. For long, nevertheless, the battle went heavily against the treaty. Even Washington, for once, stood a little while perplexed, not doubting his own purpose, indeed, but very anxious what the outcome should be. Protests against his signing the treaty poured in upon him from every quarter of the country : many of them earnest almost to the point of entreaty, some hot with angry comment. His reply, when he vouchsafed any, was always that his very gratitude for the approbation of the country in the past fixed him but the more firmly in his resolution to deserve it now by obeying his own conscience. "It is very desirable," he wrote to Hamilton, "to ascertain, if possible, after the paroxysm of the fever is a little abated, what the real temper of the people is concerning it; for at present the cry against the Treaty is like that against a mad dog;" but he showed himself very calm to the general eye, making his uneasiness known only to his intimates. The cruel abuse heaped upon him cut him to the quick. "Such exaggerated and indecent terms," he cried, "could scarcely be applied to a Nero, a notorious defaulter, or even to a common pickpocket." But the men who sneered and stormed, talked of usurpation and impeachment, called him base, incompetent, traitorous even, were permitted to see not so much as the quiver of an eyelid as they watched him go steadily from step to step in the course he had chosen.

At last the storm cleared; the bitter months were over; men at the ports saw at length how much more freely trade ran under the terms of the treaty, and remembered that, while they had been abusing Jay and maligning the President, Thomas Pinckney had obtained a treaty from Spain which settled the Florida boundary, opened the Mississippi without restriction, secured a place of deposit at New Orleans, and made commerce with the Spaniards as free as commerce with the French. The whole country felt a new impulse of prosperity. The "paroxysm of the fever" was over, and shame came upon the men who had so vilely abused the great President and had made him wish, in his bitterness, that he were in his grave rather than in the Presidency; who had even said that he had played false in the Revolution, and had squandered public moneys;

who had gone beyond threats of impeachment and dared to hint at assassination! They saw the end of his term approach, and would have recalled their insults. But they had alienated his great spirit forever.

When he had seen parties forming in his cabinet in the quiet days of his first term as President, he had sought to placate differences; had tried to bring Hamilton and Jefferson to a cordial understanding which should be purged of partisan bias, as he meant his own judgments to be; had deemed parties unnecessary and loyalty to the new Constitution the only standard of preferment to office. But he had come to another mind in the hard years that followed. " I shall not, whilst I have the honor to administer the government, bring a man into any office of consequence knowingly," he declared in the closing days of 1795, " whose political tenets are adverse to the tenets which the general government are pursuing; for this, in my opinion, would be a sort of political suicide;" and he left the Presidency ready to call himself very flatly a " Federalist "—of the party that stood for the Constitution and abated nothing of its powers. " You could as soon scrub a blackamore white," he cried, " as to change the principle of a profest Democrat "—" he will leave nothing unattempted to overturn the Government of this Country."

Affairs fell very quiet again as the last year of his Presidency drew towards its close. Brisk trade under the new treaties heartened the country more and more; the turbulent democratic clubs that had so noisily affected French principles and French modes of agitation were sobered and discredited, now the Reign of Terror had come and wrought its bloody work in France; the country turned once more to Washington with its old

confidence and affection, and would have had him take
the Presidency a third time, to keep the government
steady in its new ways.

But he would not have the hard office again. On the
19th of September, 1796, he published to the people a
farewell address, quick with the solemn eloquence men
had come to expect from him. He wrote to Hamilton and to Madison for advice as to what he should
say, as in the old days of his diffident beginnings in the
great office—though Hamilton was the arch-Federalist
and Madison was turning Democrat—took their phrases
for his thought where they seemed better than his own ;
put the address forth as his mature and last counsel to
the little nation he loved. " It was designed," he said,
" in a more especial manner for the yeomanry of the
country," and spoke the advice he hoped they might
take to heart. The circumstances which had given his
services a temporary value, he told them, were passed ;
they had now a unified and national government, which
might serve them for great ends. He exhorted them
to preserve it intact, and not to degrade it in the using ;
to put down party spirit, make religion, education, and
good faith the guides and safeguards of their government, and keep it national and their own by excluding
foreign influences and entanglements. 'Twas a noble
document. No thoughtful man could read it without
emotion, knowing how it spoke in all its solemn sentences the great character of the man whose career was
ended.

When the day came on which he should resign his
office to John Adams, the great civilian who was to
succeed him, there was a scene which left no one in
doubt—not even Washington himself—what the people

thought of the leader they had trusted these twenty
years. A great crowd was assembled to see the simple
ceremonies of the inauguration, as on that April day in
New York eight years ago; but very few in the throng
watched Adams. All eyes were bent upon that great
figure in black velvet, with a light sword slung at his
side. No one stirred till he had left the room, to follow
and pay his respects to the new President. Then they
and all the crowd in the streets moved after him, an
immense company, going as one man, " in total silence,"
his escort all the way. He turned upon the threshold
of the President's lodgings and looked, as if for the last
time, upon this multitude of nameless friends. "No
man ever saw him so moved." The tears rolled unchecked down his cheeks; and when at last he went
within, a great smothered common voice went through
the stirred throng, as if they sobbed to see their hero
go from their sight forever.

It had been noted how cheerful he looked, at thought
of his release, as he entered the hall of the Representatives, where Mr. Adams was to take the oath. As soon
as possible he was at his beloved Mount Vernon once
more, to pick up such threads as he might of the old
life again. " I begin my diurnal course with the sun,"
he wrote, in grave playfulness, to a friend; " if my
hirelings are not in their places by that time, I send
them messages of sorrow for their indisposition; having
put these wheels in motion, I examine the state of
things further; the more they are probed the deeper I
find the wounds which my buildings have sustained by
an absence and neglect of eight years; by the time I
have accomplished these matters breakfast (a little after
seven o'clock, about the time, I presume, that you are

taking leave of Mrs. McHenry) is ready; this being
over, I mount my horse and ride round my farms, which
employs me until it is time to dress for dinner. . . . The
usual time of sitting at the table, a walk, and tea bring
me within the dawn of candlelight; previous to which,
if not prevented by company, I resolve that as soon as
the glimmering taper supplies the place of the great
luminary I will retire to my writing-table and acknowledge the letters I have received; when the lights are
brought I feel tired and disinclined to engage in this
work, conceiving that the next night will do as well.
The next night comes, and with it the same causes for
postponement, and so on. Having given you the history of a day, it will serve for a year, and I am persuaded that you will not require a second edition of it."
He had kept his overseers under his hand all the time
he was President; had not forgotten to write to Dr.
Young upon methods of cultivation; had shown the
same passion as ever for speeding and regulating at
its best every detail of his private business; but matters
had gone ill for lack of his personal supervision. He
was obliged to sell no less than fifty thousand dollars'
worth of his lands in the course of four or five years to
defray the great expenses he was put to in the Presidency and the cost of bringing his estate into solvent
shape again. He did not try to begin anew; he only
set things in order, and kept his days serene.

A spark of war was kindled by the new administration's dealings with France, and Washington was called
once more to prepare for command, should the fighting
leave the sea and come ashore. But formal war did not
come. The flurry only kept him a little nearer the
movements of politics than he cared to be. He was the

more uneasy to see how the Democrats bore themselves
in the presence of the moment's peril; doubted the expediency of assigning men of that party to places of
command in the army ; approved the laws passed against
aliens and against those who should utter seditious libel
against the government; showed again, and without reserve, how deeply his affections were engaged on the
side of the institutions he had so labored to set up and
protect ; was intolerant towards any who sought to
touch or question at any point their new authority—
imperious as of old in question of action.

But it was his home that chiefly held his thought
now. He had not changed towards his friends through
all the long years of public care and engrossing business.
An old comrade, who had come in his rough frontier
dress all the way from far Kentucky to Philadelphia to
see the President, had been told " that Washington had
become puffed up with the importance of his station,
and was too much of an aristocrat to welcome him in
that garb." But the old soldier was not daunted, pressed on to make his call, and came back to tell his friends
how the President and his lady had both seen him and
recognized him. from the window, and had hurried to
the door to draw him cordially in. " I never was
better treated," he said. " I had not believed a word
against him ; and I found that he was ' Old Hoss ' still."
'Twas the same with his neighbors, and with strangers
too. He was the simple gentleman of the old days. A
strolling actor, riding Mount Vernon way on a day in
July, stopped to help a man and woman who had been
thrown from their chaise, and did not recognize the stalwart horseman who galloped up to his assistance till
the overturned vehicle had been set up again, they had

dusted each the other's coat, and the stately stranger, saying he had had the pleasure of seeing him play in Philadelphia, had bidden him come to the house yonder and be refreshed. "Have I the honor of addressing General Washington?" exclaimed the astonished player. "An odd sort of introduction, Mr. Bernard," smiled the heated soldier; "but I am pleased to find you can play so active a part in private, and without a prompter."

Those who saw him now at Mount Vernon thought him gentler with little children than Mrs. Washington even, and remembered how he had always shown a like love and tenderness for them, going oftentimes out of his way to warn them of danger, with a kindly pat on the head, when he saw them watching the soldiers in the war days. Now all at Mount Vernon looked forward to the evening. That "was the children's hour." He had written sweet Nelly Custis a careful letter of advice upon love matters, half grave, half playful, in the midst of his Presidency, when the troubles with England were beginning to darken; she had always found him a comrade, and had loved him with an intimacy very few could know. Now she was to be married, to his own sister's son, and upon his birthday, February 22d, 1799. She begged him to wear the "grand embroidered uniform," just made for the French war, at her wedding; but he shook his head and donned instead the worn buff and blue that had seen real campaigns. Then the delighted girl told him, with her arm about his neck, that she loved him better in that.

The quiet days went by without incident. He served upon a petty jury of the county when summoned; and was more than content to be the simple citizen again, great duties put by, small ones diligently resumed.

Once and again his anger flamed at perverse neglects and tasks ill done. Even while he was President, he had stormed to find his horses put to the chariot with unpolished hoofs upon a day of ceremony. But old age, and the consciousness of a lifework done, had added serenity now to his self-control; and at last the end came, when he was ready. On the 12th of December, 1799, he was chilled through by the keen winds and cold rain and sleet that beat upon him as he went his round about the farms. He spent the evening cheerfully, listening to his secretary read; but went to bed with a gathering hoarseness and cold, and woke in the night sharply stricken in his throat. Physicians came almost at dawn, but the disease was already beyond their control. Nothing that they tried could stay it; and by evening the end had come. He was calm the day through, as in a time of battle; knowing what betided, but not fearing it; steady, noble, a warrior figure to the last; and he died as those who loved him might have wished to see him die.

The country knew him when he was dead: knew the majesty, the nobility, the unsullied greatness of the man who was gone, and knew not whether to mourn or give praise. He could not serve them any more; but they saw his light shine already upon the future as upon the past, and were glad. They knew him now the Happy Warrior,

> " Whose powers shed round him, in the common strife
> Or mild concerns of ordinary life,
> A constant influence, a peculiar grace,
> But who, if he be called upon to face
> Some awful moment to which Heaven has joined
> Great issues, good or bad, for humankind,

Is happy as a Lover; and attired
With sudden brightness, like a man inspired ;
And, through the heat of conflict, keeps the law
In calmness made, and sees what he foresaw.

*   *   *   *   *   *   *

A soul whose master-bias leans
To homefelt pleasures and to gentle scenes ;

*   *   *   *   *   *   *

More brave for this, that he hath much to love:—
* * * the man, who, lifted high,
Conspicuous object in a nation's eye,
Or left unthought of in obscurity,—
Who, with a toward or untoward lot,
Prosperous or adverse, to his wish or not,
Plays, in the many games of life, that one
Where what he most doth value must be won."

INDEX

action of colonies in dealing with, 25–26 ; indecisive wars with, in America, 27; movements of, in the West, 1752, 59–60 ; aggressive efficiency of, 60; warned from the Ohio by Dinwiddie, 64–66 ; at Fort Le Bœuf, 65 ; claims of, to the West. 66 ; seize fort at forks of the Ohio, 71 ; increase their force on the Ohio, 72; build Fort Duquesne, 73; attacked by Washington near Great Meadows, 73–74; profess friendship for the English, 80–81; send reinforcements to Canada, 81 ; force of, against Braddock, 87 ; lose Louisbourg, 93, Duquesne, 94, Quebec, 95 ; volunteer for service in America, 200; respect of, for Washington, 215.

French and Indian War, begun by Washington, 73–74; action in, at Great Meadows, 74–75 ; Braddock made commander-in-chief in, 81; Braddock's defeat in, 86 ff.; goes heavily against the English, 90; drags upon the frontier, 91 ; goes against the French, 93–95; effect of close of, on colonies, 113; close of, 114.

French Revolution, beginning of, 289; progress of, 292; Washington's attitude towards, 290–292, 296.

Fry, Colonel Joshua, made commander of western expedition, 72 ; dies, 73.

Fur trade, early rivalry of French and English in the, 23–25; effort of the English to control, at Oswego, 61.

GAGE, General, 170.

Galloway, Joseph, leader of Pennsylvania delegation, 164: proposition of, in Congress, 164.

Gardoqui insists on closing the Mississippi, 254.

Gaspé, schooner, destruction of, 146.

Gates, General, 198 ; defeated at Camden, South Carolina, 205.

Genet, Edmond Charles, minister from France, 297 ; conduct of, in America, 298 ; plans of, defeated by Washington, 298 ; recall of, 300.

Georgia, prevented by governor from sending delegates to " congress " in New York, 134; overrun by British, 204; fails to send delegates to Annapolis conference, 255.

Germans, in Pennsylvania and Virginia, 18 ; settle in valley of Shenandoah, 61; Pennsylvanian, oppose war with France, 63 ; attacked by Indians on Virginian frontier, 91 ; volunteer for service in America, 200.

Germantown, battle of, 197.

Gist, Christopher, agent of Ohio Company, 65; goes with Washington to warn the French, 65 ; solicitude of, for Washington, 66.

Gooch, William, Governor of Virginia, 40.

Grafton referred to, 139.

Grasse, Count de, co-operates with Washington before Yorktown, 209.

Great Meadows, Washington encamps at, 73; "a charming field for an encounter," 73 ; Washington attacked by Villiers at, 74–75 ; bought by Washington, 144; referred to, 161.

Greene, General, surrender of Fort Washington by, 190 ; harasses Cornwallis in North Carolina, 208.

Greenway Court, built by Lord Fairfax, 50 ; Washington at, 55–56; referred to, 107.

Grenville, George, Prime - Minister, favors direct taxation of colonies, 119; attempt of, to enforce collection of port dues, 122 ; proposes Stamp Act, and billeting of troops in colonies, 123 ; referred to, 139.

Gunston Hall, centre of sport, 109.

HAMILTON, Alexander, address of, to the states, 255 ; previous rec-

at, 237, 243; Washington's correspondence at, 250; meeting of Potomac commissioners at, 252; Washington leaves, to take presidency, 265; retires to private life at, 309.

Moustier, Count de, French minister to the United States, presumption of, 276.

Murray, John, Earl Dunmore. *See* Dunmore.

NATIONAL Bank, foundation of, 293.

Navigation Acts, policy of the, towards the colonies, 20; evasion of the, 21; irritation wrought by the, 22; advantages gained to the colonies by the, 22.

Nelson, Washington's horse, 241.

Nelson, William, president of Virginia Council, 145.

New Brunswick, British stores at, 193.

Newcastle, Duke of, aroused on the French war, 80.

New England, peculiar character of population in, 9–10; persistent character of, amidst change, 10; modification of, 10–11; a body of churches, 11; population and condition of, at end of seventeenth century, 11–12; separate life of, 11–12; difference between, and Virginia accentuated under the Commonwealth, 13; emigration of congregations from, into New Jersey, 19; astir in the French war, 84.

New Hampshire, fails to send delegates to Annapolis conference, 254; rebellion in, 256.

New Jersey, establishment of, 18; emigration of New England congregations to, 19; sends delegates to Annapolis conference, 254.

New Orleans, growing French village at, 60; Genet's plans against, 298.

Newport, D'Estaing sails against, 204; Rochambeau lands at, 206.

New Providence, in the Bahamas,

headquarters of colonial pirates, 22.

New York, establishment of colony of, 17; early preponderance of the Dutch in, 18; a rival of the French in the fur trade, 24; Assembly of, questions English claim to the Ohio, 70; Independent Company from, fails to join Washington against the French, 76; Independent Companies from, under Innes at Will's Creek, 78; astir in the French war, 84; Independent Companies from, with Braddock, 85; legislative powers of Colonial Assembly of, suspended, 139; majority in, opposed to revolution, 163; opposes motion for declaration of independence, 187; delegates from, to Annapolis conference, 254; struggle in, over Constitution, 260.

New York City, cosmopolitan character of colonial, 19; a centre for pirates, 21; delegates of colonies assemble in, 134; Washington's plans for defence of, 186; British arrive before, 188; withdrawal of Washington from, 190; Clinton retreats to, 203; D'Estaing's fleet appears off, 203; Washington's welcome in, as President, 268; Washington takes oath of office in, 269.

Niagara, a French post at, 61; Governor Shirley to lead attack upon, 84; failure of Shirley's expedition against, 90.

Nicholas, Robert Carter, member of House of Burgesses, referred to in connection with debate of Stamp Act, 131; opposes Henry in convention, 170.

Nicola, Colonel Lewis, proposal of, to make Washington king, 219–220.

Norfolk, Virginia, burned by Dunmore, 187.

North, Lord, Prime-Minister, repeals taxes, 144.

ence at Philadelphia, 257 ; opposes compromise in conference at Philadelphia, 258 ; chosen president of conference, 258; returns to Mount Vernon, 259; intense interest of, in discussions of Constitution, 259 ; congratulations of, to Chastellux on marriage, 260; reluctance of, to accept presidency, 261 ; accepts presidency, 262 ; bids farewell to his mother, 265; leaves Mount Vernon, 265; feelings of, on leaving home, 266; financial troubles of, 267; journey of, to New York, 267; present journey contrasted with former ones, 267; welcome of, in New York, 268; takes oath of office, 269; emotion of, during inaugural address, 270–271; inexperience of, in administration, 272–273; fitness of, for office, 273 ; dignity of, in office, 274–276 ; illness of, 277 ; familiarity of, with affairs of government, 278; choice of cabinet by, 278; care of, in federal appointments, 281; makes tour of eastern states, 281–282 ; sympathy of, with Hamilton's policy, 284; attitude of, towards French Revolution, 290–291, 292, 296; object in national policy of, 291 ; sanctions National Bank, 294 ; frontier policy of, 295 ; neutrality of, between France and England, 297; frustrates plans of Genet, 298 ; demands recall of Genet, 300 ; elected to second term, 301; sends John Jay to England, 302; puts down Whiskey Rebellion, 303 ; favors Jay's treaty with England, 305; abuse of, by the people, 305; behavior of, under abuse, 306; wisdom of, recognized, 306; attempts reconciliation of Hamilton and Jefferson, 307; declines third term, 308; farewell address of, 308; emotion of, on retirement from office, 309; retires to Mount Vernon, 309–310; connections of, with public life, 310; treatment of old comrade by,

311 : gentleness of, with children, 312 ; attends marriage of Nellie Custis, 312; sickness and death of, 313–314

Washington, Colonel Henry, holds Worcester for the king, 14, 48–49.

Washington, John, emigration of, to Virginia, 14–15 ; ancestry of, 14–15 ; settlement of, in "Northern Neck" of Virginia, 16–17 ; life of, in Virginia, 40; fortunes of descendants of, 40.

Washington, Rev. Lawrence, rector of Purleigh, 15, 41.

Washington, Lawrence, emigrant to Virginia, 14–15 ; ancestry of, 14–15; settlement of, in "Northern Neck " of Virginia, 16–17.

Washington, Lawrence (half-brother of George), estate and education of, 46 ; service of, at Cartagena, 47 ; in the storming of Fort San Lazaro, 48 ; head of the family and adjutant - general of the colonial militia, 48 ; marriage of, 48–49 ; member of the House of Burgesses, 50; influence of, upon George, 50–53, 57 ; illness and death of, 57; makes George his executor and residuary legatee, 57–58 ; member of Ohio Company, 61; president of Ohio Company, 64 ; correspondence of, with Dinwiddie, 64.

Washington, Lund, 181 ; management of Mount Vernon by, 233.

Washington, Martha, outings of, with Washington, 111 ; at Washington's headquarters at Cambridge, 184; at Valley Forge, 190.

Washington, Mary, courtship and marriage of, 47 ; keeps George from going to sea, 51 ; attends ball with Washington, 228 ; Washington's deference to, 229 ; Washington bids farewell to, 265.

Washingtons, the, fortunes of, in the Northern Neck, 39–40.

Wentworth, commander of land forces at Cartagena, 47.